THE DISUNITED STATES

D1052875

THE
DISUNITED
STATES

VLADIMIR POZNER

Translated from the French by Alison L. Strayer

SEVEN STORIES PRESS

NEW YORK • OAKLAND

Copyright © 2009, Lux Éditeur
Originally published by Éditions Denoël, 1938.
English translation © 2014, Alison L. Strayer

Cet ouvrage publié dans le cadre du programme d'aide à la publication bénéficie du soutien du Ministère des Affaires Etrangères et du Service Culturel de l'Ambassade de France représenté aux Etats-Unis. This work received support from the French Ministry of Foreign Affairs and Cultural Services of the French Embassy in the United States through their publishing assistance program.

Cet ouvrage a bénéficie du soutien des Programmes d'aide à la publication de l'Institut français. This work, published as part of a program of aid for publication, received support from the Institut Français.

Seven Stories Press
140 Watts Street
New York, NY 10013
www.sevenstories.com

College professors and high school and middle school teachers may order free examination copies of Seven Stories Press titles. To order, visit www.sevenstories.com/textbook or send a fax on school letterhead to (212) 226-1411.

Book design by Jon Gilbert

Library of Congress Cataloging-in-Publication Data
Pozner, Vladimir, 1905-1992.
  [États Désunis. English]
  The Disunited States / Vladimir Pozner ; translated by Alison L. Strayer.
    pages ; cm
  ISBN 978-1-60980-531-9 (paperback)
  1. United States--Description and travel. 2. United States--Social conditions--1933-1945. 3. Pozner, Vladimir, 1905-1992--Travel--United States. I. Title.
  E169.P8613 2014
  973.917--dc23
                                    2013050806

Printed in the United States

9 8 7 6 5 4 3 2 1

CONTENTS

"The era of philosophical twaddle is over. That of photography has arrived."
—Jules Vallès, *Le tableau de Paris*, 1882

"The cause of America is in a great measure the cause of all mankind. Many circumstances have, and will arise, which are not local, but universal, and through which the principles of all Lovers of Mankind are affected, and in the Event of which, their Affections are interested."
—Thomas Paine, *Common Sense*, 1776

A DAY LIKE ANY OTHER

. . . yes, but the sun goes faster. It springs from the Atlantic, sets off at 5:26 in Portland, Maine, near the Canadian border, at 5:30, it's in Boston, twelve minutes later, in New York. At 5:47, it's reported in Philadelphia, Quaker City, 5:48 in Wilmington, capital of the DuPont de Nemours, 5:54 in Washington, the seat of government. At 6:06, it's the turn of Pittsburgh steel, at 6:10, the turn of Miami palms, at 6:18, that of the automobiles of Detroit. Not a second behind schedule, the sun arrives in Atlanta, Georgia, at 6:24, in Cincinnati, Ohio, at 6:25, in Louisville, Kentucky, at 6:29. The blast furnaces in Gary spot it at 6:35, the Chicago stockyards a minute later. From sixty seconds to sixty seconds, from city to city it moves, 6:46, Memphis, 6:47, Saint Louis, 6:48, New Orleans. Factories in the East are up and running, southern plantations humming; now, the Midwest farms and herds appear, Des Moines at 7:00 sharp, at 7:04 Kansas City, 7:10, Omaha. On the trails of French explorers, Dutch traders, British governors, the paths of the American pioneers and trappers. Desert cacti now, and Indians (7:17, Oklahoma City), Mexicans (7:50, Santa Fe), Mormons (8:13, Salt Lake City). An ocean appears on the horizon; Los Angeles to the south, Seattle to the north; and at 8:57, the sun pulls into San Francisco.

September 21, 1936, begins in the United States of America.

The legacy of the night weighs on the continent. The morning is gorged with strikes, conventions, deaths, speeches.

The Colorado River hauls its swollen yellow floodwaters across the plains of Texas, and in the deserted backcountry towns, water takes the place of men, enters their homes, their workshops, their offices, their . . .

In Milwaukee, the gangster Cesare Cortese goes to the window of the café where he's been sitting, peers at the lone car that's just pulled up in front: a salvo of bullets rakes the glass, the car roars away, Cortese crashes down among shards of . . .

A nurse at a hospital in Memphis removes a bag from around the neck of a baby who has just been brought to her, and takes out a shred of rattlesnake skin. "What's this for?" she asks. "To prevent the teeth from coming in too early," says the mo . . .

In Akron, Rubber Town, non-unionized mechanics come to repair a machine at the Goodrich factory; but seeing them arrive, the workers cross their arms and the machinery is paralyzed, and meanwhile the morning fog drapes itself around the Michigan highways, cars pull onto imaginary roads, four dead and six wounded by the time President Roosevelt arrives in New York.

7:30. This just in. The governor of Louisiana, following his counterparts in Alabama and Mississippi, agrees to participate in governors' regattas in the southern states, while Reverend Crown in his Illinois town, sifts through contest answers—five dollars for the person who can name the most horrible sin. *It's murder*, says a schoolgirl, *it's tobacco*, claims a doctor, and a Chicago resident, *it's communism!*

> On his sixty-first birthday, Walter Scott, a.k.a. Death Valley Scotty, divides his time between the gold mine, his hut, and his two mules Betty and Slim. He never comes across a sign of life save for the prints of his heavy boots and his animals' hoofs in the dirt. About his family: he's heard nothing of them since the day he ran away from home as a boy. He has been a muleteer, cowboy. The new century caught him by surprise in this California valley. He wanted to be rich and became a little richer each year, extracting gold.

Scotty had built a wall around his domain. One day he would emerge, powerful as Rockefeller.

Fourteen years ago, he believed the time had come. In a California canyon, he built a $2 million castle. Once the work was done, he went out for a visit, toured the rooms, turned on the bathtub faucets, fiddled with the light switches. All this belonged to him. He tiptoed out, moved by so much wealth, and bored to death. The next day he was at his mine.

Today he turns sixty-one. He will live for a long time yet, but will never have yachts, servants, women. There's only one thing in the world he enjoys: leaving for his *placer* at dawn between Betty and Slim, and returning in the evening with a little bit of yellow dust, a little bit more each time.

In West Virginia, one hundred workers hired to put in a pipeline go on strike.

In a Newark hospital, a police officer approaches a nurse. "You've got a casualty who lost his nose in a car accident? Well! We found the nose stuck to the car radiator. I've brought it for you."

A black boy in St. Louis flees at the sight of detectives who suspect him of theft: THEY SHOOT TO KILL.

Mrs. Johnson of Washington filed for a divorce: she drank too much one night and the next morning woke up in North Carolina, married to a Mr. Johnson.

Samuel Insull, renowned crooked banker who recently merged twenty-two radio stations, offers his resignation as president of the new trust, of which he remains a director.

10:00: the New York Stock Exchange opens its doors.

In an Akron hotel (at the Goodrich factory, the strike is spreading from shop to shop), Preston Harless, Dragon of the city, confers with James Colescott, Grand Dragon of Ohio: the Ku Klux Klan Convention is a few days away, the presidential elections are approaching; "*We'll limit ourselves to informing voters of the candidates' religion*," says Colescott.

Casimir Cazale dies in New Orleans; in 1887, he left his home in Basses-Pyrenees for Louisiana.

"*America for Americans,*" replies Harless.

Ellen MacGeary dies in a Pennsylvania backwater; sixty years ago, she gave up her native Ireland for the United States.

Says Colescott, "*We must elect men who will deport the fifteen hundred thousand foreigners living illegally in this country and stealing jobs from real Americans.*"

Peter Stephen dies in Atlanta; in 1899, he left his village in Greece for the plantations of Georgia.

The Grand Dragon announces the good news to the Dragon: HIRAM W. EVANS, IMPERIAL WIZARD, SUPREME HEAD OF THE KLAN, WILL SPEAK IN AKRON.

10:30. In St. Louis, the director of the Great Eastern Oil Corp, terror-stricken, opens his vaults while looking down the barrels of revolvers that two men are pointing at him— Boyd's City Dispatch, the oldest direct mailing agency, puts up for sale a list of 13,183 millionaires— In Hollywood, costume designer Adrian has just reconciled Greta Garbo with sound engineers by inventing a "noise absorber," thanks to which the star may—FINALLY!—wear the taffeta dresses she loves but whose rustling, until now, drowned out the actors' dialogue— In Chicago, a member of Congress holds forth at the Credit Jewelers Board of Trade Convention: "*The business world,*" says he (in Port Huron, Michigan, Mrs. Parish, eighty-four, kills herself by opening the gas valve), *the business world must feed the unemployed, or fight them.*"(An unemployed man dies in the hospital in Youngstown)—

11:00. 640,000 shares have been traded on the Stock Exchange since it opened—

> 3,200 lettuce growers are on strike in Salinas, California. The police have just searched the home of the union secretary, in his absence and without a warrant, and found evidence of conspiracy. That is, some communist newspapers, a

volume of the works of Lenin and a letter whose recipient is addressed as "comrade," signed "Fraternally yours." Two thousand citizens, vested with police powers, take over from each other at the Salinas Barracks. "We're in a virtual state of war," said a municipal employee. And the sheriff: "Whatever the purpose of the strike, order must be maintained. I have faith in democracy and trade unionism." Strikebreakers work under police protection. Some strikers are in prison for hitting back, blow for blow. Others who did not are in the hospital.

Noon. 970,000 shares were traded on the Stock Exchange— In St. Louis, Hickman Holloman, eighty-three, walks out of his own funeral: he wanted to know how the ceremony would go, a pastor friend was able to satisfy his curiosity— At the Texas Centennial Exposition, the audience is introduced to the mysteries of banknote manufacturing. "SEE THE ONE MILLION DOLLAR BILL!"— The Women's Club of Youngstown hurries through lunch in silence, eager to start the bridge tournament— In a Detroit home, cream-colored candles with pink tulle bows rise from silver candelabras: engagement party— Chicago City Hall advises that starting October 1, twelve inspectors will be in charge of counting the sheets on toilet paper rolls; if the number is inferior to the one marked on the label, the seller will be prosecuted for fraud— The Florida Weather Service announces that at 1:00 p.m., the cyclone raging in the Atlantic was four hundred miles northeast of the Bahamas and heading for the American coast—

Reverend Coughlin, the famous RADIO PRIEST of Detroit meets the press at a St. Louis hotel. "I lead the crusade for democracy," he says.— "If democracy failed and you had to choose between communism and fascism?" a reporter asks.— "I could never choose communism," Coughlin says. "It denies the existence of God."— "So you support capitalism?"— "Careful, my friends, careful! We must make a distinction between plain capitalism and modern capitalism. The latter is unconstitutional and anti-Christian. The former is the best economic system the world has ever produced. CHRISTIANITY, DEMOCRACY, AND CAPITALISM ARE IN PERFECT AGREEMENT. In fact, they form the only triumvirate that can possibly function."

2:00. The Stock Exchange has traded 1,450,000 shares— In Detroit, the lawyer Winter is preparing the talk he will give the following day at the Masonic Temple: "The arrest, trial, and conviction of Jesus Christ"— Spike O'Donnell, *ci-devant* beer king of Chicago and rival of Al Capone, presses charges against the district attorney who recently had him arrested, undermining his reputation as a businessman— The five Republican councilmen of Braddock, Pennsylvania, accuse their six fellow Democrat colleagues of illegally electing, in a secret meeting, a seventh council member, also a Democrat— In Pittsburgh, the Mothers of Democracy hold a card game—2:19: Start of the first race at the Havre-de-Grace racetrack (Maryland)— The Order of the Rainbow Girls of Akron elects its officers: Mrs. Willems, *Mother Advisor*; Miss Werntz, *Charity*; the Renner sisters, *Hope and Faith*; Miss MacGinley, *Treasurer*— 2:40: Start of first race at the Detroit Race Course— THE UNITED STATES' MOST BELOVED CHILD, Shirley Temple, has lunch with an admirer, the wife of the governor of California, and a group of Boy Scouts—
CALL-ING ALL U-NITS! Sighted near Cleveland, the Browe baby, missing for two weeks, and his kidnapper: blond, stocky, scar on left cheek— Two Whites and a Black escaped from the chain gang of Georgia: calling all units— In Chicago, two priests taking $500 to the bank are attacked by three bandits: this is an alert, this is an alert— Bang! 4:37: start of the fifth race at Havre-de-Grace— Bang! A tanker blows up in Dubuque (Iowa)— Bang! The farmer

Stutz, seventy years old, of Wooster (Ohio), shoots himself in the head— Bang! Miss Winslow breaks a bottle of champagne over the bow of the new destroyer named in honor of her grandfather, the vice-admiral— 6:45: start of the sixth race in Detroit. Bang! Bang! Bang!

The mayor of Pittsburgh is there, surrounded by police officers and reporters. Day-before-yesterday evening, gangsters visited the "Amerito" Club, headquarters of City Councilman Verona. Club management did not file a complaint.

An inspector rounds up the doorman. The mayor himself conducts the interview. "Had some trouble at your place on Saturday?— Sure.— But when the police questioned you, you claimed nothing had happened!— Sure.— What exactly happened?— Someone rang the doorbell. Strangers. I opened the door to ask if they were members. Yes, they said, and one of them stuck a gun in my gut. The other went upstairs, lined up the players and emptied their pockets.— And why didn't you report it?— What for?— And your bosses?— That's their business.— Who was there that night?— What do I know?— Was Verona there?— Oh! No.— But he's a member of the club?— So they say.— And did you recognize the gangsters?— I have a lousy memory for faces.— Looks to me like you're covering for someone.— What an idea!— Is it Verona you're covering? Or the gangsters?— I don't understand.— Maybe both?"

Thousands of tons of salmon leave Alaska; in the Hawaiian Islands, the crowd lays siege to grocery stores; from Los Angeles to Seattle, cargo ships load and unload bananas, coffee, furs, grapefruit, oil, cement: in nine days, the Pacific sailors go on strike. The police chiefs are already conferring in the shipowners' offices— Roxana (Illinois). Restaurateur Fairbanks is pressing charges against the management of Shell Petroleum: he's demanding the $15,000 they owe him for meals he provided for scabs locked in the company factory during a recent strike— Atlanta. Mrs. Smith celebrates the seventeenth birthday of her Airedale Miki with twenty dog friends: they serve cake and ice cream— St. Paul. 1,700 strikers from Public Works Administration are forced to return to work: defeat— Toledo. Workers from eighteen dry-cleaning establishments, on strike for three weeks, sign an agreement with the bosses: victory—

(*Now in turn the night sets out*) In a small Ohio town, Mrs. Dobson recites a poem about friendship at the Pleasant Grove Club— (*It springs from the Atlantic and invades Portland . . .*) The football player Russel, nineteen, is buried in a small town in Texas (*night engulfs Boston . . .*), operated on for appendicitis, he died the day before (*. . . New York . . .*) As he lay dying, he was delirious: (*. . . Philadelphia, Washington . . .*) "Let me out of here, I want to get back to the team"— (*it grazes the Miami palms . . .*) Mary Pickford finally admits to reporters that she spoke these words: "I'm not engaged, at least not yet"— (*and the steelworks of Pittsburgh . . .*) In a village in the state of New York, Doris Purcell, sixteen, learning that the man she was in love with has gotten married (*Memphis follows at 7 p.m. sharp . . .*) takes her own life— (*. . . after St. Louis and before New Orleans . . .*) The Roosevelt family is celebrating the eighty-second birthday of the president's mother— (*an ocean appears on the horizon . . .*) The Excelsior Lodge meets in Louisville— (*Los Angeles to the south, Seattle to the north . . .*) The daily greyhound races start in Dallas— (*. . . and at 9:09 p.m., night pulls into San Francisco and the sun plummets into the Pacific . . .*)

> Now that the journalists who dogged him with their questions have been left behind, the car peacefully cruising through the Pennsylvania night, Charles Margiotti, district attorney, can finally stop smiling. There is nothing to be cheerful about. Monaghan was murdered by police, and

that's a fact. One more time, the judge reviews the case. Ten days earlier, the chief of detectives was found with his throat slit. A few hours later, three policemen arrested Frank Monaghan, sixty-four, a hotel manager whom they suspected of the crime. They took him to the basement of the police station, and when he did not confess, they beat him all night. The D.A. thinks of the blood splattered on the basement walls: he would not have believed an old man's body could contain so much. Monaghan didn't talk, but he screamed until dawn, and the crowd gathered in front of the station listened to his cries. Too much noise, too many witnesses. They'd had to arrest the officers, alert the journalists, the photographers, the experts. A dirty business. "THIRD DEGREE, THIRD DEGREE." Luckily, it rarely ends in death. Rarely, Mr. D.A.? Rarely?

Now the numbers are rolling in from all directions. Three injured in Pittsburgh, two killed in car accidents— Saint Louis slaughter-houses took in 7,000 heads of horned cattle, 8,500 sheep, 11,000 pigs— In Washington, thirty-eight births, twenty-one marriages, thirty-one deaths— At the Detroit Stock Exchange, 16,934 shares changed hands, in other parts of the city, there were thirty-seven deaths and eighty-nine births— 53,000 shares were traded on the Chicago Mercantile Exchange, two gazelles and a monkey were born in the Chicago Zoo—

The clicker at the *Baltimore Sun* is doing layout for the Classifieds: "LADY (white) economical, gentleman's home preferred." "WOMAN (negro) looking for any work at all." From *The Globe-Democrat*, St. Louis: "YOUNG MAN, situation, anything. Strong, 20, good driver." From the *Times-Picayune* of New Orleans: "WE want to encourage prayers to St. Joseph and faith placed in him for the great favor he granted us. Mrs. Jourdan and her son Charles." From *The Detroit Free Press*: "Wanted: PRIESTS to sell, in spare time, *The Treasures of the Doré Bible* against payment of

fifty cents a week." From the *Chicago Herald*: "Christian Industrial League. Send us used clothing, furniture, newspapers to help
rebuild men"—

> There is not a single free bed left in Cleveland. The
> American Legion is holding its annual convention. Time
> to see who's shown the most imagination: they've had a
> year to think about it, in the shop, at the office, or chafing
> under lack of employment. One Legionnaire has made
> a miniature cannon that shoots firecrackers into the legs
> of pretty passersby. Another member offers a sandwich to
> any woman in the street, two slices of bread with a baby
> alligator in between. It's a September 21 they won't forget
> any time soon. Eighteen years ago they were young, they
> experienced adventure and didn't die of it. How beautiful
> war is in peacetime, it gives the chance, once a year, to
> escape the family, money problems, the boredom that
> weighs heavy on the continent, heavier than the deepening
> night. (New York falls asleep.)

In a Chicago hospital, a woman is screaming and crying. She
is only twenty-two, and her newborn is dying. Due to a malfor-
mation, the baby cannot expel food. "We can operate," says the
doctor, "put in drains."— "And then what?" the father asks.—
"Without surgery, he'll die for sure," the doctor replies.— "I don't
want him to live as a cripple," the father says.— "I do, I do," cries
the mother. "Operate!"— "I can't without the father's consent,"
says the doctor. Chicago falls asleep. In his cot, the child grows
weaker by the hour. Around him, a half-dozen newborns snore and
digest.

> Minneapolis falls asleep. Slowly the floodlight moves
> over the factory roofs and walls, the deserted yard, the
> compound, the bolted door, the armed men standing

guard, and outside, the workers. There's a strike at Archer Daniels Midland Co.

The forty mills of Minneapolis are on strike. Minneapolis truckers are on strike. Minneapolis factories are about to go on strike.

Again the floodlight beam moves over the roofs, the walls, the picket lines. Armed guards protect the factory, patrol the city streets, knocking down isolated strikers. They know how to kill but they don't know how to operate the machines. The shops close for lack of supply, and only a hundred railway cars come through the freight yard a day instead of two thousand, like before.

That floodlight again. A bullet fired in the dead of night lodges itself in the eye of the guard turning the floodlight, the eye of the bosses goes out, and shadow engulfs the factory, the yard, the compound and picket lines.

At his home in Joliet (Illinois), watched over by two doctors, Patrick McFarland, who once was one of the best boxers in the world, is dying of heart disease—

John Sweeney—twelve years old, nine-time runaway, escapes from his father's house, gets off the bus in downtown New York, skulks around Times Square, goes into a shop, buys tobacco and a pipe, a real pipe like an old sailor's—

Denver falls asleep— At the hospital in Chicago, the mother cries, and the father says: "I'd rather the child die"— Pat Mac-Farland is raving on his deathbed— John Sweeney lights the new pipe, a policeman comes up to him. "Nice pipe you got there."— "Yes, it's good, and the tobacco is strong." He wants to vomit, but life is worth living. "Do you live around here?" asks the policeman.— "No, I ran away from Philadelphia"—San Francisco is going to sleep—

MacFarland's heartbeat slows, the boxer sees his life in the ring, the brewery he owned . . .

At the police station, the officer makes his report, and the sergeant greets John, an old acquainta . . .

The child grows weaker at the hospital in . . . A gangster approaches the cash booth of the Chicago Skytrain— The radio dreams of jazz— Unemployed people are sleeping in parks—The Rocky Mountains: airplane flies— The rotors rotate: news flies— Chicago: gangster flies off with his loot. All along the telegraph wires, from cloud to cloud, telegrams fly.

Yes, but the sun goes faster. It springs from the Atlantic and sets off at 5:27 in Portland, Maine, near the Canadian border . . .

September 22, 1936, will begin in the United States of America.

This chapter is a summary of news items from thirty US newspapers dated September 22, 1936, covering the events of the day before: a day like any other. All time references are in Eastern Standard Time.

CONVENTIONAL AMERICA

I. LIFE

The elevator they took from the platform at Pennsylvania Station deposits the two travelers in the hotel lobby: green plants, all alike, white columns, identical, and at the foot of the columns, blue employees with arms folded across their chests, all exactly the same. The room is crowded: the Suspenders Manufacturers Union has organized a dinner, the Daughters of the American Revolution (Bronx Chapter) is having a celebration for a Presbyterian minister, the Deaf Mute Association their annual convention. A great deal of running back and forth, fluttering, talking on the phone and shouting, except for the deaf-mutes who keep to themselves in a forest of raised arms.

An employee takes the two travelers to a counter; they book a room on the sixteenth floor; at the next counter they claim the mail that's been held for them; further on, they exchange francs for dollars, forgo examining the ten or twelve other counters, all in a row, that each provide a different service, and head for the express elevators. Three bellboys follow with the suitcases. They go up to the sixteenth floor, walk along corridors, turn the key in the lock that has been set above the doorknob so it can easily be located, and enter the room.

The first bellboy turns on the overhead light, which eases the reading of normal-sized lettering (as certified by the Scopometer), the second bellboy rotates a switch on the light fixture over the bedside table, powerful enough so that Everyman can make out even the smallest writing (as certified by, etc.). The third bellboy ignites a lamp by the armchair that facilitates the reading of a newspaper (as certified, etc.). Then he goes into the bathroom and, having switched on a bulb over the mirror, thanks to which one is able to perform the most delicate operations, shaving or putting on makeup (as, etc.), he runs the hot water tap, the cold water tap, the ice water tap, while his two pals lower the blinds in unison. Now bellboy number one is checking in the table to confirm the presence of letter-size paper, personal stationery, large envelopes, small envelopes, cards, telegraph forms and order forms for the laundry service; number two inspects a pincushion on the dresser adorned with a safety pin, three straight pins, a black button, a white button, a small pearl button and two needles, threaded: one with white and the other with black; bellboy number three slips over to the pedestal table, turns the handle of what appears to be a drawer, and jazz leaps out like the devil from his hole.

It has all taken only a minute. The boys in uniform have performed their little ballet with the precision of three billiard balls that a pool champion sends rolling across the felt, hitting the frame strips, hurtling past each other and colliding with an identical clack, which reunites the bellboys at the door, bends their heads down, stretches their arms out, and has them disappear down the hallway, thanking and thanking away.

Hotel management of the Pennsylvania, 2,200 rooms, 2,200 bathrooms—"the hotel where the customer is always right"— has thought of everything, and you can be born in this bed with its horsehair innerspring mattress and, as it happens sometimes, die without ever leaving the house or feeling a need that was not instantly satisfied.

Radio and telephone connect the room to the outside world. Just turn a knob and you can hear the daily jazz or the Sunday sermon, the closing price on the Stock Exchange and weather forecast. Just pick up the receiver to order a meal, get the flight schedules or a shoeshine, or book a passage on an ocean liner. Each time a different employee answers and a new voice provides the information.

A panel opens in the valet closet, also the front door (under which a newspaper is slipped each morning); just slide your suit in, and the next day it's back, cleaned and pressed. Relinquish your dirty laundry before nine, and there it will be in the afternoon, stray buttons sewn back on, snags whip-stitched.

In permanent residence: a doctor and a notary, a chiropodist and masseur, stenographers and interpreters, a financial advisor and a travel consultant; it is rare for a lawyer and priest not to be on the premises. Seven restaurants are there for the picking, according to whether visitors wear a suit or jacket and want to eat, drink, talk business, or dance. In the summer, they go up to the roof garden that crowns the hotel's twenty-two floors with its well-trained plants, in the winter they go underground to the dance hall where jazz drowns out the din of three subway lines and the panting locomotives of Penn Station.

There is a hospital and a gymnasium, a library and Turkish baths, beauty salons, swimming pools, hairdressers, stores selling cigarettes and candy, druggists, haberdashers: they sell everything from suede shoes to the latest novel by Sinclair Lewis, from orchids to vaginal douche bulbs, from jewelry to artificial sun. But mostly they sell the two great American myths: the myth of *efficiency*, which means competence and performance, and the myth of *service*, which does not mean anything at all.

Fifteen years ago, the Hotel Statler Company, owner of the Pennsylvania, the biggest in the chain, published and many times reprinted a booklet entitled *The Statler Service Code*, including the following exordium:

"LIFE IS SERVICE. The One who progresses is the one who gives his fellow human beings a little more—a little better SERVICE."

The *Code* continues:

"Hotel Statler is operated primarily for the benefit and comfort of its Guests. Without Guests there could be no Hotel Statler. These are simple facts, easily understood.

"So then it behooves every man and woman employed here to remember this always, and to treat all Guests with courtesy and careful consideration.

"Any member of our Force who lacks the intelligence to interpret the feeling of the Good Will that The Statler holds toward its Guests can not stay here VERY LONG.

"New Customers are just as valuable as Old Customers— remember that. Remember that each New Customer is an Old Customer in the making. See that you do your part to give him the desire to come back to us bringing his family and friends.

"Never be perky, pungent or fresh. The Guest pays your salary. He is your immediate benefactor.

"Snap judgments of men are oftentimes faulty. A man may wear a red tie, a green vest and tan shoes and still be a gentleman. The Unpretentious man with soft voice may possess the Wealth of Croesus. The stranger in cowhide boots, broadbrim and rusty black hat and an old-fashioned suit may be the president of a railroad or a senator.

"Have everyone feel that for his money we want to give him more sincere service than he ever before received at any hotel.

"The employee who helps to perpetuate this plan is never out of a job, nor does he escape the eye of the Man Behind the Scenes— the Boss.

"At rare intervals, some perverse member of our force disagrees with a Guest on the rightness of this or that.

"He maintains that the meat is well done when the guest says it isn't. Or that THIS sauce was ordered when the guest says the other.

"Either way may be right. But these are PERMANENT INSTRUCTIONS. No Employee of this Hotel is allowed the Privilege of arguing any Point with a Guest. He must adjust the matter at once to the Guest's satisfaction.

"A hotel has just one thing to sell.

"That one thing is Service.

"The hotel that sells Poor Service is a poor hotel. The hotel that sells Good Service is a Good Hotel.

"It is the object of Hotel Statler to sell its guests the VERY BEST service in the world.

"The Service of a Hotel is not a thing supplied by a single individual. Hotel service—that is—Hotel Statler Service—means the limit of Courteous, Efficient Attention from each particular Employee to each Particular Guest.

"When the room clerk says, 'Thank you, Mr. Robinson, the bellman will show you to Room 1252,' instead of yelling, 'Front, Room 1252,' the Guest immediately gets a warm feeling of being welcome. To be able to give a Guest this feeling adds dollars to the income of the house and dollars to the salaries of the clerks.

"An operator who is quick to answer telephone calls and does not keep a Guest holding a cold telephone to his ear and listening intently to nothing can swell the Guest's appreciation of Statler Service—and increase Statler's appreciation of her.

"A waiter who can say 'Pell Mell' when the Guest says 'Pell Mell,' and 'Paul Maul' when the guest says 'Paul Maul,' can make the Guest think himself right—and makes us think the waiter is All Right.

"Take heed, that in all Discussions between Statler Employees and Guests, the Employee is Dead Wrong—from the guest's point of view and from Ours.

"Any Statler Employee who is wise and discreet enough to merit tips is wise and discreet enough to render a like service whether he is tipped or not.

"And he is wise and discreet enough to say 'thank you' if he receives a tip.

"In this connection let it be said: the man who takes a tip and does not thank the tipper does not feel that he has earned his tip any more than a blackmailer feels he has earned his blood money.

Any Statler employee who fails to thank the guest who gives him something falls short of the Statler standard. We will thank any Guest who reports such a case to us."

How much easier it is to exploit those who have fallen hook, line, and sinker for the myths of *service* and *efficiency*. They must feel proud of opening their mouths to say thank you in one of the greatest hotels—the hotel where the employee is always wrong—in the greatest city in the world. Life is service. The One who progresses is the one who services his fellow human beings a little more, a little better, by working a little more, enslaving themselves a little better all the time.

It is no coincidence that in each of the 2,200 rooms in the Pennsylvania, management has placed next to the phone a copy of *The Statler Hotel Service Code* and a Bible.

HARLEM

To James and Mary

Do you think the Negro who sweeps your streets, cooks your meals and waxes your shoes is your equal? If that's what you believe, join the Communist Party. And beware: the Klan rides again.

From a shorthand transcript of a Ku Klux Klan meeting held in January 1936 in Atlanta (Georgia).

He bent his white horse head toward me.

"And where do you live in New York?"

The hallowed rituals of a cocktail party carried on around us: docile, invoked by the tinkling of ice in the shaker, the man-who-never-drinks, the young-woman-who-never-gets-drunk, and other mythological figures emerging from the clouds of smoke.

I answered:

"Starting tomorrow, I'm going to live in Harlem."

"Sorry?"

"Harlem."

He'd understood perfectly well but thought he hadn't.

"You know," he said, "we never think of them."

"Really?"

"No. We don't think of those people existing."

"And yet 'those people' represent nearly one-seventh of the US population."

"Yes, yes, I know," he said absently. "So you found yourself a decent hotel in Harlem?"

"I'll be living with a family."

"With Negroes?" He was appalled.

"Yes. Or actually, the husband is black and his wife is white."

"Oh . . . You know, that's very, very rare. I hope you won't go telling people in France that it's common. That's really tough luck," he added in a woebegone voice.

He was quiet for a moment and then small talk, once again, got the upper hand on dismay.

"So what do you think of this *other* American institution, the cocktail party?"

For the next few days, I entertained myself telling people I was going to live in Harlem. Here are some of the replies:

"*They'll* never let you live with them."

"You could stay at the Hotel Theresa in Central Harlem. They don't let Negroes in."

"Be sure not to carry personal belongings. The bare minimum. Otherwise, *they'll* clean you out."

"Watch out, you're asking for trouble."

"Be careful: they all have syphilis."

Most White New Yorkers do not know Harlem, or despise and fear it. If on an evening they go to some Cotton Club where black customers aren't allowed, all the way there, through taxi windows, they study this reservoir of crime and jazz and think they're having a big adventure. In American mythology, Blacks fall into three categories: "big kids" (example: *Uncle Tom's Cabin*), gangsters (example: the Scottsboro defendants), and simpletons (example: black servants as seen by Hollywood). Respectively they spend their time singing spirituals, raping white women, and saying, "Yessir." And when they're not, they're polishing footwear, opening car doors, and operating elevators. The shoes, cars, and elevators belong to Whites.

SLAVES

The subway trains and buses that travel up the island of Manhattan have disgorged their white passengers by 110th Street. Vehicles crammed with black cargo continue the journey along Fifth and Seventh avenues, Madison and Lenox.

James Ford sits across from me in the tiny office of the Harlem Division of the Communist Party. His grandfather Forsch, first name unknown, a railway worker by trade, was lynched in Georgia at the end of the last century for "being cheeky to a white woman." His father, Lymon Forsch, was a miner. On the envelope that contained his first paycheck, his name was spelled "Ford." The supervisor said, "So what? As if a nigger name had any importance!" That is why the communist candidate for the vice-presidency of the United States is called Ford, James Ford. He takes a sheet of paper and draws a rectangle.

"Harlem is located between 110th and 155th streets; to the west, not far, is the Hudson; its eastern boundary is the Harlem River: all in all, about a quarter of Manhattan. Lower Harlem—up to 125th Street—is inhabited by Black Caribbeans and Central Americans: most are Puerto Rican. Black Americans occupy Upper Harlem, except for a small enclave of Finns and Estonians. The black bourgeoisie keeps to the west, in Washington Heights. In total, almost three hundred thousand inhabitants: the largest black community in the world."

Ford's pencil on the paper sketches a diagram as he speaks.

"At the beginning of the century, Harlem was white. But as the years went by, misery and terror drove the southern Blacks north. The war that drained the mines and factories of white workers sped the emigration along. Today, Harlem is black. You'll find two or three very rich Blacks, a handful of well-off bourgeois, a few thousand lower middle class and intellectuals. The rest are workers."

The pencil draws a period, a thin line, a thick line, and a big square.

"The main problem in Harlem is unemployment. About three-quarters of the population is unemployed: three out of four men."

The first time I entered Harlem was at night. Two o'clock in the morning. The crowd surges down Lenox Avenue. A Black calls out in a gravelly voice:

"I'm hungry. If you're a decent guy, buy me a sandwich."

He insists. He shouts.

"I'm hungry. When a man's hungry, he's hungry."

Since then, I have walked Harlem many times. Nowhere in the world are the streets so alive, night and day. The crowd rambles, or parks itself at intersections; bellows, sings, swarms around the hawkers, collects cigarette butts or old newspapers, pokes through trash cans, or stands for hours by windows plastered with signs reading "For Rent" or "For Sale," and we don't know if they're referring to the shops or the men.

"Three out of four men are out of work," says James Ford, "but one out of four receives benefits. The average monthly relief per family is forty-two dollars in New York, it's only twenty-eight dollars in Harlem, where food is of inferior quality and costs 10 percent to 20 percent more than anywhere else. Harlem is the most congested part of the city; it has the most slums and the highest rents, typically 20 percent more than the going rate. The landlords know very well that Blacks can't go live someplace else. It is rare that a black family isn't forced to sublet one or more rooms; often five or six people sleep in the same room, and still the rent amounts to a third or even half of salaries."

The front door opens by itself: the self-closing mechanism is out of order. Puddles of water have frozen on the tiles in the front hall. I knock on a door: there isn't a bell. Mae sits by a pale fire burning low in the fireplace.

The central heating hasn't been working for two weeks. Ice burst the pipes, water got into the apartments. Outside, it is 5°, and slightly less cold inside.

Mae has been unemployed for eight months, she gets benefits: enough for the rent plus twenty cents a day to feed herself and her little girl.

"Only one hot meal, canned food, half a bottle of milk every two days. Today, I bought a pack of eight logs. I paid twenty cents, that's a whole day's food."

Mae takes me to see other units. Her neighbor uses a small stove to cook meals and keep her newborn warm: a little scrap of brown flesh, six weeks old, grave and indifferent. On the second floor, parents and four kids are squeezed into two rooms: the father earns sixty dollars a month and spends half of it on rent.

Cold has ravaged the place. Burst pipes, water dripping into the pots and pans on the floor, ceilings cracked, walls peeling. The building is coming apart piece by piece: door handles, faucets, light switches come off in your hand.

Everyone in this house is unemployed, all the tenants know each other and enter each other's homes without knocking: since the apartments are as cold as the stairways, a front door is a door like any other.

At night, everyone goes to sleep at friends' homes: the house sits empty, dark, frozen, deserted by even the cats.

"The Black suffers as a worker," says James Ford, scribbling away on his piece of paper. "He suffers as an unemployed person. He also suffers as a Black. He pays more for everything he buys, he receives less for everything he provides. He is the first to be fired, the last to be hired. He is not allowed into most hotels and restaurants outside of Harlem. For a judge, a black defendant is guilty from the start. Black jurors are extremely rare. Even in New York prisons, Blacks are locked up apart from the others. It's only in cemeteries that they are buried with Whites, poor Whites, of course."

A white woman married to a black man told me:

"I'd like to have a child, but I don't dare. There's the money. That could be arranged. But then there's race. It's so terrible, that eternal feeling of hatred and contempt that surround Blacks, the feeling that they're condemned for life to the dirtiest, most degrading work, that nothing can be done. The circle of terror around them . . ."

In Harlem itself, in windows we often see the sign: "Apartment for rent. Whites only."

And at the entrance of employment offices: "Wanted: *white* cook." Or, at most:

"Wanted: a good Negro driver (*very light-skinned*)." A crowd of unemployed black men are studying the ads.

"Terror, terror," says James Ford, slashing the pencil across the paper. "In a year, the Harlem police killed five Blacks without the slightest provocation, including a boy of eighteen suspected of stealing sixty-eight cents. Police threw teargas grenades into a crowd gathered to listen to Ada Wright, the mother of one of the Scottsboro defendants. Three boys accused of stealing thirty-eight cents were beaten and sentenced to a total of ninety years in prison: twenty-eight months in prison for each cent. None of the policemen were ever charged with murder. And nowhere are the policemen as numerous as in Harlem. They send in the officers fired up on racial prejudice. There are also a few black police officers: they're the most ferocious. An eight-year-old was arrested for allegedly attacking an officer who weighed a hundred and seventy-six pounds. Our children . . ."

A black child comes into the world . . . A black child comes into the world . . .

Sally is sitting across from me. Her baby is sleeping.

"I arrived at the Harlem hospital at midnight," she said. "There was no space in the delivery rooms: they put me in a hallway. After an hour, I was wheeled into a little room where a fifteen-year-old girl was in labor. She was in a lot of pain and the doctor told her: 'If you're old enough to have kids, you're old enough to give birth.'

"They put me on an operating table where I lay until three in the morning. A doctor came in and said that they'd deliver me in an hour. He left, and I stayed there alone on the table in pain. At seven o'clock in the morning, the baby still wasn't born and the doctor cursed me, saying I wasn't giving birth because I didn't want to. He gave me nothing for my pain.

"A new nurse came in and asked what church I belonged to. I answered: 'None.'—'None? That's perfect. If you die now, nobody will pray for you.' I was in so much pain I barely understood what she was saying.

"Another doctor came in, and I promised him money if he would stay with me: I didn't know what I was doing anymore. He stayed with me for half an hour. Then other doctors came and said they had to deliver me with forceps. They came back at nine-thirty, examined me once more, and disappeared until noon. I lay alone on that table, a table so hard that eleven months later, my lower back still aches. Finally, at half past twelve, I was put to sleep and the baby was delivered.

"They transferred me to a ward of forty beds where there were sixty women. Nobody changed my clothes. The narcotic they'd given me made me vomit on the bed and on the floor; nobody paid attention. I slept in the same sheets until the day I left.

"They shouldn't have taken blood for the Wassermann test because I'd had it done three times already. I told the doctors, but they didn't listen. It was because years ago I had malaria, and the blood of people with malaria is used to make serum. Usually they have to pay for that blood, but me . . . They took four samples and I was very weak.

"They're supposed to keep you ten days. But there's no room. They put you on the floor, in bays, on bunks without a mattress. I went home on the seventh day, and I realized that at the hospital, they hadn't even thought of putting a dressing on my little girl's navel."*

"There are 325 beds in the hospital in Harlem," James Ford continues, "and an average of four hundred patients. Tuberculosis patients are not isolated; syphilitics are examined in the presence of other patients. Recently, a surgeon performed a very bloody operation in front of thirty-some children screaming with terror. It's the only hospital in Harlem.

"The birth rate among Blacks is higher than among Whites, but there are twenty-one times more births than deaths among Whites as compared to Blacks. Puerperal fever takes twice as many victims among our women than among theirs, and compared to the general population, two black children for every white child die before the age of one. This two-to-one proportion is the same for deaths from typhus and lung congestion, it is five to one for tuberculosis, nine to one for syphilis. All because of poverty, overcrowding, lack of hygiene and medical care. This is how our children grow up."

---

* See "Yesterday, the Parks Department announced, with considerable pride, the birth of a monkey, in Central Park Zoo, of a species prevalent in India. This pride is excusable, given that such an event has never occurred in the history of Central Park. The little monkey, a male, was born on Monday, at nine o'clock in the morning, and is thriving, Dr. Nimphius, the zoo veterinarian, reported yesterday. He is 6 inches long and weighs 15½ ounces. His mother, Gertrude, acquired by the zoo in February 1935, has spent most of the day at the gate of the baby's cage, but this has not prevented her from going to get her rations of potatoes, milk, bananas, oranges and lettuce. The baby was born at the hospital in the monkey house, but mother and child were transferred to the cage because there, the air and the light were better." *New York Times*, November 3, 1936.

They grow up in the street. If the parents work, the house is locked up until evening. There are no parks in Harlem, just two small squares. Hardly any playgrounds. Only one free swimming pool. And there are more than fifty thousand children.

They go to school: the most recent were built before the war, there are no schoolyards, and several groups of students come and go in shifts from morning to night. The schoolbooks are dirty and ragged; the washrooms are often outdoors; in the cafeteria, there are five kids to one seat.

Just as Black doctors are kept away from Harlem Hospital, it seems that Black teachers are seldom chosen for these schools. They send in Whites they want to punish. In mixed-race classes, children make friends without regard for skin color, but parents and teachers keep a close watch.

"I do not want you bringing that dirty little pickaninny into my home."

"Don't make friends with Jimmy, darling, you'll regret it later."

The authors of a *Study on Criminal and Abandoned Black Children* cite the following case:

"A fifteen-year-old boy was taken to juvenile court by the Child Protective Services because he was bothering his classmates. He told them that in the hospital, he'd donated blood for a transfusion to a white girl. Questioned by investigators, he admitted that he had wanted to brag. He was placed under observation and transferred to another school, where there have been no further complaints about him."

Children go to school, but they do not stay long: two or three years, rarely more than five. They take up ranks on the sidewalks and the middle of the streets to play gangsters and G-Men, baseball, Joe Louis, Ethiopian soldiers, and they get run over like cats. The parents have a few lines printed in a black Harlem newspaper:

He suffered without a murmur
And endured his pain with the smile of the Elect.
And the Angel of the Lord spoke:
Dear Eddie, come home, suffer no more.

And other children who have escaped tuberculosis and cars grow up to be shoeshiners, to play dice, open automobile doors. They are hungry and cold; they shoplift; they are arrested and go to prison; they've had only a few days' work in their entire lives; they sell what they have: girls, their bodies (in a doorway for twenty-five cents), boys, their strength and dexterity; often the wooden pistols they brandish in play as children, in their larger hands become automatic revolvers; these kids have never had a family or a home; so through years of misery far beyond their age, and years of unemployment exactly their age, children in Harlem disappear into the adult population.

"Slavery was abolished by the Civil War," says James Ford, "but freedom hasn't followed. Slavery's still there in the plantations of the South and the factories of the North, in schools, courts of law, health centers, in the street. Judge for yourself."

She will never read these lines, and yet at eighty-three, she doesn't wear glasses. She can't read.

"My little schoolteacher wanted to teach me the ABCs. But her mother caught us, she squeezed my head between her knees to spank me, I bit her, she trapped me under her chair and beat me. We were forbidden to learn to read. Once a week, a German gathered us together to recite the Bible and tell us that we must obey our masters."

Miss Pleasant is a tiny bird of a woman wearing a lacy white blouse. Two small pearl combs, a large tortoiseshell comb are planted in her gray hair. Her mouth is slightly sunken, her eyes just a detail in the hollow sockets: in this face, the skull is already showing through at the surface.

"My name is Miss Pleasant," she says in a shrill and haughty voice, "and I was born in Virginia in 1853, at the end of December. My masters gave me to their little daughter for Christmas and she was very nice to me. I did not learn to read, but I know many things. I know it's an Italian, that Columbus, who discovered America, he had a black man with him, Chris, who first sighted land. I know that you never get sick if you eat onions: I have not seen a doctor since 1865. I know there are three kinds of people: the ones who are kept poor, the ones who live in an ordinary way, and the rich. I know how to pick cotton—like this, fingers together and pulling upward."

Miss Pleasant lifts her skirt and runs her hand over the folds of her white embroidered petticoat that hangs all the way down to the floor.

"My master, Buck Walker, was very rich," she says. "He had five hundred women and children and I don't know how many men. All his friends had a hundred head of slaves. There was one cook in the morning and another in the evening; each of the master's children had his own servant, and when poor people came to talk to Buck Walker, he answered through the door to prevent them from seeing his face. I started working at the age of seven, and when I was ten, I was sent to pick cotton in the fields. I was a slave, I was beaten, and God knows, I had to work hard.

"My uncle, my mother's brother, escaped to Canada. Some dressed as women to flee, they went to Boston, from there it was easy to cross the border.

"I was six years old when John Brown came to talk in Lynchburg. He spoke very well, that man. He said, 'God didn't allow anyone to have slaves.' All the slave owners, Buck Walker, James Bruce, and the others got together and said that John Brown was ruining the country. They went to get him and took him away, and us kids, we ran after them. In 1859, they hanged John Brown at Harper's Ferry. He climbed up onto the scaffold and died like a gentleman because he was a gentleman. He stretched out his arms over the black crowd and said: 'You will be free.'"

Stepping daintily, Miss Pleasant meanders through History and its embroidered legends. She'd seen John Brown, the great revolutionary. She'd heard the first shots of the Civil War.

"The blacks were fleeing the plantations and hiding in the woods. They stopped by Yankee homes and showed them the way. We children marched with sticks over our shoulders, and we sang the White song:

> *Hep! Hep!*
> *I'll kill this Negro if he misses his step.*

Then we learned other words to sing to the same tune:

> *Hep! Hep! Hep ! O!*
> *We ain't slaves no more.*

"You couldn't sing those words in front of Whites, or say the name John Brown. But they made us pray for a Confederate victory.

"I saw the Civil War, my son fought in the Cuban war, my grandsons in the Great War, I had fourteen children, thirteen of them are dead, and in a minute my great-granddaughter will be home from school: the government should give me a pension, don't you think?"

She bends effortlessly, opens an old suitcase, and spreads out on the bed a treasure trove of lace and tulle, skirts, miraculously voluminous.

"This one I bought it in 1877, and this one I wore in 1880. It took six meters of cloth to make a skirt."

She adds: "When I was young, Blacks and Whites thought I was beautiful. It was after the Civil War, Confederate money was worthless: I made a folding screen with their banknotes. That's when I saw my master Buck Walker again. He had nothing left, and I was able to offer him tea and a clean bed. And I said (Miss Pleasant's voice is contemptuous, pitiless): "I'm happy to be able help my enemy."

Mary Lou is home from school. She clutches her great-grandmother's skirts and looks at us questioningly.

"Miss Pleasant, are blacks today free?"

She laughs a fierce and mocking laugh.

"They are more slaves than we were," she said. "We at least were dressed and fed. In my day, blacks were beaten, today they kill them."

Slaves more than ever. Cross the Harlem River, go up Jerome Avenue in the Bronx. At the corner of 167th Street, on Burnside Avenue, at about eleven in the morning, you will see a slave market.

Dozens of black women from Harlem are crowded on the sidewalk. There they are, each clutching a bundle, leaning against the lampposts and walls, like prostitutes on 116th Street. Waiting.

A white woman comes by. She approaches slowly, examining the black women, appraising the width of their shoulders, the thickness of the joints. Having completed the inspection, she approaches the woman who looks the most robust.

"Twenty cents an hour," she says. "For the afternoon."

The white woman is not rich, she does the housework herself. But from time to time, help is needed: one of these beasts of burden, who in three hours will clean three weeks of accumulated filth.

"I'll go up to twenty-five cents," says the lady, and with an over-familiar gesture, lays her hand on the unemployed woman's arm to furtively assess the swell of the muscles.

The slave picks up her bundle and follows her new mistress. She has not eaten today, and her shoes are full of holes. Since the abolition of slavery, there is nobody to feed or dress her.

James Ford is silent. He lays down his pencil, then carefully folds in fours and places on a stack of newspapers the piece of paper, black as Harlem.

GODS

"On a stormy, frozen night, a ragged little boy was standing in the street.

"That afternoon, the landlady had come to tell his mother that she had to pay the rent by the end of the day or leave.

"The ragged little boy knew his mother and sisters were sick. He ventured out into the street with his schoolbooks and the transaction worked well.

"A sweet old lady came by; he stretched out his hand and said, 'Please, ma'am, buy my last book so my people won't be evicted.'"

"No sooner had he opened his mouth than the lady said: 'Of course.' She put a ten-dollar bill in his hand, took the book and went on her way.

"The rent was paid! The rent was paid! And that night, before bed, the ragged little boy prayed that the sweet old lady would be blessed."

This poem appeared on the children's page of the *Amsterdam News*, a Harlem black newspaper. It was written by a little girl called Dorothy Hendrix. Such are the dreams of black children.

There is little difference, except in terms of age, between Dorothy Hendrix and the countless idle dreamers who fill Harlem with the droning of their utopias. Ghosts of sweet old ladies roam the skies of the black capital, distributing phantom ten-dollar bills.

Centuries of national pride held in, human dignity trampled, cry out for escape hatches, which act as safety valves for the white bourgeoisie. Whether the Black dreams of Africa or the Kingdom of Heaven, as long as he counts on the sweet old lady's ten dollars to pay his rent, he'll keep quiet.

Better than that, it all provides someone with an additional source of income. Nowhere can you find as many fortune-tellers and snake oil merchants as in Harlem. "Are you depressed, anxious, poor? Do you want happiness? Come see me and that will all change."

What Harlemer is not discouraged? Does not desire happiness? And what destitute person does not want to buy *The Authentic African Key of Dreams* to learn that corn in a dream means wealth, a Bible means simple pleasures, and a city, wealth. They spend their last pennies to purchase incense "made with dragon's blood" or consult Professor Gale, "Wizard of the West Indies." They pay a fortune for creams purported to whiten their skin, and lotions to make their hair long and straight, to be the equal, at least, of the most underprivileged, unemployed White.

Three-quarters of the buildings in Harlem belong to Whites. Theaters, movie houses, nightclubs in Harlem have white bosses. Stores in Harlem line the pockets of white shop owners, and the mannequins who smile out of store windows and the models on billboards are white.

And nickels and dimes become ten-dollar bills between the fingers of the sweet old lady.

There are also *numbers*, a surefire source of revenue for American gangsters since the end of Prohibition. Every evening, a number whose three figures are indicated by the results of pari-mutuel betting or the day's maximum and minimum temperatures, brings betters a return of one hundred times their stake. The win seems huge, but the player has only one chance in a thousand to guess the number that comes up, even if he's used "inspiration incense" or subscribes to *Black Horse*, a weekly paper devoted to numbers.

Each block has its *runner* who, under the guise of selling candy or cigarettes, takes bets and pays the winners. Hundred of runners are placed under the authority of a *controller*. At the top are the big bosses, the *bankers* who have divided New York into zones and are never bothered by the police.

More than half of Harlemers play the *numbers* and most days lose between five and twenty-five cents.

And the sweet old lady, surrounded by bodyguards, opens new bank accounts, and buys cars, estates, jewelry, police, and politicians.

There is also alcohol: whiskey that smacks of petroleum; and drugs, heroin the most common, some cocaine and opium; also marijuana, the *grass* whose praises are sung in the song "La Cucaracha," rolled into cigarettes called *reefers*.

Caught in this web of misery and narcotics, of *numbers* that are never the right ones, and of prophecies taking too long to come true, the girls go earn a few pennies by getting their bellies ploughed, the boys remember the gesture they perfected as children of emptying a wooden hand gun into the head of a schoolmate. They kill: to dream of killing means an inheritance; and they kill themselves: to dream of suicide means freeing yourself of a useless worry.

Other, more benign escape hatches are available to residents of Harlem. On Wednesday evenings at the Apollo Theater, a black music hall, amateurs take to the stage after superstitiously touching a log in the wings. They cling to the microphone and the singing begins. After a measure, the pianist nonchalantly lowers his hands to the keyboard, and one by one the instruments come in. The audience has brought whistles and bells. If the song is too slow or too fast by a fraction of a second, it is drowned out in a torrent of hue and cry, but if the tempo is right, if the singer's husky voice trails languorously from quarter tone to quarter tone, hands start drumming, shoulders rolling, and the applause brings the house down. Then the orchestra comes alive, and the back curtain rises on the solid frame of Louis Armstrong, handkerchief in hand, all thirty-two teeth flashing, or the silhouette of Duke Ellington, ready to pounce.

The hiccups and hoots of the jazz continue through evenings of dance, organized daily by clubs, associations, or simply neighbors raising rent money for a tenant facing eviction. Dreaming of dancing means an inheritance, and they dance the Trucking and the Lindy (Lindbergh) Hop to the sounds of one of the best orchestras in the world, from the Savoy double ballroom to a tiny café in upper Harlem where salt crunches under the couples' feet and whose pianist, also in charge of the coat check, doesn't stop playing when drunken customers smash their champagne glasses on the keyboard, but simply changes octave to keep from cutting his fingers.

Dance is an essential element of Harlem "high society" life, as well as bridge: dreaming of cards means happiness. The clubs that abound in the Black capital have no other purpose. Their members are fond of French names: *The Chic Clique Club, La Gai Veuve Social Club, The Regal De Luxe Debutantes, Les Jolies Mesdames Bridge Club*. During the day, members—if they are not unemployed—head downtown to cook and clean for Whites. Evenings, rid of their aprons and uniforms, for a few hours they live the life they've only observed through an entrance door or the door of a Pullman, a sham facsimile of moving picture glamour unspooling on the screens of Harlem.

And little Bernardine Blessit writes a poem for the children's page of the *Amsterdam News* about a young Harlem girl who goes to the movies to dream about "mansions and servants . . . She's just a steno, but sees herself in an ermine cloak and married to the hero of the film."

The illusion of high society goes hand in hand with the illusion of political activity. It is concentrated in the "brotherhoods," Masonic societies and others too, simulacra of parliamentary bodies where Blacks can among themselves indulge in games of debates, elections and intrigues. These "brotherhoods" are also common among Whites, but those ones are closed to Blacks. More than a quarter of the Harlem population belong to lodges with names such as "The Morning Star," "Toussaint Louverture," or "United Sons of Oneida." Some old members have not missed a meeting in fifty years.

In front of a bookstore on 125th Street, used books are divided into three categories: novels, ten and fifteen cents; detective stories, twenty-five cents; religion, thirty-five cents. Of all the sweet old ladies who haunt the Harlem heavens, there is none more tenacious or insidious than religion.

For three centuries, the Church was the only form of social life open to Blacks. It was a meeting place, a school for slavery and sometimes revolt, a wellspring of gossip and simulacrum of equality, university and society dance-club. The Association of Protestant Churches of New York list in its directory 120 black temples of every confession. The sects long forgotten in Europe, the heresies that Rome ceased to fight after the Reformation for lack of heretics, flourish today at the top of the Island of Manhattan. The thirteen shades of baptism; the Congregationalists, grandsons of the Puritans, merged since 1929 with the Christian Church; the Lutherans; the Moravian Brethren, the disciples of Jan Hus; the African Episcopalian Methodists; the African Episcopalian Methodists of Zion; the Presbyterians; the Episcopal Protestants; the Adventists who, since 1843, have been waiting for the second coming of Jesus Christ, those of the Seventh Day who believe in the prophecies of Mrs. Ellen White, and those of the Church of God, who do not; all these hybrids and many others have churches, pastors, and faithful between the shores of the Hudson and the Harlem River. There are also Catholics, Jews, but most of all a dusting of chapels in the ditches along the roads that lead from religion to club, from Christianity to more primitive forms of superstition, from the heart of New York to the center of Africa, those infinitesimal pockets of faith with solemn and complicated names who set up shop in a dry cleaner's basement or in a room above a hair salon.

Mother Horn's Church is on the first floor of a building on Lenox Avenue. A large room. An orchestra pit in the back, next to a stage. Sitting on the chairs, the audience. Facing them, female celebrants in long white coats and little white caps: they look like nurses. A woman recites prayers on the stage. The drumming goes on without a moment's pause, the pianist plays a tune that is somewhere between a hymn and the blues, some bars repeated ten times, a hundred times.

Kneeling in front of their chairs, men and women pray, silently at first, and then quietly begin to moan, eyes closed, heads thrown back. The moans swell like a single breath, two words float to the surface: "O! Jesus!" Louder: "Oh! Jesus!" and their cries lengthen: "O-o-o-oh! Jee-suss!" and hands slowly rise, palms forward, fingers spread, arms bent, the cries dissolve into a sobbing wail: "Oh! Jesus!"

The singing begins again, punctuated by drumrolls and hand-clapping. The flock of hysterical nurses leaps, always on the spot, always vertically, and their feet pound the floor like drumsticks the skin of a drum. A tall Black lies coiled on the stage. His head forms a right angle with his neck, and we see his horizontal profile and thick lips. "Lord," the Black yells, "what a wonderful road, Lord. Open your hearts tonight. Lord. He's at the door and knocking. Lord. Praise God. Hallelujah. Lord. He is here. Lord. Hallelujah. Say, you're going to have yourself some fun tonight. Hallelujah." He recites more and more loudly and quickly, interrupting his arm-shaking to wipe the sweat from his face.

Through the virgin forest of outstretched arms, the tom-tom, hoarse and monotonous, sounds the charge. Planted on the stage, a microphone absorbs the shouting and chanting: the Mother Horn chapel is "the first radio-church in Harlem."

Mud and garbage have overtaken 115th Street, and the houses on either side are as filthy as the street. First, a Chinese laundry, then the "Iglesia de Dios Pentecostal Latino-americana Inc.," farther on, "Tipografía Puerto Rico"; then the "Democratic Vanguard Club for a better Harlem," a closed synagogue with smashed stained-glass windows, a grocery store, and the Kingdom of Heaven.

The Kingdom is dilapidated and there a crowd is gathered on the stairs. Miss Light of Day, one of the sixty secretaries, comes to meet us.

"We would like to see the Father."

"He's dictating letters."

"Will we have to wait long?"

"When we come to Him, we lose all sense of time."

"Will you tell him that we're here?"

"Even if I didn't, he would know."

"It's wonderful," chorus the black women on the landing. "Father Divine is God Almighty."

Father Divine has nearly sixty thousand followers, about half of them in Harlem. In the United States, there are 144 "annexes" of the Kingdom of Heaven. We recognize these dormitories, restaurants, shelters, garages, and shops by the words written at the entrance: "God" or "Thank you, Father," which replace the "excuse me's" and "thank you's" of life today, or "peace," which means "hello" and "farewell." These are very modest paradises where Blacks can stay warm, get enough to eat, and regain some of their human dignity.

A mulatto woman beckons. Six stenographs come toward us: the letter dictation has ended. A door opens. The word "God" has been carved all the way through the wood so the light shines through.

A man gets up to greet us. He's very slight and must be over fifty. Bald, a little mustache, slightly hooked nose, eyes very close-set and bright, high forehead, tiny ears, almost no eyebrows, plump neck nestled in the collar of a gray jacket.

Father Divine gives me a chubby little hand and sits down at the table, covered with bundles of letters. Half-buried, a booklet entitled "4,000 Frequently Used English Words." Above him a star dangles from the ceiling, bearing the inscription: "Our Sweet Father."

Miss Light of Day has come with us. She gets settled, ready to take shorthand: every single word the Father utters is committed to paper.

"The work of the Government of Justice," says Father Divine, "will be taken into account because it is very far reaching. It takes hold of men's minds, and not only from a social perspective. It is morally transforming and gives men the strength to become new creatures. The authentic *practicality* of God comes down to earth and into the hearts and lives of those who dwell here below, God becomes real, tangible, and practical, while religions, as they have been taught to you by the masters of the Faith, were unprofitable and impractical. Where is the advantage in being a believer if your religion doesn't help you achieve something in life, something for the good of humanity?"

The chirping of the canaries mingles with the gurgle of the radiator. On the right, a stuffed dove spreads its wings from the top of a miniature column. A copper platter commands: "Worship the Divine Father." Pressed against the wall, side by side, are bundles of newspapers, a metal filing cabinet, an armchair whose cushion is embroidered with the word "God," two photos, walnuts in a vase, a radio.

"I want all men to be equal," says Father Divine, "and I know I will perfect whatever I undertake, with or without the assistance of other organizations; with the Communists whose interpretation is closest to mine, with or without them I shall succeed. I will, with my millions of followers, sacrificing their bodies if necessary, as I have sacrificed my own thirty-two times at the hands of lynch mobs when I started to fight color prejudice in the South and the Midwest."

A childish smile reveals his teeth, stained black at the root, and a hole in the upper jaw: the Divine Father is missing his left canine.

This God, his name radiant with miraculous legends, his watch chain draped across his belly, is a special God, created like his peers in the image of man, and they too are special men: Blacks exploited, starving and terrorized whom heavenly paradise no longer satisfies.

The word "Black" must not be pronounced in his presence, because it is a term "that separates." You say: "so and so" or "those people."

"Whatever your profession, especially in the United States, if you are called 'so and so'—the customary expression in this part of the Western world—and the way I would be commonly designated—if that is what you are called, whatever your skills or occupation, you will receive a lower salary than another person designated by the name of a different race or nationality.

"Why is it so?" he asks. "This vulgar name was given to sell what they call 'those people' into slavery, to treat them with contempt and brutality. They were given this common name so that exploiters and capitalists could lower their value, buy the ones they could get in Africa and elsewhere, reduce them to slavery and maintain them, after so-called emancipation, and up to the present time, in a state of inferiority, preventing them, you see, from getting a normal salary and enjoying their constitutional rights."

The voice grows more solemn.

"So I ask: Which is worse, the outlaw or the one who uses the law to steal from the poor and needy?"

We go down into the great hall of the Kingdom where a blue, red, purple, green crowd disappears beneath a volley of handkerchiefs saluting the entry of the Divine Father. These winged handkerchiefs swirl and quiver to the beat of the music. Father Divine makes his way to the stage through an avalanche of handkerchiefs.

> *Father, Father, I'm in love with you,*

sings the crowd.

> *Father, Father, you are so kind and genuine.*
> *Father, Father I'm in love with you,*
> *I will shape myself to your will.*

The walls are plastered with flags and banners. "Father Divine is the Dean of the universe." "Peace. Peace. Peace." "Father Divine is the wonderful counselor, the Prince of Peace." "Father Divine is Almighty God."

Up on the stage, Father Divine shakes his watch chain: others may lose all sense of time, but not he! It's Sunday evening, songs and speeches are broadcast for an hour thanks to a toothpaste laboratory that is particular about its advertising.

A black girl approaches the microphone. The white speaker asks her with paternal affection:

"Your name?"

"Anne Davis."

"Your age?"

"Nine."

"Do you go to school, Anne Davis?"

"Yes."

"Do you know Father Divine?"

"Yes."

"And who is he?"

"God."

The applause continues even after the interviewer has started speaking again.

"Do you brush your teeth? To do it properly, you squeeze a half-inch of Laboratories Toothpaste onto the brush . . ."

Now the Divine Father is speaking, and to the rhythm of his words, a blue feather framed by the window at the back of the stage dances on a black head. He speaks in a hoarse voice, throat contracted, gesticulating, interrogating the audience. He talks to the room, addresses the 144 annexes of his kingdom, and also himself.

A murmur rises in the room: "Yes, Father. Yes, God. That is admirable."

If these men and women are there, smiling blissfully at the performance of the little fellow they call "God," it is because he talks to them about racial equality, the evils of capitalism and paradise on

Earth. They are there because the white traders stole their ancestors, made them slaves, treated them like beasts of burden when they remained docile and like wild animals when they dared to revolt, they taught them the use of alcohol, drugs, gambling, prostitution and begging, inoculated them with tuberculosis and syphilis, have lynched more than four thousand even since 1900, taught them about comfort while making it inaccessible, dangled before their eyes the sources of education only to deny them admission, and gave them a God to pray to, fear, and obey: the inexorable white God, the faithful God of the pious Rockefellers and the devout Henry Ford, Judge Lynch, and Theodore G. Bilbo, the Mississippi senator who puts muzzles on the pickaninnies he gets to pick vegetables in his garden.

MEN

"Uncle Tom" is a term of contempt. It refers to the Black who always says yes, who revels in his slavery. There are still many "Uncle Toms" in the South, fewer in Harlem.

The attitude of the Whites is the cause of black nationalism. Pitted against the so-called scholars who claim to demonstrate, through anthropology, the inferiority of the black race are scholars and poets such as Frederick Douglass, Booker T. Washington, Paul Laurence Dunbar.* The tradition of victors since Chaka, Bantu warrior, and El Hadj Omar, Toucouleur conqueror, to Toussaint Louverture,** Behanzin, Menelik, and the last of the line, Joe Louis, provide consolation for beatings and humiliations. And since it is enough to have two hundred fifty-sixths black blood in your veins

---

* Frederick Douglass (c. 1810–95), politician and writer. Born a slave, he would become one of the most famous American abolitionists of the nineteenth century. Booker T. Washington (1856–1915) was a teacher, writer, and activist who primarily defended the rights of black Americans. Paul Laurence Dunbar (1872–1906) was an African American poet. (French editor's note.)

** Toussaint Louverture (1743–1803). Leader of the Haitian revolution, he is known for having been the first black leader to defeat the forces of a European colonial empire in his own country. (French editor's note.)

to be excluded from the white community,* we will claim for ourselves great mulattos, glorious quadroons and octaroons: Alexandre Dumas or Pushkin. The complete works of Dumas are found in all the libraries of Harlem, and there's even a Dumas Hotel; every year on the anniversary of Pushkin's death, the black press devotes articles to him and publishes his portraits.

Harlem is deeply shaken by any event involving the black race. During the winter of 1935–36,** the portrait of the Negus and the Ethiopian colors were displayed in storefronts, and on lapels. Nationalist organizations gave dinners "in honor of Ras Seyoum, Ras Birru, Ras Kassa, and many other noble fighters and their valiant conduct on the battlefields of Ethiopia to defend the rights and dignity of our race." Kids with wooden guns pursued the divisions of Marshal Badoglio through the mountains of Harrar, the mirror image of Lenox Avenue snowbanks. In the *Amsterdam News*, little Clara Taylor published the poem "Ethiopia":

> *We gaze, beyond the sea*
> *Hill, plain and vale.*
> *It is a country forever,*
> *Our free homeland.*

This fierce nationalism is not without its dangers. It may further isolate the Blacks of North America. This is where labor organizations come in. The union center on 125th Street, The Pullman Car

---

* *The African-American* from February 15, 1936, published three portraits of Pushkin and an article in which we read that "Pushkin's great-grandfather on his mother's side was a black Ethiopian general in the service of Peter the Great of Russia, who had married a Russian aristocrat. Thus, the poet was at least one-eighth African . . . Pushkin is one of the immortals. Red Russia honors him today as much as Tsarist Russia did a century ago, for the poet was a champion of the people. His *Ode to Liberty* led to his deportation from the capital. Seeing how the Russian Church impoverished the people, he spoke positively about atheism and lost his job in the civil service. For his entire life, he got into trouble because he believed that ordinary people have the right to live in peace, be paid for their work and benefit from the country's prosperity." The article is followed by a version of *The Pistol Shot*, the collective work of three lacks: Pushkin, who wrote the story, Alexandre Dumas, who translated it from Russian into French, and Mercer Cook, who translated the French version into English. (Author's note.)

** The Ethiopian (or Abyssinian) Crisis—1935/36 Italy invaded and conquered Ethiopia. In 1936, Emperor Haile Selassie I was forced into exile and Ethiopia became annexed to Italian East Africa. (Translator's note.)

Workers' Union on 136th, the Harlem chapter of the International Red Aid, Harlem Chapter of the Communist Party, the Harlem Unemployed Council, the Harlem People's Library are all meeting places and organizational factors.

Every day, Merrill Work takes delegations of unemployed to the bottom of the city to face down the civil servants' courteous contempt with his firm and glacial politeness. Black and white picketers stand guard in front of shops that turn away black labor. Every week, Rosa goes to the "slave market" in the Bronx, puts a motherly arm around the waist of a young unemployed woman, and leads her to a coffee shop, saying with a smile that reveals her teeth:

"Don't let me out of your sight, my love. The union will take care of you."

And the girl responds eagerly, sipping her coffee, her first of the day: "Of course we won't let go of you."

Patterson, one of the nine Scottsboro defendants, has been sentenced to seventy-five years of prison. Beside me, a young Black tells how he was nearly lynched in Florida:

"There was a white woman who made advances to me. Except I kept my distance. I'd been warned. I'm from the South. I was scared."

His neighbor says:

"It's not their fault. It's a backward population, raised for generations by rich farmers and industrialists. The only thing that exists for them: tree, a rope, and a man."

A man, a ladder, and a blackboard. Clumps of dirty snow line the sidewalks littered with cans, waste paper, vegetable peels. An old car stands between two hand-carts; written on its door is, "God is love, John 4:8." A chilly unrelenting wind sweeps ice down the road.

The ladder stands at the corner of Lenox Avenue. A hasty hand has scribbled on the blackboard:

January 24, 3 p.m.
OZIE POWELL
Scottsboro Boy
killed in a car by a police officer
while he was leaving the "court"

Someone added the word "cracker" over the word "police."

From the top of the ladder, a Black shouts the news. His face stands out in sharp relief against the background of low opaque clouds. Passersby stop, bent double by the wind that slashes at the speaker's words; they read the news, look at the man speaking, the snow, the trash, the car, and at the bottom of the ladder, two small shivering American flags. The thermometer reads 3°.

A hundred yards farther, a leaflet is being handed out: "Protest Meeting Tonight."

The meeting is held in a room full of Blacks; here and there, the shock of a flaxen blond head: Finns. One after the other, the speakers take the stand. The murder of a Black is a common occurrence. Even Harlem newspapers rarely report them as front-page news. But Powell is different. Scottsboro is the symbol of the greatest battle since the abolition of slavery.

Coins jingle at the bottom of a hat being passed around: they're taking up a collection.

"Well! What about some bills? Dollars?"

A man gets to his feet. He is redheaded, thin, his eyes are blue, his face marked by work around the temples and the edges of his mouth. He wears a cap and an old green coat. Slowly, the Finnish worker digs into his pocket and draws out a bill, green and worn as his overcoat.

The president asks for volunteers to sell a special edition of the *Daily Worker*, just arrived, in the streets and the homes of Harlem. Hands are raised, men and women's hands, white hands and black hands.

"If you knew the South the way I do, you'd understand the meaning of the Scottsboro case. You've got the lords in their mansions, self-satisfied and confident, so sure that nothing can ever put up resistance to them or their desires. Historically they've exploited and cheated Blacks, imprisoned and lynched them whenever they saw fit. And suddenly someone put a hand on their shoulder and said: stop! It was a mighty hand, the hand of the working class. The bosses were stunned, horrified, frightened. I know it. And I also know that since the beginning of the battle of Scottsboro, every black worker, every black farmer has breathed a little more easily and held his head a little higher."

Angelo Herndon is sitting in front of me. He is only twenty-three. His great-grandmother was a slave. His grandmother was nearly lynched during the Civil War. His father was a miner. At thirteen, Angelo went down to the mines like his father. Ten, twelve, fourteen hours a day, he loaded coal into mine cars. He worked in the north part of the mine with the other Blacks; the south part was reserved for Whites.

"My parents were Republicans and they told me that Lincoln had freed the slaves and that we should put all our hopes in his party, the Republican Party. But I began to have doubts. There I was, being cheated, and the victim of color prejudice. Every two weeks, the newspapers reported a lynching in the South. And yet there was a Republican government in Washington, and it did nothing. My people told me to have faith in God: he would take care of everything. I'd read a multitude of religious pamphlets, but I couldn't believe them. I thought it was useless for a Black to go to Heaven, because he'd only be there to shine white men's shoes."

That was in 1930. Herndon was seventeen. He was killing himself at the bottom of a mine only to see his pay dissolve between the expert fingers of the cashier, and his friends die through the negligence of engineers. He lived in the Black quarter and traveled in cars that bore the inscription: "Men of color." If a White man spoke to him, he had to reply, "Yes, sir."

"One day on my way back from work, I saw some fliers posted by the Birmingham unemployed council: 'Would you rather fight or starve to death?' A meeting was scheduled for that afternoon. I arrived in the middle of a speech a white speaker was giving. I didn't understand everything, but I was struck by the little I caught: workers can't get anything without a fight, Blacks and Whites must unite to overcome. Then a Black spoke from the same platform, and I realized this was what I'd been looking for all my life. At the end of the meeting, I walked up and gave my name.

"We tried to set up an office. It was closed down by police. We saved money, one cent at a time, and printed out tracts on an old machine, in silence, with the curtains closed. At night we went out and slipped them under people's doors. Sometimes we announced that a meeting would take place in half an hour, at a certain street corner. Only one speaker went and spoke as little as possible, gave out brochures and left before the police arrived. The bosses were afraid and the Ku Klux Klan took action. Its members paraded through the Black quarter making public announcements: "Communism must be destroyed. Alabama is a good place for good niggers, but a bad place for niggers who want social equality."

Herndon presented his cause to the miners and farmers of Alabama.

"A black preacher denounced me to a black stoolpigeon. The two of them tried to terrorize me. Finally, they called the sheriff, and a crowd started gathering to lynch me. I was saved by taking the first train out of town. A white farmer gave me the money for my ticket."

The region was thrown into crisis. Armed mining company agents patrolled the roads. Angelo was arrested several times.

"When arresting me once, the police asked me the address of a white militant. 'Where's Tom?' they said. 'We'd like to get our hands on that son of a bitch.'—'I haven't seen Tom for days,' I said. One of the policemen punched me in the mouth. 'It's *Mister* Tom to you, you bastard!' he shouted."

Herndon had to leave Alabama and take refuge in Georgia. That was in 1932, when the Georgian authorities decided to close down the unemployment funds. Angelo organized a demonstration: a thousand men, Black and White. The next day, the benefit system was restored. And three weeks later, the police arrested Herndon. He was nineteen years old.

"Before I arrived at the prison, the guards told the inmates I'd murdered several people, and they handed out sticks and bottles to finish me off. I was the only political prisoner. I spoke to my cell-mates, I explained what I'd done and why I was locked up. I spoke for two hours, maybe more. They understood. Nobody used sticks. The guards took me to a cell where they'd set up an electric chair and ordered me to sit in it or tell them 'the whole truth.' I thought I was going to die, I refused to talk. Then they charged me with inciting a revolt."

There is a law in Georgia that dates from the time of slavery. "Whomsoever introduces or transports within State limits written or printed matter inciting the negroes, bonded or free, to insur-rection, revolt or resistance, is guilty of a major crime punishable by death." After sixty-eight years, this law was going to serve again.

"The trial took place on January 16, 1933. The prosecution dis-played books seized from me and read passages to the jury. These were books published in America and sold in all bookstores. I had to answer a lot of questions. Did I think the bosses and the gov-ernment should pay unemployment insurance? That Blacks should enjoy full equality with Whites? Did I feel that the working class was able to manage the factories and mines and take over the gov-ernment? Did I think we could do without bosses? I told them that's what I thought, and many other things besides."

The prosecution declared that being a Communist called for capital punishment. "Annihilate this detestable thing," the prose-cutor cried, "with a verdict that will automatically result in elec-trocution." But the jury, magnanimous, sentenced Herndon to twenty years on the chain gang. Twenty years of breaking stones and building roads for as long as the sun is in the sky, dragging chains on your ankles. No prisoner has survived more than ten years of this labor camp.

The accused spoke in turn. "You can do what you like with Angelo Herndon," he said. "Feel free to condemn him, put him in prison. But thousands of other Herndons will appear. You can kill one, two, several labor activists. But you cannot kill the working class." He was twenty years old.

"My lawyers appealed, and I ended up in prison again. I was hungry. I was sick. I wasn't allowed to see friends or read books that interested me. The guards didn't dare beat me or even insult me. They brought an issue of the *Daily Worker*, which I hadn't seen for months, and they tore it to pieces in front of me and scattered them on the floor of my cell. The months passed. Prisoners told me horrible stories about torture: chain-gang stories. I said goodbye to ten men who left the cell to sit in the electric chair."

Black farmers were organizing in the South, black workers were organizing in the North. The workers' organizations fought for Angelo's life. The courts tossed the case back and forth like a ball.

"There was a crooked banker in prison with me. He'd been released on bail of $8,000. Ten thousand was enough to pay for the release on bail of another prisoner, a murderer. As for me, the judge set the amount at $15,000: he was convinced that our organizations would never raise a fortune like that. As soon as I heard the news, I started getting ready to leave. The guards laughed at me. But I knew I was going to get out. And I got out. Black and white workers raised $18,000 in twenty-three days."

We go out into the street. Oxblood-colored houses teem with chapels and hair salons open at night. Jewish shops alternate with Chinese laundries. From corner to corner, kids pound on garbage can tom-toms and light big bonfires with old newspapers. At the door of Mount Olive Church, a sign says: "Here on earth, where all material things pass, religion remains." Material things pass in front of the temple: servants and the unemployed, beggars and prostitutes, and especially children, an essentially perishable commodity. At intersections, mounted police inspect the Avenue, twirling their clubs.

"You should go south," says Angelo. "New York—this is paradise."

I think of the little black boy across the street from where I live, his ancient felt hat with crenellations cut into its raised brim, who earns thirty cents a day shining shoes for the rare passersby; I see the ripped stockings of choristers in the Puerto Rican Theater on 116th Street, cadaverous black women diving into garbage cans up to the waist; I think of the Mulatto Dumas, and Pushkin, the great-grandson of an Abyssinian general, who, if they came to New York today, would be forced to live in Harlem, because of their black blood.

We've passed the Kingdom of Heaven and the head office of the International Red Aid, Mother Horn's Church to the right, the People's Bookstore to the left. We can already see Harlem Hospital and the Savoy sign. Suddenly, at the entrance of the Unemployed Council I see God Sabaoth. Like everyone in Harlem, he is black. White beard flowing over his chest, a nebula of gray hair forming a halo. He is huge, has to be six feet six inches. With indifference, he walks barefoot over the frozen mud sidewalk.

"That's Martin-Goes-Barefoot," says Angelo. "He was a slave when he was young."

I try to picture the road from slavery in 1860 to unemployment in 1936. The old man sees us. He comes toward us, smiles at Herndon, turns to me, asks:

"Are you a comrade?" He holds out his hand. "I'm a comrade, too," he adds.

NOTEBOOK

JANUARY 1936

New York. Midnight. I'm waiting for the bus at the corner of Forty-Second Street. A man approaches, mutters a few words. He
squeezes the coin I gave him in the palm of his hand, but cannot
make up his mind to leave. I ask: "Unemployed?" He nods. "What
do you do?"— "Auto mechanic. I worked for Ford in Detroit."—
"How do you get by?"— "I eat at a city refuge. I sleep in the
subway. For five cents, you take the Brooklyn line to the end, you
come back, you start again, all night. You wake up at the stops
when they slam on the brakes."— "Where are you going now?"—
"Anywhere."— "So let's walk. Is that all right with you?"— "Sure.
I haven't talked to anyone for a long time."— "No friends in New
York?"— "Yeah . . . guys like me. Others got married and you don't
see them anymore because you're ashamed."— "Have you been
unemployed for long?"— "Eighteen months. I haven't always been
like this." He points to his beard. "What are you going to do in
a month? In a year?"— "My future? I don't think I'll ever have
work again."— "Are you looking for work?"— "Why bother?"—
"So?"— "Lie down in Central Park for a policeman to wake me
up with a kick and chase me out. At least in New York, I can walk
around the way I am. In Chicago, if you're shabby, they send you to
jail for vagrancy. You get out, they put you back in again."

January 2. Read in the *New York Times*: "Henry Ford expects the return of prosperity. 'People are tired of doing nothing,' he says, 'and they go back to work.'"

The solitude of New York.

January 7. David Rubin, a thirty-three-year-old mechanic, was arrested today. Firemen discovered him in his smoke-filled room. Rubin explained that he had tried to set the furniture on fire. He was alone and very sad. He thought the fire would draw people to his room. "Either that or death," he said.

The Daily Worker published the following letter from a reader:

"I'm twenty years old, I'm a virgin and I have normal sexual impulses. Seeing as men don't find me particularly attractive and promiscuity is wrong, I am faced with the problem of the sexual life of the single woman. What do you recommend?"

A café on Forty-Second Street. Beside me, a made-up young woman is drinking a malted milk. Across from her, a young man eating a plate of vegetables says to her in a low and expressionless voice:

"I'm talking to you. I don't know you. I don't want to know you. Don't think I want to get to know you. I don't give a damn about you. But I'm talking to you. I need to talk to someone. You don't interest me. When you leave, I won't follow you. But I have to talk. I have to talk and I'm talking. I'm talking to you."

The woman doesn't even raise her eyes to look at him. She finishes her milk and goes. The boy stops talking. He's young. He's not ugly. He doesn't look unemployed.

A check is displayed in the front window of the Times Square Mission, at the corner of Forty-Third Street and Sixth Avenue:

No: Rom. 8, 32.   Anywhere. Any time.
THE BANK OF RICHES IN JESUS CHRIST
(RESOURCES UNLIMITED)

Pay to the order of bearer on demand
$ all your needs according to his riches in glory by
(Signed) Jesus Christ

January 10. Newspapers describe in detail the quadruple execution that just took place in Sing Sing. Robert Elliott, Sacco and
Vanzetti's executioner, arrived at the prison one hour before. Then
witnesses—reporters, policemen, doctors—took their places in the
room. Raymond Newman was taken in first. The youngest of a
family of eleven, said to have been an obedient son. The chaplain
escorted him to the chair. The executioner sent 2,200 volts through
the boy's body, which pitched forward but was restrained by the
straps. The guards laid the corpse on a white ambulance gurney,
and the next prisoner, Angelini, was strapped in. He kissed a cru-
cifix and said "My father." Two minutes later, he was gone. The
third, Gilbride, plodded in, cast a look of indifference at the witnesses and dropped his cigarette butt on the floor, where a guard
crushed it out with his heel. He died with one eye half-closed, the
other wide open. Next was the gang leader, Orley. His father died
in a mine accident, his mother remarried, and as a young kid, he
had to leave home to make a living. He fell under the influence of
Nelson Clark, an important person, former candidate for governor
of Massachusetts, the "brains" behind the gang and currently in
prison for possession of stolen property.

The four boys, barely of legal age, were discovered by a policeman
while burgling a store. Orley killed the officer. The amount stolen
was forty-seven dollars.

On the independence of the freelance professions:
January 12. Two ads in the *New York Times*:
"Lawyer seeks position: trusts, agencies."
"Architect wishes to make contact with real estate agency."

Another ad in the same newspaper:

"To solve your problems with workers. Buy a New Jersey plant with non-unionized staff. Fully equipped."

Sign in a storefront for a power tools retailer, Lower Manhattan:
    "Church accessories: red light-bulbs with filaments in the shape of crosses."

At the Public Library.
    All day long, in the stairways and on the marble benches, women, mostly men. Some read newspapers they have picked off the ground, others sit doing nothing or dozing. Neatly dressed: hats and white collars, even starched collars, but the shoes are down-at-heel. Some know each other and quietly converse. Unemployed.

A young New York woman who is ill goes to see a healer. The healer tells her about a certain "Aunt Josephine," a witch who lives in a bungalow on a hilltop on Seventh Avenue and is on intimate terms with the devil.
    After several months the fraud is exposed.
    The girl said, "How was I supposed to know there wasn't a hill in the center of New York? I've never been there."

January 20. The governor of Indiana has just declared martial law in two counties where strikes are in progress. This is nothing new. In Vigo County, also Indiana, martial law has been in effect for six months for the same reason, and in Sullivan County for over two years. Strikers had better behave themselves.

A judge who found an Adventist guilty of not respecting the Sabbath received a letter from a resident of Knoxville. He offered a duck to anyone who could quote passages from the Scriptures that named Sunday as the Sabbath.

The *News* of Englewood reports that a hundred poor families of this rich Jersey City suburb eat straight from the trash cans, concluding: "This is a state of affairs that must be rectified at once, a state of affairs that any red-blooded citizen will want to put a stop to, even if it costs him his bottom dollar. The necessary amount must be raised immediately to build a waste incinerator that will put an end to these revolting practices."

To encourage readers to publish a few lines in the Classifieds on the umpteenth anniversary of the death of a relative, the *San Francisco Chronicle* publishes this ad:

> *IN MEMORIAM*
> *Revisit cherished moments*
> *by resurrecting the memory*
> *of days gone by.*
> *Fee: 30 cents a line.*

Posters in the subway (drawings and captions):

NO MORE CORNS! PAINLESS!
THE FIRST DROP STOPS PAIN INSTANTLY
(A blonde in a pink shirt, stretched out on her
stomach, feet in the air.)

DON'T LET BAD SKIN
RUIN YOUR COMPLEXION
(A blonde in profile.)

HAVE YOU FOUND THE SECRET
OF POPULARITY?
SUNNY HAIR THAT FRIENDS ADMIRE. IT CAN
BE YOURS, THANKS TO *SUNNY HAIR* BY . . .
(A blonde cheek-to-cheek with a fox.)

HAVE BREATH THAT STAYS SWEET.
(A couple kissing.)

THE LIP APPEAL OF MOVIE STARS.
(A couple kissing.)

SUCCESS IN LOVE IS GUARANTEED WHEN
SHOES ARE POLISHED WITH . . .
(The feet of a couple who beyond the shadow of a
doubt, are kissing.)

In Newton, a well-to-do suburb of Boston, Reverend Barth of the Unitarian Church delivered a five-word sermon: "Why hast Thou forsaken me?" The follow-up was performed by dancers.

January 30. Paul Di Bari, unemployed for two years, killed his wife with an ax and threw himself out the window. The Di Baris' two little girls told police that lately their father had been acting strangely. He'd scolded them when they laughed too loudly and thought they were laughing at him.

Here, the unemployed person is ashamed of his condition. In the country of "boundless opportunities," a jobless person must be inept, or, at best, a man with rotten luck. He sees only his personal case. Rockefeller made a fortune, but me, Di Bari, I'm good for nothing. My own daughters make fun of me.

To accept a cash unemployment benefit is to admit that one is inept. This mind set is starting to disappear, at least among the unemployed. But what years of misery it's taken for people to comprehend that twelve million cases of bad luck and ineptitude is due to something other than sheer coincidence.

Some time ago, John Jacob Astor III, heir to the financial dynasty of the same name, accepted an office job for twenty-five dollars a week in the offices of one of his companies. He wanted to "start at the bottom of the ladder and make his way to the top." It did not last long. He left today for a pleasure trip to Europe. Reporters questioned him on the change of heart.

"The job took all my time," he said. "I had to work eight hours a day and get to the office at nine in the morning. Impossible to get home before six in the evening."

"Are you in favor of the thirty-hour week?" a reporter asked

"Of course. Thirty hours is much easier than forty-eight."

40,000 BATTLE THE SNOW
(8 INCHES THICK)

40,000. Read: "people." Huge headlines sprawl across the front page of newspapers. Snow piles up in the streets. In the Bowery, the corpse of a barefoot man found by a patrol. A stranger took refuge in the doorway of a house and died. An old man was discovered, his body already cold, under heaps of old newspapers— his blankets. In an apartment, police found the frozen bodies of two retired schoolteachers; the women had been lying for four days without food on the kitchen floor next to a portable stove with no fuel. Etc., etc. The living stay warm as best they can. Every day, fires break out in Harlem, the East Side, Brooklyn. There are always victims. It would seem that fires compensate for the deficiencies of central heating. Millions live crushed together in the slums of New York. *Millions.* Read: "people."

A DELUXE VACUUM CLEANER

To Miriam and George

There are three kinds of garbage in Hollywood. By dint of sorting it, every resident becomes something of a rag picker. Dry combustible garbage: newspapers, cartons, paper bags, which everyone burns at the back of the yard in an incinerator resembling a small termite mound. Non-combustible dry garbage: ashes, tin cans and empty bottles, packed in boxes that are removed every two weeks. Wet garbage ferments for three days, is collected twice a week by the city of Los Angeles and sold to pig farmers, so they say.

Through the window of his office, where a large fly is buzzing, the screenwriter observes the open truck driven by a Black, inching along the avenue lined with Seville orange trees. Another Black follows on foot. In a single movement, he picks up the garbage cans, empties them into the truck, and pitches them behind him. They roll on the sidewalk with a metallic hullabaloo. Garbage cascades over the top of the truck and onto the road, the orange trees and the Black.

A sedan stops in front of the house. The man who emerges is tall and boney. He goes up to the door, rings the bell.

Jane, the new maid, is not there: ten times a day, she escapes to the corner of Sunset Boulevard in the always-disappointed hope of seeing a celebrity. The screenwriter opens the door.

The visitor introduces himself. His real name does not matter; let's call him Mr. Knight. He has a small white mustache and baby blue eyes. Seen up close, his suit is slightly frayed.

"He's back," he said, as if reciting the words by heart. "The War is over: he came back."

Hollywood farts through silk, nowhere in the world are there so many silk merchants, but there are even more hot-air floggers, from psychoanalysts to Theosophists treating diseases, all imaginary, all incurable.

"Who's come back?" the writer cautiously inquires.

The Parker 51 or Jesus? He remembers that after Pearl Harbor, Lucky Strike packs, then green, turned white; the winds of economics and patriotism were blowing down on advertising, and one fine morning the country learned that "Lucky Strike Green had gone to war." The war now over, could it be that the Green will be back, loaded down with scars and medals?

Mona, the little girl next door, is playing hopscotch among the overturned garbage cans, trails of orange peels and coffee grounds. Her blond curls dance on her head. Mr. Knight has returned to his car. He opens the trunk, takes out a box and a bag.

"If I may?" He enters the office and kneels on the carpet. Chrome tubing glimmers in his hands. He gets up.

"Look," he says.

A cylinder on steel runners, a hose, nozzles, tubes, elongated, triangular, round brushes. "If I may?" Mr. Knight plugs in the device, which starts humming. Under the visitors' fingers, the hose comes alive, slithers along the floor, climbs the furniture, snakes up the walls, hurtles down the curtains from whose folds a big fly escapes and buzzes back and forth over an old suitcase, open in the middle of the room.

Outside, Mona stops jumping and disappears, as if vacuumed into her house.

Dust rushes into the cylinder, scraps of paper, cigarette butts, bits of wool—"my wife knits, too," says Knight—tufts of feathers, pins, petals, crumbs, a marble—"I have two daughters," says Mr. Knight, "but they're big now."

Telephones in the posh districts of Hollywood do not ring, they whisper. The screenwriter picks up the receiver. It's Mrs. Brighton, Mona's mother. She could have gone to the window and called out to him, but she feels that phoning is more dignified.

Mrs. Brighton has just received a call from Central Casting, where every Hollywood extra has a file. Mona must report to the studio in two hours, it's very important, but how are they to get there without a car? The screenwriter promises to drive her there with her daughter and hangs up. In Mr. Knight's inattentive hand, the pipe is sucking only air.

"Film," he said. "I did that, too."

The screenwriter thinks of his grocer's wife, once a dance teacher with a studio, and of the Chinese waiter in Ching How restaurant who once a year plays bit parts for Orientals in spy movies.

"Really?" says he.

Memories—he can see them coming, he can already hear the man confiding (as in brothels, all the girls are daughters of commanding officers), he's guessed it right down to the gestures: the hand disappearing into the pocket over the heart, drawing out a dog-eared wallet, smoothing out the three-line clippings and faded photos.

He takes the clipping Mr. Knight is handing him. Times Square New York, as it was circa 1920, and in the foreground the neon marquee of a movie theater.

"You're too young to remember," says the visitor.

Too young to remember, but not to recognize the film's title and the name of the director above the entrance.

"Are you Peter Knight?"

No Griffith of course, nor even a Borzage or a Cruze, but one of those fine craftsmen you read about in silent-film histories, who discovered stars more famous than himself, and nonetheless famous enough to have his name in sizzling letters in Times Square.

"Yes, they all came to my place," said Knight. "I, too, had a villa in Santa Monica, on the beach, near Marion Davies. Good food, drank champagne. French champagne. We only went there weekends. I had another house in Beverly Hills, a few doors down from Douglas Fairbanks."

"Those were the golden days," says the writer.

"Those were the good days."

He tugs at the cuff of his shirt, studies the suitcase at his feet, envelopes and cards spilling out of it. A brief silence. The buzzing of the fly fades into the hum of the motor. Mr. Knight pulls himself together. With a brittle gesture, he extends the hose and snaps up the fly on the wing.

"I had two cars and a swimming pool," he says.

He turns off the switch, opens the cylinder and pulls out a bag that he makes to empty—"If I may?"—at the bottom of the steps: a fleecy, fluffy little mound. He puts the bag back, presses a button. The vacuum cleaner is running, manufacturing emptiness.

"You can buy with confidence," Mr. Knight says, and you can't tell whether he's singing the praises of the merchandise or the salesman. "This is the deluxe model," he says.

Jane, the maid, is back. The writer watches her through the dining room door. If he called, she wouldn't hear; if he walked in front of her, she wouldn't see him. The real world no longer exists. Jane is completely absorbed. Her long horseface is grave, only her lips move. She is reading the gossip column in her newspaper.

There are a few dozen Hollywood gossip columnists lurking in studio corridors, slipping coins to the Maître D's of fashionable restaurants, buying a drink for the secretaries and accosting the servants of stars. Anything goes: dry and wet garbage, combustible and noncombustible.

Those are the small-time tattlers. Big columnists don't go to the trouble. They have secretaries who claw through the garbage for them.

At a friend's place, the screenwriter met one who works for the most powerful of these *Madame-Pipis*. This man with the well-groomed mustache came to ask intimate details about a star who was a friend of the hostess.

"Greta is already getting bad press," he reminded the screenwriter. "Her silence won't get her the sympathy vote."

The screenwriter reflected on the dangers of incurring the rancor of these slops-mongers, whose trough is nothing less than the entire American press.

The lady of the house studied the visitor with incredulity.

"Have you no shame?" she said quietly. "You, a healthy man who could be doing an honorable job: sawing wood or planting vegetables—how can you sink so low?"

The visitor stood up.

"Very well, Madame."

He bowed, went to the door. Hesitated, turned back. The blood had rushed to his forehead, his ears. They could hardly hear what he said.

"A man has to earn a living," he said. "I have five children."

In the dining room, Jane is still reading. The screenwriter looks down at the suitcase that Mr. Knight has swiped with the vacuum hose. Long ago he'd seen the suitcase, coated with dust, in an actress's dressing room. She was tired: she'd been on set all day. Tired and furious: two days earlier she asked the studio director that in future he give her films that bore some resemblance to reality; he'd offered her a raise that she refused; the next day he sent her a basket of flowers and half an hour later, a psychiatrist.

"Fan mail," she said, pointing to the suitcase.

Three thousand letters arrived in the past month, never opened; dry and combustible: ripe for the incinerator. The writer didn't have to beg to take them away.

He bends down, picks up a postcard:

"Dear Louise,
I collect portraits of stars and I would like to have yours.
Maxime A., Kankakee (Illinois)."

He picks up another:

"Dear Louise,
My name is Nancy Jean R. I live in Royal Oak (Michigan).
I have a sister. Her name is Margaret. Please send me a portrait
of you."

The phone rings. Mrs. Brighton and daughter are ready.

Through the window, from where he is sitting, the writer sees his neighbor hang up the receiver and head for the door.

He passes in front of Jane. The maid is still reading.

"Jane, what would you say to a new vacuum cleaner?"

She looks up at him absently. She's heard nothing.

In a sky where clouds are more rare than airplanes, the sun beams down on a two-dimensional set in Technicolor.

The writer's car cruises along spacious palm tree-lined boulevards. Left and right, tucked at the very back of impeccable lawns, white villas sprawl under red tile roofs. In the shadow of double and triple garages, outsized automobiles mysteriously shimmer. Against the backdrop, silent silhouettes come and go: the Japanese gardeners, black chambermaids and Filipino valets finish polishing Beverly Hills. Beverly Hills, where, in the evening, police stop pedestrians, suspects by definition, and where Mr. Knight too had a villa. Beverly Hills, the only place in the world that actually resembles the world as it appears in a Hollywood movie.

"That's the home of Joan Fontaine," says Mrs. Brighton.

She is sitting next to the writer. Once slender, she is verging on scraggy, her blond hair bleached before it turns white, the blood from her cheeks receded and waiting to return as red patches of broken veins.

To her right, Mona, slender, pink, and blond.

"It's annoying," says Mrs. Brighton, "you never know beforehand what it's going to be. The last time they made Mona smear chocolate all over her face."

She shrugs, runs her fingers through the little girl's permanent wave.

"And when you just get regular extra work, it's an entire day for five and a half dollars."

The car turns down Rodeo Drive. In front of the Romanoff restaurant, autograph hounds are ready to pounce, notebook and pen in hand.

"Only," Mrs. Brighton says, "you never know."

"I refused," said Mona.

"She didn't let them smear her face," said her mother. She repeats: "But you just never know. Maybe today."

She sinks into a pipe dream.

Beside her, Mona smiles her silly smile.

And so, ten times a year, mother and daughter head off in search of Paradise.

In the studio courtyard, in front of a white building, twenty other mothers are waiting, and as many children. Forty pairs of eyes take Mona in, envy her smile, hope that her nose is too upturned. A woman paws her little girl's permanent, another arranges her daughter's kiss curls. Mrs. Brighton returns their sidelong glances, feigns indifference.

They wait. Nobody talks, nobody moves.

A boy whistles, imitating various birds. A little girl walks on pointe along the asphalt: they watch her every move. She is very white, the faintest touch of makeup and the graceful, polished gestures of a dancer.

A woman approaches with her daughter and a three-year-old toddler, chubby-faced and curly-haired.

"I brought him just in case," she says, amidst general indifference. "You just never know."

A new mother arrives. Her daughter wears overalls and two braids down her back. Panic! Why didn't anyone else think of pigtails! What if *this* was the secret of success! Look at Margaret O'Brien. The permanent waves are starting to look tired—obsolete. The newcomer smiles: she's missing two teeth. The others breathe a sigh of relief.

There they are, wives of employees, of shopkeepers, small-property owners, doctors—every one of them resigned, like the insects that die the moment their eggs are laid.

A door opens. A man appears, looking at a list. The white girl marks out a dance step. The boy imitates a black bird. Another boy, a redhead, tap-dances: his steel-tipped soles clickety-click on the asphalt.

The man calls a name without looking at anyone. A child steps forward. His mother follows him with her eyes. As he passes, all the women assess him. The door closes. The waiting begins again.

"I should have guessed," says Mrs. Brighton, on the way back. Four children, including Mona, were chosen; tomorrow they'll do a day of regular extra work for $5.50.

The car drives through Beverly Hills. The midday sun makes the scenery flatter than flat. The palm trees are tinplate cutouts against the indigo sky. In front of the Romanoff, the autograph scavengers have multiplied.

"Sometimes the director will spot you on the set," says Mrs. Brighton.

"Did you see the dress of the dancer girl?" Mona says.

"It comes from Magnin's," says Mrs. Brighton. "Twenty-nine dollars."

"I want one like that for Christmas," says Mona.

"She believes in Santa Claus," says the writer.

"At her age it would be unfortunate," says Mrs. Brighton, "if she didn't."

"*Dear Louise,*

I am an admirer, and I've always wanted a photo of you to keep it as a sort of souvenir.

Zelda B.

Edenville, Orange Free State."

"*Dearest Louise,*

I would be thrilled if you would be so kind as to send me your photo, which I would like to frame for my bookshelf.

Mrs. G.

Malacca."

"*Dear Louise,*

Please give me your photo. I think you are very pretty. Very pretty. I have no money. I am poor. I cannot buy your photo. I love you very, very, very much.

Your friend Lola A.

Rio de Janeiro."

"*Miss,*

Could you find it in your heart to send me your true image? I would like to put it on my dressing-table so I can look at it and think of you. I'm sure it would chase all my worries away.

Candelaria T.

Iloilo. Philippine Islands."

Mr. Knight has come to deliver the vacuum cleaner. He carefully unwraps the parts, puts them together and tests that they are working. He would have liked to re-do the demonstration of the chrome triangle that sucks up the most stubborn threads, but the carpet is littered with letters. Mr. Knight counts the tubes and brushes one last time. All that's missing is the vaporizer to remove stains from the carpet. Mr. Knight apologizes: there were no more at the store, the part will be sent directly from the factory. He examines at length the signature on the writer's check.

"Was that you who worked on Olivia de Havilland's last movie?"

"Yes."

"In my day, we didn't write film-scripts, they were improvised on set. And it was the director who did everything. I had notes . . ."

He indicates the cuff of his shirt, but does not specify if that was where he wrote down his ideas.

"Times have changed," he said. "For three years I've been working on a story. I could go tell it to a producer, I know them all. But you know how people are. Last week, I ran into X on the street. I had him as an extra in a lot of my films, but I hadn't seen him since he became a star. We were talking about old times when a bit-part actor we both knew called in passing: 'Hi, Knight. How're the vacuum cleaners?' X jumped a little in surprise: 'What vacuum cleaners?' I told him the truth. He left without saying goodbye."

Mr. Knight smiled indulgently.

"He was afraid of being seen with me: a guy who earns fifty dollars a week and whose daughters have to work. People are superstitious, they believe bad luck's contagious. And they're afraid of wagging tongues."

"Tomorrow," says the writer. "Tomorrow afternoon, if you want. You'll tell me your story. I don't know if I can be of any help."

"You need ideas," says Mr. Knight. "We always do. My story is chock-full of ideas."

The writer accompanies him to his car. Mrs. Brighton comes toward them with her bag of groceries.

"I wanted to buy steak for tonight," she said. "The price of meat has gone up again."

"So, did things work out for Mona?" asked the screenwriter.

The neighbor shrugs.

He goes back into his house. The vacuum cleaner stands in the middle of the office, its chrome surfaces mirror a sea of envelopes.

The writer calls Jane. She does not answer. She must be out star-gazing at the corner of Sunset Boulevard.

From New York:

"I collect my favorite celebrities and I would like to have your photo. I'm sick in bed and I am waiting for it so I can paste it in my album. Dorothy G."

From Pince Grove (Pennsylvania):

"Will you autograph the attached photo and return it to me? Please do, I'd be infinitely grateful, because I'm just a poor invalid boy. Clarence M."

From Kansas City:

"My son, aged 14, suffers from heart disease, the result of scarlet fever, and has been bedridden for two years. If you would like to write him a few words and sign them, you would make him happy and make me happy too.
Walter C."

Every time you enter the producer's office, he shouts:

"Close the door!"

It is nice and cool in the office. The screenwriter drops into a chair and observes, beyond the air conditioner that purrs by the window, two gardeners mowing the lawn, their naked torsos glistening with sweat.

"This'll be a poor family," the producer continues, addressing his assistant, the son-in-law of the studio president. "The father, a bottom-of-the-ladder employee, the mother, who's sick, and two young children."

"Three children," the assistant says.

"Two or three children. What I really want is the ring of truth, like you get in some foreign films. Show realistic detail, how these people dress, their way of life. Let's say the father earns seventy-five dollars a week, and take it from there."

The writer's eyes follow the gardeners: they talk as they push their mechanical mowers, but we hear nothing: no outside noise reaches the office.

"It's something that's never been shown," continues the producer, "and I think the public is ripe for it—close the door!" he interrupts himself.

The secretary enters the room, bringing in a blast of hot air and the clatter of typewriters. She puts a bundle of letters on the desk to be signed, and withdraws. A studio secretary earns from thirty to sixty dollars a week.

"We need a good story, of course," says the producer. "But the key thing here is atmosphere."

"What if the father only earned sixty dollars?" suggests the assistant.

"Nobody'd believe it," says the producer with the conviction of a man who lives in Beverly Hills. He turns to the writer. "What do you think of my idea?"

"I heard a good one," says the screenwriter. "Want to hear it?"

The producer's eyes light up.

"It happens in a private school in Beverly Hills that only children of celebrities go to. One day, the teacher asks them to write a little story on a subject of their choice. One boy wrote a story that began: 'It was a very poor family. The father was so poor. The mother was so poor. The valet was so poor.'"

There is a silence.

"And then what?" asks the producer.

From Bath, in England:

"*. . . perhaps you will find me impertinent for writing you, but I've seen you so often on the screen that I've started to consider you a friend.*
    Joan S."

From Montreal (Canada):

"I am writing so you will answer me and so we become friends, good friends. You see, I live alone with my grandmother, who is seventy-five, and my mother is dead, and I feel alone. Please write to me and send me your picture. Please say you'll be my friend.

Your friend, Millie N."

From a village in Northumberland (England):

"You will think I'm stupid but whenever I see you in a movie, I start to cry. I don't know what makes me do that. I live in a village in mining country, and the cinema is our only entertainment. If you knew how much it means to us!

Your sincere admirer, Jimmy McB.

I am 21 years old."

"I know what's what," says Mr. Knight. "I see new movies. And I guarantee, none of them holds a candle to mine."

He is sitting in front of the screenwriter, very straight, very proper in his gray suit: he looks like a retired officer.

"I was inspired by reality," he says. "It starts out with a real showstopper: humanity is destroyed by the atomic bomb. Of the entire population of New York only one girl is left: Betty Grable or Veronica Lake. At the time the bomb went off, she was in the vault of her father's bank, that's how come she's alive. Next we're underneath the Arizona desert. A shadow moves. A boy: Dana Andrews or Burt Lancaster. After many twists and turns, they find each other. They thought they were alone on earth. They have no idea they're being watched by enemies: foreigners. Of course, we won't name any country but . . ."

He goes into detail, becomes animated, loses track, gives the cameraman hell, puts the star in her place, ad libs dialogue, adds a set, hires a thousand extras, throws the producer off set, spends $1 million, $2 million, $3 million.

In the next room, the vacuum starts to hum. The writer peers at Mr. Knight. He hasn't heard a thing. He's on the last reel of his movie.

"The couple is in shadow with the sunrise in the background," he says. "The music swells. Fade out."

He blinks as if the lights had just come on in the theater, his eyes on the writer.

"If you want it, take it," he says. "You're sure to make a lot of money."

In the silence that follows, the voice of the vacuum cleaner grows louder. Mr. Knight appears to be thinking.

"Running like a charm," he observes. "Are you satisfied?"

"Very."

"I forgot to tell you. My wife had this great idea. All those brushes lying around, it's a nuisance. So she sewed a sort of apron with pockets where she puts them when she's not using them."

The screenwriter wants to scream that *this* is what life is, an apron with pockets for vacuum cleaner brushes, and a woman who sews and knits, and two big daughters who have to work, and the groceries, the smiles, the flattery, all day long, to make a sale, and doors slammed in your face, and time marches on.

He looks Mr. Knight in the eyes, his baby-blue eyes, transparent, empty, and mumbles a few vague promises.

From Lancaster (South Carolina):

"Last night I saw you in . . . , first movie I've seen in over a year. For many reasons, I cannot go to the movies often. But yesterday I decided to see the great film that I'd read so much about in the magazines a friend gives me when she doesn't need them anymore. I said I was sick from the typhoid vaccination so I could get the night off—I also work nights in a small restaurant. Seeing you, I completely lost myself. Yes, I forgot who I was.

Nancy G."

From La Crosse (Wisconsin):

"*There's seven children in my family. I'm eighteen and the eldest. If I could work, things would be better, but I'm sick. Everything makes me tired, and the least effort makes my heart beat so hard that I almost suffocate. I'm more tired of living than ever and I don't know who to talk to. Despair is making me bitter. What am I going to do? Have you ever felt this way, Miss?*

Nora K."

From Council Grove (Kansas):

"*I'm just a night clerk in a hotel. I know you will find it ridiculous to receive a letter from a poor person, but you know that people who live in our kind of world need to choose one of you movie people and of course we all love to write and tell you how much we think of you.*

There's a guy here who just said I might as well write to a telephone pole but I told him he was wrong and that you people are human beings just like us and some of you talk to people like us if you are not too busy, and so I can finally say I have written to tell you how much I love you in your films and I hope you will make many more so I will say goodbye for now wishing you the best of luck and many happy days in movie-land.

Benny S."

Jacket folded over his arm, collar unbuttoned, the screenwriter leaves the studio and a colleague who's agreed to write the poor-family story. "I'm not a writer," he said, "I'm a pencil on the producer's desk."

A few months later, the screenwriter will discover that the pencil is used to write police reports for the Commission of Inquiry on Un-American Activities. But he does not know that yet, and if he avoids shaking his colleague's hand, it is only because it is hot.

He passes picketers who have been walking back and forth for months in front of the studio. Two sailors approach him:

"Is this where the stars are?"

He does not understand.

"Is this where the stars go by?"

He gets into his car and drives off.

"Are you going to Hollywood?"

The man, who spoke with a foreign accent, must be pushing fifty. Gray eyes in a leathery face. He is sweating profusely. Settled in the passenger seat, he wipes his forehead, says:

"Hot!"

"As usual."

"The heat's killing me. Because of my curls."

The screenwriter looks at him: flaxen hair, cut short, turning white at the temples.

"Are you an actor?"

"I'm Norwegian. They needed Dutch soldiers for their film, so they took me because of the accent."

"And the curls?"

"It's a historical film."

"Do you have a good role?"

The man hesitates, then:

"No. Two sentences."

"Do you work often?"

"It depends. The last time was in . . . "

He names a movie that is ten months old.

"Have you lived here long?"

"Fifteen years."

"Do you have a job?"

"I make movies."

They've turned onto Cahuenga Pass, a freeway that connects the San Fernando Valley to central Hollywood. Innumerable cars, filling four lanes in both directions, sparkle in the sun. In any other city in the world, we return from a five-minute walk to the corner diner having seen a thousand faces, gestures, words, sounds, and smells. In Hollywood, when evening has fallen, we note: today I drove by 72 Cadillacs, 49 Lincolns, and 252 Buicks.

"Before, I was a sailor," the man says. "In the Norwegian Merchant Navy. In '28, my boat stopped here in San Pedro. I liked it so much that I decided to come back at any cost. I went back home to Tromsø, and applied for an immigration visa for the United States."

"You've never regretted it?"

"Never."

"Did you want to be an actor?"

"I wanted to make movies."

"Extra work?"

"Until something better came up."

He grows animated.

"It won't be long now. I wrote a script, and I know a producer who's promised to read it. That's why I stopped you: I'm in a hurry to get home. I have to copy the script to show it to the producer."

"Is it your first script?"

"I've written several. But this is the first time a producer has promised to read it. They're very busy, you know, producers."

He lives alone in a furnished room, has a sandwich for lunch and dinner in a tavern. All day, he runs around looking for extra roles, which he lands two or three times a year, as does everyone like him. At night he writes screenplays. That's how it's been for fifteen years.

The screenwriter stops the car at the corner of Franklin Boulevard. The man gets out: he seems to be in a hurry to return home.

"Tell me," the writer asks, "do you enjoy life here?"

"Of course."

The screenwriter looks him in the eye, insistent:

"You really like it?"

Discomfort clouds the Norwegian's eyes, gray as the fog of Tromsø: malaise and nostalgia. He looks up at the palm tree etched against the indigo sky.

He lowers his voice as if afraid of being heard.

"I don't like the weather," he whispers.

On the doorstep, the screenwriter finds a package left by a delivery boy. Absentmindedly, he opens it: his thoughts are elsewhere.

Night-time Lotion for Dry Skin. Invisible foundation. Holy Water of the Stars. Daytime Moisturizer. Each bottle boasts the trademark *Hollywood Girl*.

The screenwriter examines the label. The package is for Jane.

"Dear Louise,

My wife and I live in Harlan County (Kentucky). We live at the foot of Pine Mountain, which separates us from mining country. The first trappers crossed the mountains on foot with their dogs, bringing only axes and guns. They lived by hunting bear, buffalo, and other wildlife that were plentiful at the time. The men were quick to exterminate all but a few squirrels and snakes. Forestry companies took the land right out from under the feet of the settlers they employed to fell trees, paying them, until recently, a dollar a day. Now there are no more forests on the hillsides, the rain washes the soil away, and it's as if my friends were caught in a trap.

Some children bring empty bowls to school. They still have their pride and do not want others to know that all they have for lunch is corn bread. The other day a boy arrived at our home with a broken arm. He's been having accidents like this for his entire life: he even broke his hip from just a light fall. It's because he's got rickets from lack of milk.

Recently, a woman walked twelve miles with a big bag of vegetables she wanted to exchange for clothing. She had to leave without the clothes, because the small reserve we'd collected had run out. One of the most hardworking men in our valley cannot send his children to school because they have no shoes.

In all the visits I've made in the region, I don't think I've ever seen toys. From a young age, children need to help collect wood and carry water. The houses are breeding grounds for infection. Many cabins have no windows: they are dark, stinking huts, overcrowded, with catalog pages stuffed in the cracks in the walls to keep the cold out. Beds are heaps of corn leaves where three or four boys and girls sleep every which way. There are no toilets, and children must relieve themselves in a corner. They do not take baths until spring, when it starts to warm up. Most often, people, young and old, sleep fully clothed. A few days ago an old woman died, and we had to find clothes to bury her in, she didn't have any."

The screenwriter is having the most sordid meal he's had in his life. He's alone in his car, in the middle row of a kind of car park. A boy in uniform came to take his order and brought him a tray with a clamp to hang on the door. A sandwich, a glass of milk, a knife, a fork, a paper napkin. The screenwriter chews, listening to the radio and the falsely cheerful voice of Hollywood's most famous gossip columnist.

She says, "I was the first to tell you last week that the marriage wouldn't last. Well, once again, I was right. Just now, Mary called me herself—because she wanted me to be the first to know—to tell me she'd decided to ask for a divorce and that the matter is now in the hands of her lawyers."

Other radios echo in the darkness; in other cars, other people chew their sandwiches. You can see them everywhere, even in the rearview mirror.

"Mary spent many sleepless nights before making the decision," the columnist coos, "and I know her too well to doubt . . ."

The screenwriter snaps off the radio, pays, and starts the engine.

Lights are on in his office. Through the open window, the story of Mary's divorce unfurls into the rustic silence of Hollywood.

Mr. Knight gets up to greet him.

"Excuse me. I turned on the radio while I was waiting. I knew Mary as a young girl: this is her third divorce."

He immediately adds:

"I apologize for getting here so late. I didn't go in to the office today. But I left instructions, and as soon as you phoned, a colleague came to tell my wife."

You can feel he is nervous, impatient, almost anxious.

"I didn't phone you," says the screenwriter.

"But . . ." Mr. Knight takes a little gulp of air. "They told me at the office, and seeing as you were going to see about my script . . ."

"Wait."

The screenwriter goes in search of Jane.

He's guessed right. It was she who called to ask when the factory would be sending the carpet vaporizer. As Mr. Knight was out of the office, she simply asked that he call back.

Mr. Knight is standing. He pulls on his cuff.

"I'm afraid there's been a misunderstanding," says the screen-writer.

The visitor listens in silence. His eyes are expressionless.

"I understand perfectly," he says. "It's completely natural. I'll make the necessary arrangements for the vaporizer."

In the doorway, he stops.

"If you ever have the chance to mention my story . . ."

The screenwriter would like to talk to Jane, but she has vanished, and he exits in turn. A couple is coming up the walk.

It's Mrs. Brighton and her husband. He's an underwriter for an insurance company: every morning, he travels an hour by bus to get to his office. On Sunday he plays golf. He's a pretty boy, a bit soft, and his wife despises him, mostly because he is not Clark Gable.

"We're going for a walk," says Mrs. Brighton. "Maybe we'll go to the El Mocambo: we haven't decided."

She knows that if they ever entered that celebrity nightclub, they'd leave behind a week of her husband's salary. She knows they'll walk to the corner, just as on other nights, and go home to bed. There are many things she knows and would prefer not to.

Jane is back.

"I thought it was best to call them," she said. "I can clean the office carpet now you've finished reading all these letters."

He's read every one, the whole lot. The letters from the Fort Dodge (Iowa) boy who collects autographs of stars on postage stamps, and the girl from Camden (Ohio) who collects them on chewing gum wrappers. The letter from a grandmother in Evanston (Illinois) who for years has been piecing together a "History Quilt" with bits of their clothing. The letter from a Cawker City (Kansas) mechanic who collects stars' buttons. A letter from a resident of Yankton (South Dakota) who collects their bras, pants, and used stockings. Hundreds, thousands of letters from around the world, all the same.

Who has not dreamed of virgin forest, flowers in the hair, and tropical birds? There are names of seas and promontories that open out on adolescence and the futures we longed for as children. The screenwriter found those names printed on envelopes, and he grasped their meaning. What is Elsinore waiting for? Photographs. What does Waikiki wish for? Autographs. What does Surabaya dream about? Signed portraits.

In a rage, he stuffs the envelopes back into the suitcase. No one else but he will read them, no one will answer them, no one could. What can you say to the Bethlehem (Pennsylvania) milkman who, when he gets home from a movie theater to which his friend sometimes takes him, takes refuge in the yard and stands alone in the moonlight miming the part of one of the actors on screen? How can you answer the young girl from Little Rock (Arkansas) who goes to see movies and weeps to see the stars in their beautiful dresses because she has no money to buy a decent coat or even a star photo?

The screenwriter closes the suitcase and carries it outside.

The incinerator is hunkered at the back of the yard: a little concrete termite mound crowned with an iron mesh cone. Next to it grows a palm tree. Just behind, the land sharply drops.

From here you can see all of Hollywood: square miles of lights that intersect at right angles, a gigantic deluxe miner's village. Here and there, neon starbursts of red, green, and blue; searchlights erected at the doors of movie palaces sweep the sky as if promoting their movies to the angels.

But on high, all you can see, as on other nights, is a red-winged horse jerkily galloping in the night.

The letters are piled high in the incinerator. *Voudriez-vous me favoriser en m'envoyant une de vos jolies photos?* It would please me so very much to have your picture . . . *Ich wäre sehr froh, wenn ich Ihr Bild mit Unterschrift bekommen könnte . . . Sarei felice se potessi avere una Vostra foto con preziosissimo autografo . . . para solicatarle una foto de su tan distinguida y reputada persona . . . desejando possuir uma photographia sua para a minha collecaõ . . .* The touch of a match, ringlets of smoke: a universal prayer, huge, primitive, rises into the Hollywood sky.

A spotlight lingers on the winged horse, reveals the contours of a blimp with an oil company's neon logogram on the flank.

The screenwriter thinks back a few months to other crisscrossing beams, dozens of them, sweeping over that hybrid edifice, half-circus half-temple, home to the annual Oscars ceremony, happening that evening, the distribution of those little gold statues that are the highest award for Hollywood filmmakers.

The boulevard was jammed with cars. Arms weighted with bracelets emerged from backseats of Cadillacs to caress a tuft of orchids on the lapel of a mink coat, or briefly illuminate, with a gold lighter, a famous face and dangling cigarette. Agents posted every ten feet stood torn between doing their job and curiosity, which made them perform futile gestures.

Only trams moved against the current, headed for one of the city's black ghettos, and as it was the hour when maids go home, the trams were filled with black women. They sat slumped on the benches, faces haggard, each with a bundle on her knees, collapsing into themselves as people do when they have backaches, sore arms, sore legs. They still had the evening meal to prepare, and the traffic jam would get them home late. Resigned to the wait, some dozed, fatigue stronger than curiosity. But most watched the procession from a distance: the luxury sedans and their cargoes of jewels and fur.

Sitting by a rolled-down window, a white girl, also a maid began talking. She was addressing no one in particular.

"Look at them," she said. "Go on, look at them. They go around in cars, giving themselves airs, when everyone knows they don't have one red cent. When everyone knows all you need is a few dollars to rent a car with a driver."

She was blond, poorly dressed; hardness in the face, and in her voice all the bitterness and rage in the world. Black women around her unsteady on their feet, gray with fatigue. She did not see them. Her eyes full of hate and greed searched deep inside the cars. Her voice grew louder.

"When everyone knows that two bucks will rent you an evening gown."

You sensed she was about to snap her jaws or burst into tears. Suddenly she stopped talking.

The flames roar in the incinerator. The writer stuffs in armfuls of letters pell-mell. Through the wire mesh, the smoke carries shreds of burnt paper to the palm tree. Maybe the letter of the English governess from Norwich who reads star lore aloud to her charges. Or the one from the Englewood, New Jersey, woman whose greatest ambition is to go to Hollywood. Or from the young Brazilian girl: the greatest wonders of this world, she has seen them on screen.

Spotlights dance in the sky. There are at least two revolving at the entrance of Grauman's Chinese Theater where, all day long, tourists bow low over the cement slabs where stars have left their footprints and signatures. All of them are there: living and dead, the great deaths of American cinema.

Not far from here is an art gallery where the screenwriter went not long ago to rewatch old Griffith movies. The gallery was so cramped that the projectionist had to stand outside to put enough distance between his machine and a makeshift screen hanging on the wall. The director was expected to attend.

Outside, the crowd milled by. Long lineups in front of the huge first-run palaces, where brand-new films in color are shown, films that cost millions of dollars, awaiting release to be consigned to oblivion.

In the gallery, three dozen spectators sat elbow-to-elbow, shoulder-to-shoulder. There was not even a piano to drown the drone of the projector. On a trembling screen, in a deluge of stains, Lillian Gish and Richard Barthelmess went off to meet their destiny.

After the films, a man in the back of the room stood up.

He was asked questions, technical, historical. His answers were curt, impatient. In the first moment of silence, he jumped at the chance to say: "Well, what are you waiting for? It's late. Time to go home. Go on, get out, it's over!"

The screenwriter can still see him: David Wark Griffith, without whom movies would not be what they are today, nor Hollywood what it has ceased to be, and who, for the past seventeen years, for lack of producers, no longer makes movies, Griffith, tense, malign, identical in his rage to the blonde in the tram, driving people to the exit with his bursts of fury:

"It's late! It's over!"

The suitcase is empty. He throws in the last handful of letters. Flames lick through each hole in the wire net, rise hissing to light the lower branches of the palm, point to the cloudless sky where Pegasus of Hollywood rides on.

NOTEBOOK

FEBRUARY 1936

Mr. Eaton, Methodist and Conservative, is filing for divorce and custody of his two children, whose mother has committed the reckless act of *thinking*. The trial has just taken place in Newark, New Jersey Judge Grosman. Here are some excerpts from the interrogation of Mrs. Eaton by the judge and the husband's counsel, Mr. Tiffany.

Judge: What are your views as to the existence of God?

Mrs. Eaton: God is a power that lies within each individual. It is not something separate from man.

Judge: Do you believe in the existence of a God separate from man?

Mrs. Eaton: No. Man is related to God.

Judge: Do you believe that every man is his own God?

Mrs. Eaton: I do not believe so.

Judge: Do you believe in the divinity?

Mrs. Eaton: No.

Mr. Tiffany: Are you interested in the maintenance of religion in this country?

Mrs. Eaton: Yes, but not the maintenance of the Church.

Mr. Tiffany: Do you believe in the Immaculate Conception?

Mrs. Eaton: No.

Judge: Do you believe in the afterlife, be it Heaven or Hell?

Mrs. Eaton: Oh! No.

Mr. Tiffany: So you do not believe in an afterlife?

Mrs. Eaton: Yes I do.

Mr. Tiffany: What?

Mrs. Eaton: I believe in eternal life.

Mr. Tiffany: In what form?

Mrs. Eaton: I cannot imagine the disappearance of life; therefore, I do not know what form it will take.

Mr. Tiffany: We believe that we move from one life to another. Is this your opinion?

Judge: Madam, if you cannot answer these questions, say so.

Mrs. Eaton: I do not think anyone can answer them.

Mr. Tiffany: When you say that the Church does not count for you, does that imply that you have no interest in your children's education?

Mrs. Eaton: On the contrary, I am very interested.

Mr. Tiffany: Do you belong or have you ever belonged to organizations said to be "red"?

Mrs. Eaton: Never.

Mr. Tiffany: Have you ever participated in a subversive movement?

Mrs. Eaton: Never.

Mr. Tiffany: Or attended a meeting in the street?

Mrs. Eaton: No.

Judge: Do you believe in the Marxist theory of religion?

Mrs. Eaton: I do not know it well.

Judge: What do you think of religion and its present influence on people?

Mrs. Eaton: Well, the religious spirit is found in everyone. I shall speak about it as briefly as possible: my duties to myself, to my neighbors, and to God. It embraces everything.

Judge: Is that not the Marxist definition?

Mrs. Eaton: I know nothing of religion in relation to Marx, who was an economist and not an exegete.

Judge: What do you think of the institution of marriage?

Mrs. Eaton: Well! I'm married like everyone else.

Judge: Do you believe in the institution of marriage, as it exists now, or in the Marxist theory of marriage?

Mrs. Eaton: I do not know Marx's ideas on the subject.

Judge: Do you believe in private property?

Mrs. Eaton: Yes.

Judge: Do you believe the family and the raising of children should be controlled by the government?

Mrs. Eaton: They are, in part.

Judge: Do you believe they should be completely?

Mrs. Eaton: No.

And here are Judge Grosman's conclusions:

"It is common knowledge that the principles of communism are the antithesis of those generally held by most Americans. These principles scoff at belief in the Supreme Being, in the brotherhood of man, in the virtue of women, in the institution of marriage, as well as the personal relation between parent and child. The petitioner, of course, is 'the mistress of her soul,' but she has no right to instill in the minds of her young children, against the will of the father, these doctrines which she has embraced and which are looked upon with abhorrence by the vast majority of people living under the protection of our laws . . ." Therefore, the divorce is granted in favor of Mr. Eaton, to whom the children's care is entrusted. Their mother cannot see them unless she renounces "all attempts to instill her atheistic and communistic beliefs in their minds."

This occurs in an American city of half a million inhabitants, some eleven miles from New York, in 1936.

A White goes to a black brothel in Brooklyn where the going rate is twenty-five cents a trick. He is taken upstairs and beaten so badly that in court, he is unable to recognize his attackers. The judge says:

"And what did you think you'd get for twenty-five cents from Blacks? The next time you're looking for that kind of service, choose a decent sort of place."

A Harlem bank. Between the tellers' windows on frosted glass a sign reads: "Have you made a will?"

February 1. Under "Lonely Hearts" in the black newspaper *New York Age*, the following letter from a reader:

"I hope with this letter you will find me, or help me find someone who will keep me from feeling so alone. I work hard, I go to church, I work more, and I go home.

"From time to time I go to a dance and I love shows, but I have no one to escort me. I am good-natured. I do not drink or smoke. I'm thirty-five and I would like to meet a man aged thirty-five to forty, provided he is kind and respectable. I am five feet three inches, my skin is brown, I weigh 123 pounds. I will answer all letters."

This ad was published in a newspaper in Stockton, California, where single men are not entitled to unemployment benefits:

"Seeking wife. Veteran, denied unemployment relief, must marry or starve."

February 7. Chicago psychiatrist Dr. McMurry believes that 20 to 30 percent of employees and employers in the US are suffering from nervous ailments. Here are the symptoms: tendency to daydream, insubordination, ill health not accompanied by organic disease, exaggerated suspicions with regard to colleagues and superiors, defensiveness, lack of resistance to fatigue, too-frequent errors and accidents. Nervous disturbance is also prevalent among bosses personnel, "probably because they have more ample opportunity to express their eccentricities. Symptoms identified include pedantry, cruelty to subordinates and extreme greed."

Associated Gas & Electric Company,
on the one hand,
deducted 4 to 10 percent of staff salaries, requiring them to buy
company shares in exchange;
and, on the other hand,
instructed seventeen brokers to buy back these shares from its destitute employees at a rate of fifty-five cents on the dollar.

For details, contact the State Attorney of New York, who has just
released these facts to the press.

February 17. Fragment of a letter from a reader in the *Daily News*:

"I suggest that instead of granting new privileges to criminals,
repeat offenders be sterilized. Then will we have done something to
combat crime."

A newspaper from Chattanooga, Tennessee, publishes the statements of the director of the city's Department of Education:

"Principals of black schools inform me that several hundred
black children do not attend class, most owing to the fact that they
have no lunch. God knows how many poor white children do the
same: pride prevents them from admitting it."

February 22. Today, in the papers, two short items. In New York, a
policeman surprised a thief in a shop and shot him on the spot. A
small-time crook, not a dangerous bone in his body. In Syracuse, a
policeman spotted three boys escaping from a school, shot at them,
killing one. "I wanted to scare them," he said.

"Shoot to kill." As long as the gun is loaded, why waste bullets?

Camp 217 is in Alabama, near the town of Goldsboro. Immersed
all day in freezing water, eighteen black prisoners drain the
swamps. At night they are locked in a steel cage with canvas
stretched over the top. To warm up, they have a little stove and
a shovelful of coal. If they get sick, they are given castor oil or

Epsom salts. An inmate died of appendicitis: he had been administered salts.

America being a civilized country, prisoners are entitled to a
shower every Saturday. But as they also must be punished at least
once a week, business is combined with pleasure: they are whipped
while they shower.

The unemployed man is black, but the worker is white,
The laborer is black, but the skilled worker is white,
The journeyman is black, but the foreman is white.
Bread is white, but misery is black.

Blacks pick the cotton, and Whites gussy up,
Blacks clean the Pullmans, and Whites travel,
Blacks do the cooking for the Whites, who eat,
Blacks play jazz for the Whites, who dance,
Like bread and misery
Never the two shall meet.

The black baker at his oven is white,
The white miner in his mine is black,
Winnie Williams was black, and Sam Arsenti white.
They were unemployed and they asked for food.

The police killed them, and the blood of the black woman was red
As the blood of the white man,
Red as the flags at their funeral, in Cleveland, in the month of July,
One thousand nine hundred and thirty-four.

CONVENTIONAL AMERICA

II. BUSINESS

The blouse was born at 2:02 p.m. in the beam of a fifty-watt bulb, life breathed into it by a wheezing Jewish laborer, tubercular and unionized. It was white and unique, or so it thought. It didn't know that another blouse, equally white and unique, had emerged into electrical daylight at 2:00 p.m. sharp, and that a third, fourth, and fifth would alight at two-minute intervals.

Each was packed in a box. Then they were piled into a truck. A flood of new clothes surged up Seventh Avenue, heart of the garment trade, New York's biggest industry. Other garments, used, clothed the crowds that barreled down the sidewalks.

Arriving at the thirties, the truck veered and careened through a carriage door. An elevator swept the boxes up to the fourteenth floor, while the delivery was recorded in triplicate.

The unique white blouses, from the moment they entered Macy's, the world's largest department store, opened a wellspring of tags and cards, soon to flow into the mighty river of paperwork that rolled and pitched its signs and figures throughout house.

Upon reception, a serial number torn from a counterfoil book was pasted on the invoice; the same number accompanied the merchandise. A slip providing the supplier's name, the quantity of items delivered, and the total price was dispatched to the twelfth floor, Accounting. There, the blouse department was debited the amount of purchase. The invoice, adorned in the interim with the department director's signature, was sent to the tenth floor for verification and then to the twelfth for a second inspection. A machine printed a check, examined twice and finally signed.

While these papers traveled across the company premises, according to a pre-established schedule and itinerary, on the fourteenth floor, one by one, the blouses were unpacked and inspected to ensure that no button had gone astray, no seam come unraveled. To the unique white fabric a little machine appended a tiny double tag bearing the price and a series of numbers, and all was whisked away by another elevator to the third floor, the blouse department.

Macy's occupies an entire neighborhood. An entire population throngs in the shadow of its nineteen floors and ever-changing-windows on Broadway, Seventh Avenue, Thirty-Fourth and Thirty-Fifth streets, shoeshiners, newspaper vendors, police and loafers, hawkers selling orangeade and malted milk. From the first basement to the ninth floor, the object is selling; from the tenth to the nineteenth, stocking and calculating; below ground, it's shipping. Housewives who learn to compose a menu on the eighth floor in Groceries go down to the basement and a model kitchen enveloped in aromas and steam. Satisfied, they are borne back up to the sixth to learn the mysteries of inserts and buttonholes at a row of sewing machines. There is a department that sells only dresses from five to seven dollars, and another where dresses are eight to fifteen, a doormat department and oriental carpet department, a department of small toys and department of big toys, departments for skirts, clocks, orthopedic shoes, cigars, adult games, corsets, 168 departments in all, 328,000 square feet crisscrossed by elevators and the inclined planes of escalators.

The upper floors are offices. The Comparison Office, which ceaselessly monitors competitors' prices for any given item so that all Macy's items are sold is 6 percent cheaper than anywhere else, for the company does not give credit and maintains a mystique of cash, offset by the 6 percent reduction, its own special formula for *efficiency* and *service*. The Advertising Bureau, which every day of the year comes out with twenty-five pages of ads: copy, drawings, and photos that are pitched and hauled in New York newspapers from morning to night. At the Bureau of Standards, behind a glass wall, a room bristling with retorts, generators, pipes. Electrical bulbs of all dimensions burn on a battery. A baroque machine sets a weight in motion and drops it onto a leather cushion. Elsewhere, a tennis ball bounces nonstop. All this is because the company is bound to telling the truth in their ads. A silk blouse must be made of real silk. At the Bureau of Standards, they study the resistance of leather cushions under future sleepers' heads and the number of times a tennis ball will rebound from future players' rackets.

Up to one hundred thousand customers pass through the store every day. They wander through the departments, looking for a gardening hat or oak dining set. Nervous, indecisive, distracted, angry, hesitant, they are the only element of disorder in a perfectly regulated world.

As soon as a frilly collar or a ukulele is sold, the bits of paper begin to multiply again. Twelve operations must be performed if the item is a cash sale to be taken home: 1) record name and price of goods on first line of bill, drawn up in triplicate; 2) if item is taxable, calculate amount and enter separately; 3) fill in other columns of the bill; 4) enter total transaction in cash sales column of summary statement of goods to be taken home by buyer; 5) state aloud, in an intelligible voice, amount paid by customer and enter it in space reserved for this purpose. Six, seven, eight, etc., up to twelve. If the merchandise, paid in cash, is to be delivered to the customer's home, the number of operations is increased to eighteen. When the customer has a current account with Macy's and makes a take-home purchase, thirteen steps suffice, but are increased to nineteen if the item is to be sent.

And so there are three different counterfoil books, plus three corresponding summary-statement slips. There are also pink, white, and blue forms, each with its own precise meaning. The money paid by the buyer is enclosed in a metal container, first the change, then the bank notes, folded, with the bill on top. For cash transactions, they use a hemmed gray felt recipient, for current account sales of under ten dollars, the felt is red, and blue if the amount is higher. The little messenger is inserted into a tube for pneumatic transport. The entire house is crisscrossed in all directions by tubes that converge upon cash stations. Each group of tubes are assigned to a belt that conveys the metal containers to fingers that empty them, and stamp the bill, which they return to the tube along with the money. The messenger glides on the moving carpet to the other end of the room, where other fingers stuff it into a return tube. Every ten fingers dispatches three hundred containers per hour, five per minute, one every twelve seconds, and it takes scarcely a minute for the little metal collection box to make its voyage across the store and back.

All orders to be delivered are placed in a bag with an inside pocket for the duplicate bill. The bags make their descent on inclined planes to Basement Number One, where the goods are packed. The packages are placed on one of the six conveyor belts, according to destination, and taken to Basement Number Two, to fall into a frameless car which, when filled to capacity, will be placed on a platform and delivered to the desired address.

How well organized it all is, so finely tuned and synchronized, from the arrival of the cargo in ships and trains from Europe and America until the final departure of the delivery trucks, the so very precise turnover of customers, merchandise, invoices, and bank notes in the circuit of elevators, freight elevators, escalators, inclined planes, and pneumatics, all enveloped in a network of numbers, statistics, and regulations in this nineteen-floor unit built on a skeleton of money-bearing tubes that flow into a large armored heart made of conveyance equipment and crates.

There are also nine thousand six hundred employees.

THE RAPE

On March 25, 1931, at 1:30 p.m. nine black boys between the ages of thirteen and twenty, accused of raping two white women, Ruby Bates and Victoria Price, were arrested and incarcerated at Scottsboro Prison, Alabama.

The newspapers

"My parents were sharecroppers in Alabama, where I was born. My father drank and we didn't see much of him. It was my mother who raised us—my sister, my three brothers, and me. When life got too hard, we moved to Huntsville. There are a lot of factories there. That's where my mother worked, and so did we kids once we got a little older. I was hired on in 1928, I was fourteen. Apprentices earned five cents an hour. Management had a system: as soon as you learned to operate a machine, they moved you to a different shop and you started as an apprentice again. I worked for three years at the factory and never made more than five cents an hour. I worked eleven hours a day and earned $2.75 for a five-day week.

"The factory was where I met Victoria Price. She was twice my age and a lot more experienced. She drank and was familiar with men. She's the one who took me to parties and made me drink. I was really scared.

"Victoria Price had a friend, Tiller, a married man. The police caught them together one day in an apartment that wasn't theirs, and Tiller was sentenced to six weeks in jail. Victoria they let go: the police knew her well.

"During his detention, Tiller made friends with a boy, Lester Carter, arrested for vagrancy. One day Victoria Price took me to the prison, and Lester Carter and I got on well.

"That was 1931. The mills shut down in Alabama, so we decided to look for work in Tennessee. On March 23, the two men got out of prison, we celebrated their release, and the next day Victoria Price, Carter, and I went to Chattanooga, where Tiller was supposed to join us after. When we got there, they told us the plants were closing in Tennessee too and there was no work for us. We didn't know what to do because we had no money and didn't know anyone in the city. A guy we met suggested we spend the night in the 'jungle,' a field where vagrants sleep, and go back to Huntsville the next day. That's what we did.

"So on the twenty-fifth, we jumped a freight train back to Alabama; it's easier than hitching a ride: drivers don't want to stop when they see three people. We traveled in a trash car. In another car, black boys were fighting with white boys who called out to Carter and he left to go help them. The train was traveling slowly, and the Blacks, who were stronger, began to throw the others onto the tracks. Then the train speeded up. The last white boy, who'd stayed on the flatbed, wanted to jump onto the grade but the Blacks prevented him because he could have hurt himself.

"I watched all this from a distance and I couldn't say if those Blacks were the same guys I was to meet in prison.

"Later we were told that the white boys who were thrown off the train went to complain at the nearest station, and the operator telegraphed ahead to Paint Rock, the next stop, to warn them.

"But then we didn't know anything about it, and we were really scared when the train stopped at Paint Rock and the platform was packed with people. Victoria Price and me ran off to hide until the train started up again. We hightailed it for the locomotive: it was crowded up there too, so we backtracked, and two deputy-sheriffs spotted us, chased and arrested us. We knew they were going to charge us with vagrancy; I think in Alabama it's ninety days. For Victoria Price, it could be more serious: there's a law against bringing minors across state borders, and I was only seventeen.

"They made us get into one car, and the black boys in another, and they took us all to Scottsboro Prison. The white boys who'd fought in the train were there too. The judge and the sheriff came to ask us questions. They just asked if we'd seen the fight, and we said yes. Then one of the sheriff's men told Victoria and me that if we agreed to accuse the Blacks of raping us, we wouldn't have to go to prison. I refused because it wasn't true. But Victoria Price had more experience and right away she said yes. They took us straight to Dr. Bridges. He and another doctor—I forget his name, wait, I think it was Lynch, that's it, Dr. Lynch—they examined us and didn't find anything because there was nothing to find.

"Dr. Bridges only asked if we'd seen the fight and we said yes. But he didn't ask us anything about a rape, because he saw that there had been no rape.

"When we returned to prison, the guards began to terrorize us. Especially me, because, Victoria Price, she had said yes right away. They threatened us so much that in the end I saw no way out except to repeat what they told me to say. I was seventeen years old and I had no one in the world to look out for me.

"The prison was small, white men and women were locked in the same cell, and Blacks in another. We were never alone, ever. In the morning we got a slice of meat and a piece of bread, and sometimes a cup of hot water they called coffee. At dinner we had peas or beans and a glass of milk, and in the evening another glass of milk with a slice of cornbread.

"The sheriff and his assistants came by the prison often. They would take Victoria Price and me into a separate room where there was a crowd of men, they forced us to undress in front of everyone and threatened to beat us. The guards on duty in front of our cell pushed their guns through the bars and said they'd kill us if we changed our testimony.

"We stayed in prison for sixteen days, including the trial, and during that time, crowds often gathered under our windows. People shouted and threatened us, and I was even more afraid of them than of being arrested. I didn't know what they wanted, I didn't understand they wanted to lynch the Blacks.

"The day before the trial, the guard told us we'd get a decent meal. Just eggs and bacon, but it tasted pretty good to us.

"The trial began in Scottsboro, April 6, 1931, a Monday, and it lasted three days. Victoria Price and I were the witnesses for the prosecution. The Blacks had a defense attorney appointed by the Court, who had advised them to plead guilty and place themselves at the mercy of the judges. They had refused: they had nothing to take the blame for, they were innocent.

"Victoria Price testified first. She spent three hours in the witness box, or maybe more. She told the story we'd been taught in prison. Then they called me and asked me to tell them everything. My story must not have matched Victoria Price's, because the prosecutor stepped in. He answered instead of me and advised me just to say yes or no. So I didn't tell my story, they asked me questions and I said yes or no.

"When it was all over and the boys were sentenced to die in the electric chair, we were released. The last day of the trial, Wednesday, the courtroom was packed, and there were thousands of people outside. When the sentence was read, the audience shouted: 'We knew they'd burn!' and the crowd outside heard them and repeated the words, everyone chanting, 'We knew they'd burn!' The Ku Klux Klan had brought in a brass band, and they all paraded around the courtroom, playing and singing the national anthem.

"Then the sheriff sent in some men to take a collection for 'the two white girls.' They collected a lot of money, but they only gave us thirty-five dollars, and if I am not mistaken, fifty cents. That was the reward for our testimony. They also promised us work for the rest of our days and told us that if we were ever unemployed, they'd get us benefits.

"When I got home to Huntsville, I starved. Nobody wanted me. I'd been blacklisted and couldn't get work. The authorities refused to give me benefits. There were sewing workshops for the unemployed but I wasn't allowed in.

"Victoria Price went back to the factory where we had worked. And when the factory closed, Victoria Price got benefits.

"My whole family was persecuted because of me. When I realized I wouldn't ever find work in Huntsville again, my mother and I went looking in the textile mills in Alabama. We managed to get taken on. I stayed for six or seven weeks. Then one of the guards from Scottsboro who'd seen me during the trial, came to work in the same shop as me. He recognized me and went to the boss to tell him who I was. I was called to the office and fired. There were three factories in the city, my mother and I were put on the blacklist for all three.

"We left again, and in August—this was still 1931—we found work in another mill. I stayed two and a half months, I was a winder, a spinner, I did everything. But a man who'd worked with me at the other factory and lost his job arrived at the hostel where we were staying. He recognized me and went to see the boss. He asked:

"'Do you know who's working for you?'

"The boss replied:

"'I have fifteen hundred workers, I can't know them all.'

"'One of them is Ruby Bates, the one from Scottsboro.'

"The boss called me in and told me that I had to leave because there wasn't enough work at the factory. My mother was also sent away.

"We went back to Huntsville, but I left again in January 1932. I wandered around the region and went back home in May because my mother was in hospital, and the doctors thought she wouldn't survive. But she got out in June, and in July I went into hospital.

"At that time unemployment benefits had been suspended and the Red Cross took care of the unemployed. But they didn't want to do anything for us. They refused to give us money and food. All they gave us was a bag of flour, two pounds of meat and three pounds of lard: that's what the four of us had to live on for a month.

"My mother and I were still sick and couldn't eat that kind of heavy food. At the Red Cross, they didn't speak to me openly about Scottsboro, but they did their best to remind me of it. They said, 'If you hadn't left home, you'd be working today.'

"There were two black families on our street: one next door and the other a few doors down. When we were sick, these Blacks—despite the prejudice against them, and in spite of the Law, because if they'd been caught visiting Whites they didn't work for, they'd have been beaten, maybe killed—despite all that, those people brought us vegetables from their garden through the back door. They helped us for two months, and without them, we'd have been in the cemetery a long time now.

"These Blacks knew who I was, and they spoke to me often about it. They were convinced the Scottsboro Boys were innocent. But I was too scared to talk, I told them nothing. I would've liked to do something, but I was just too scared.

"I tried to tell the truth, once, in January, in a letter that I asked a friend to deliver. But the man got in a fight; he was arrested and the police found my letter. The sheriff arrested me and forced me to sign a statement saying I'd lied because I was drunk. I wrote what the police told me to and said that I'd written it on my own. I was afraid to talk about Scottsboro even with my mother. It seems strange to be afraid to confide in your own mother, but you can never be sure you won't be discovered.

"At the end of September I found work: I was going to sell house-wares door to door. It didn't last: whenever I walked into a home, people threw Scottsboro in my face. I never understood why Victoria Price had so much better luck than me. Probably because at the trial, she did and said everything she'd been ordered to say and do, and I didn't.

"I learned that the accused hadn't been executed yet, and I knew if there was a retrial, I would testify in their favor. I wasn't going to let them die because of me. I should have done something sooner, but I was scared and there was no one in the world I could talk to about it.

"In 1932, there were rumors that they were going to kill Victoria Price and me, because the defendants still hadn't been electrocuted: people believed we'd contacted the International Red Aid. I didn't even know the International Red Aid was involved in the case. The authorities stationed guards around Victoria Price's house and had a policeman everywhere with her. I got nothing. They just gave me permission to carry a revolver if I was ever attacked.

"The trial was coming up for review at the end of March or the beginning of April, we didn't know exactly when. In the end of January, Attorney General Knight called a meeting in Birmingham. Victoria Price and I were summoned: he wanted to refresh our memories. The day before the meeting, I left home.

"When they saw I wasn't coming, they came to question my mother. She told them she didn't know where I was. I hadn't said anything to her when I left. I didn't know myself where I'd go.

"I traveled for a month, stopping cars on the road or jumping freight trains, when I wasn't too afraid to do so, and on March 5 or 6 I arrived in New York City.

It was my first time and I was completely lost. I didn't know where the streets would take me: I'd never been in a big city before. I ended up finding a room somewhere on the East Side, I think, but I couldn't tell you where: even now, I still don't know much about New York.

"I looked for work and one day met a friend from the South who I hadn't seen for two years. She knew someone who could set me up, and I went to work in Upstate New York.

"I was still there on March 27 when I read in the papers that the second trial had begun in Decatur, Alabama. I decided to go and tell the truth. But I told myself that someone had to know the whole story before I left: I didn't know what could happen to me.

"I'd read an article in the *New York Times* about a certain minister, and I went to see him. I introduced myself, I told him who I was, I sat down and told him the whole story. Then I asked him:

"'What would you do if you were me? Would you go testify or keep quiet?'

"Because the newspapers had reported my disappearance, and if I wanted it, no one would have been able to find me.

"He talked about the Church and the Bible, and he quoted the Scriptures. Do unto others as you would have them do unto you, and so on. You know it? He told me to go to Decatur and tell the whole truth. That was the only person I asked for advice and told my story to before heading back south.

"I arrived in Decatur on April 7, the last day of the trial, a few hours before the end. All the town could think about was lynching, the word came up in every conversation, it's all I heard between the station and the courthouse.

"The entrance was on the courtroom side, and a bay led to the judge's bench. I arrived when they were reading from my Scottsboro testimony. When the district attorney saw me, he was happy, relieved, and immediately invited me to come testify.

"I went up to the bar—I didn't know anyone in this room—and the judge told me to tell my story.

"I told it.

"It wasn't what the district attorney or the judge wanted to hear. They called Victoria Price again, along with Tiller, who'd been her boyfriend, and Lester Carter, and they ordered me to identify them. It was the first time I'd seen Victoria Price again, face to face. She looked at me, turned red and mumbled something. I didn't catch what she was saying—I still don't know what she said—and didn't answer. I didn't know what was happening to me, I didn't know if the defense would protect me, I just told the truth.

"After my testimony, I was placed in the room for defense witnesses. If I'd been sent to wait with the witnesses for the prosecution, I don't know what would have happened. I entered the room, and that's where I met the mothers of the accused for the first time, and I will never forget it. There was Mrs. Jenny Patterson. She looked at me and asked me if I'd testified for or against her son. When I answered that I'd told the truth and testified for him, she collapsed in my arms—I'll never forget, she kissed me and thanked me.

"She said, 'I knew my son was innocent.'

"I'll never forget it.

"That night in Decatur the lawyers got wind that the crowd was marching through the city to kill the accused, their counsels, and witnesses. The National Guard stepped in and saved our lives. After the trial, the lawyers took me back to New York, and since then I've stayed at the International Red Aid.

"I didn't go to the third trial in November 1933, because I was in the hospital in New York, and the doctors thought I was dying. I didn't go to the fourth trial this past winter either; it would have been too dangerous for me. Anyway, I'm not going back South any time soon.

"I don't know what'll happen to the accused. All I know is that the courts of Alabama will never grant them a lawful judgment. If they can't kill them, they'll keep them in prison, which amounts to the same thing.

"I've known Blacks since I was born. There were three or four at the Huntsville plant where I first worked. I had a kind of *inferiority complex*, I thought they were inferior to Whites. I learned that at school, I'd have never thought it up myself. We were told that life in the South would be easier without Blacks. And meanwhile Blacks were told they'd be better off if Whites did not break strikes. Those two black families who helped my mother and me, they made me think; they changed a lot of things for me. Here, in New York, I began to read and understand.

"My family is still in Huntsville. My mother is unemployed. We write to each other; she thinks I did the right thing. My little brother had to go work in a textile plant, he's thirteen today. I'd have done anything to keep him from working, but life is so hard.

"My sister has also been working for five years, and she's twenty now. She works in the same factory where I did my apprenticeship, and she earns what I did: five cents an hour. But the workweek has been shortened. I earned $2.75, and my sister only makes $2.40.

"As for me, I go to meetings here in New York and other places, wherever people want to know the truth about the Scottsboro defendants, and I tell them the truth.

NOTEBOOK

MARCH 1936

Vertical strike in New York, where elevators transport more people more miles than subways, buses, trams, and cars put together. One hundred and twenty-five thousand elevator operators, janitors, boiler supervisors, etc., are unionized. They are demanding an increase of eight dollars per month, a forty-eight-hour week, and the exclusive use of unionized labor.

During the night, a good half-dozen "employment agencies" popped up; hotbeds for scabs. Low-level gang members from Philadelphia, Jersey City, Pittsburgh flock to New York. Newspapers publish ads:

GUARDS
brawny, neat appearance,
good salary, labor dispute.
Phone . . . night or day.

In one of these agencies, a brawl broke out because an employee wanted to take the men's fingerprints: police intervention was required. Scabs are paid six to twelve dollars a day (strikers' average salaries were sixty dollars per month).

It has become difficult to enter companies and plants. The doors are closed. You are examined at length before being granted entry. Men sit in the lobby, playing cards or reading newspapers. Next to them on a bench lie batons and cudgels.

Walking on Park Avenue. The majestic doormen, who are usually seen in front of entrances, have traded in their gold-braided livery and caps for old overcoats and felt pens. They pace back and forth, sandwich men whose signs back and front read STRIKE in big red letters.

Garbage is not removed. Along Park Avenue, there is more per capita than anywhere else. But as Robert S. Allen, Municipal Public Health Services, told journalists: "We distinguish between good and bad trash. In Park Avenue, it's good."

In "bad trash" neighborhoods, tenants mingle with picketers, bring strikers sandwiches and hot coffee.

March 6. Mark Goodger of Chicago announced that he had just completed his thirty-fifth reading of the Bible. He stressed that this was not a record, while remarking that to his knowledge, no one else has done as much.

The strike continues. Spoken with strikers. Of the picketers, two had finished high school, the third was an engineer on roads and bridges, the fourth a journalist. The crisis has made elevator operators of them all.

Later, a man carrying the union sign told me his name was William Jordan, forty-five, a graduate of the University of Pennsylvania. Now an elevator operator.

"What do I know how to do? Teach political economy. I have two kids and I'm afraid I'll never teach. For now, I want my children to eat."

March 10. In Zion, Illinois, the Prophet Voliva predicted today on his seventy-sixth birthday that Mussolini would probably become dictator of the world.

Voliva had already achieved a certain notoriety by asserting the earth was flat.

March 13. Dr. Albert Brundage just died. The famous toxicologist, an authority in his field, gave his health to science and his fortune to charity. Six weeks ago, he was evicted from his house, which the IRS had seized. He died in the hospital at the age of seventy-four.

Earl Browder, secretary of the Communist Party, spoke on the radio for fifteen minutes. *The Daily Worker* published some of the letters sent in from listeners.

"Bettie, Texas.

Dear Mr. Browder,
Please send me some literature. I heard you on the radio last night. I'm an old socialist. I'm 81. I want to do everything I can for the class of the poor because I am one of them myself."

"Saint Louis, Missouri.

Dear Sir,
Your speech on the radio tonight gave me great pleasure, and please put me in touch with communist organizations in St. Louis. I would also be happy to get more information.
I was converted to Communism by the Acts of the Apostles, Chapters 4 and 5, as recorded by the men our Savior taught about how things should be here on Earth."

"Erie, Pennsylvania.

Dear Mr. Browder,
I hope I am writing your name correctly. My radio is as miserable as myself. I listened to your speech with great interest. I wish you could have talked for an hour. My husband and me are two old victims of poverty and need. I require medicine and a doctor's care. I need food to get my strength back.

We have been evicted from our home for the third time in five years, and this time, I think we'll be out on the street for good. I've cried all my tears. Where will we go? I do not know, and I am too ill to do anything about it.

If I were able to speak in public, I think I would be arrested. Do you have any literature on communism you could give me to read? I would be delighted to have it. I would like to have a badge. I would be proud to wear it. You are for the rights of man."

March 16. Yesterday, in a park in San Francisco, a young woman asked passersby:

"Do you want a baby? My neighbor wants to give away her baby."

We eventually learned that she was sent to the park by a friend, Linda Jones, mother of two children, who told reporters:

"I was distraught. I'm separated from my husband. If my daughters stay with me, they'll never know anything but misery. The basement we live in is dark and cold. My little ones don't get enough to eat."

The children were adopted by two different families. The mother lives on alone in her basement.

Met with John Dos Passos.

He moves across the room with a peculiar gait, a slight limp, lights a cigarette, pour drinks, hesitates before answering a question, searching for words as if he were writing rather than talking.

I ask:

"Do you live in the United States?"

"Yes."

"And in 1936?"

"Yes, yes."

He thinks a moment and adds:

"Certainly."

"It is not like that for all writers. There are some who'd prefer to live on the moon."

"Not me. The books I write are more factual than novels and they are mixed up with reality."

"What is American reality today?"

"It's always hard to tell, especially at the present time. The situation of workers and the unemployed are certainly what's most important. We also have to consider a recent development of ideas, very difficult to follow. A movement that doesn't include intellectuals."

"What sort of movement?"

"I don't exactly know. Capitalism is undergoing transformations. Events escape and outstrip all theories. These events don't have names, they haven't been named yet. And theories are extremely rare in this country. The habit of not having ideas, pragmatism, is so strong in the United States: it's a real disease of a kind. It's as if at the train station, everyone had agreed to get on without asking where the trains are going. I'm like that myself. It is the very basis of American life."

Dos Passos crosses the room, takes a cigarette, digs into his pockets, goes looking for matches, returns inhaling smoke.

"We live in a barbarous country," he says, "the most barbaric of all. The very cradle of fascism. Germans have borrowed a lot from certain American ideologues. The anti-civilizing influence of the United States in Europe was much more powerful than anyone thought. I think of the emigrants—and there were a lot of them— who returned to Europe after living here, taking with them the cult of Might makes Right, losing track of European traditions in the process. The Ku Klux Klan was the first example of organized fascism. Compared with our large industrial cities, Hitler's Germany is a haven of freedom. The word "freedom" itself was appropriated by the ruling class, who called its most reactionary organization The Liberty League. Fascism is so common among us that in a way we are immunized against it. And besides, the country is so big and so chaotic that industries will never agree among themselves, they've got too much power. I don't think we'll ever have a single, centralized fascism. And there's this too: the organizations that exploit fascism are so dishonest. When there were $50,000 in the coffers of the Ku Klux Klan, the head of the organization disappeared with the money. The words that those men use have no meaning. They are businessmen, wordmongers, but they forget the nature of their merchandise: the words they're trading in mean nothing to them. What matters is selling. Fascism can come after the next war."

"An imminent war?"

"Definitely. It's as if we were playing baseball with balls of dynamite. Something's got to blow up somewhere. It'll break out later in the United States than in Europe, but it's inevitable. One would have to be very naïve to believe that we can stay out of another war."

"Seems to me your people don't want to."

"No more than in 1917. Remember that class-consciousness is very undeveloped in the American worker. And our workers don't have the tradition of solidarity that's so powerful in Europe. In some trades, we've had magnificent solidarity movements, but they don't last. Yes, we've had some splendid strikes. San Francisco in 1934, the Vermont marble workers, as we speak. But these movements are sporadic. In a modern factory, there is no necessary, indispensable trade: you don't have to know very much, and the learning period is shorter and shorter. There are engineers, technicians—a handful of people, generally well paid, and for this reason they're always on the bosses' side. The production line and a few experts, that's it."

"So that's how things stand now, in America?"

"Yes, and at the same time, in our barbaric and violent America, there is an old democratic tradition. The question is whether or not we can revive it."

He fills our glasses, reaches for cigarettes, decides against it, speaks again:

"Today, for the first time, traditions of a kind are beginning to emerge from American chaos. There is a lot of vitality in this country.

If we managed to salvage something from all the confusion, that would be perfect. Washington and Lincoln have been appropriated by the reactionaries. Will we be able to get them back? There's a movement forming with that in mind. Especially among miners. These are rough men, often illiterate, living in the mountains and who know that their forefathers fought for this land. Their parents have told them the family history, the country's history. Those men have preserved an oral history of our revolution."

He lights a cigarette, inhales the smoke, says:

"Politics in the United States has become a kind of ball game. There are professional politicians the way there are professional ball players. It's a job. Another business like so many others in America."

He thinks for a moment.

"Yes," he says, "we live in very complex times."

March 24. Ad in the *Boston Evening Transcript*:

"Idealist seeking a worthy cause for career."

A Black is dying in a hospital in Birmingham, Alabama.

Two police officers on routine patrol had tried to question the man. He didn't stop. The police opened fire and wounded the black man in the head, arm, hip, and leg. Shoot to kill.

Nothing is known about the man, not even his name, only his ability to be a target.

In the train that takes me back to New York. In the dining car, a man sits down across from me: fifty years old, glasses, clean-shaven, cold Anglo-Saxon face, slurred speech. He orders a martini.

Then he speaks to me:

"What terrible weather. This rain."

His eyes avoid mine. I don't answer. Indicating our neighbors, he says:

"Such vulgar conversation. What can the future of America be?"

I hazard a vague smile.

The man laughs stupidly, beatifically. A trickle of clear saliva escapes from his mouth.

"You have to know about people and things," he says. "Sex is everything. The falling rain is sexual."

March 31. Conrad Mock, rubber craftsman, had been working eighteen years. Then his profession disappeared: machines worked better, cheaper, and faster. At fifty-three, he had to start life again. Learning a new profession was blatantly useless. Conrad Mock swindled charities at the municipal shelter in the dregs of the Bowery. Last night, he picked up a stone and smashed the window of an empty shop, then sat on the curb and patiently waited for a policeman to arrive. He was going to be able to eat and sleep in a warm place.

CADAVERS, BY-PRODUCTS
OF DIVIDENDS

PREAMBLE

The *New York Times* of January 4, 1936, published an ad on two-thirds of a page, paid for by the Ralph H. Jones Advertising Co. The agency offered free publicity to benefactors from whom they hoped to acquire paid business:

THE BUSINESS WORLD IS NOT BAD

The recent Depression resembled war in many respects. But wars breed tales of alleged atrocities. Atrocities magnified with every retelling.

The main tale of so-called atrocity in the Great Depression portrayed the business world and businessmen as inhuman, selfish, parasitic—interested in profits not men, in property not progress. *And yet, is there anyone in the world who has shown more interest in mankind and the problems of individuals than the American businessman?*

Consider the case of public utility companies. While countless stories of their atrocities made the rounds, the price of home electricity steadily declined. Can we say that millions of dollars for better lighting and a better life were sacrificed for profit alone? If anyone believes these companies are only in it for the dollars and have no soul, let that person call upon their services on some dark winter night. He will get what he needs without fail, quickly and easily, and will not even have to tip. *Because public utility companies work for society as much as for profit.*

Without being forced at sword's point by the Law, the business world fixes its attention on other things besides the dollar. It is profoundly human. But it has made a mistake.

The business world has not told its story. The business world is not *bad*, it is simply too modest. But the day will come when it will make humanity aware of its point of view. And on that day the sowers of discontent will find fewer listeners.

The story of the construction of the Gauley Bridge tunnel, far from a tale of atrocity, is precisely one of those stories that American business in all its modesty has not yet made known to humanity. It is a very simple story about men, and silica, and dollars.

PRESENTING THE CASE

First, the dollars.

Union Carbide & Carbon Co., New York, with which the Morgan and Mellon families are indirectly involved, are among the one hundred largest corporations in the United States. Its many subsidiaries work in electrometallurgy, electrochemistry, and synthetic chemistry. Its products are sold worldwide. Worthy of note is acetone, used for artificial silk production as well as the manufacture of smokeless powder, certain alcohols used in explosives, and special charcoal for gas masks. In short, Union Carbide is related to the war industry, and its stocks unfailingly rise on the Stock Exchange whenever armed conflict is about to break out somewhere in the world.

Union Carbide has capital stock of about a quarter of a billion dollars and is administered by eight directors who occupy eighty-eight company management positions. Its profits totaled over $15 million in 1934 and almost $20 million in 1935.

One of the biggest branches of the trust is the Electro Metal-lurgical Co., the largest US plant to manufacture particular steel alloys, located, as it happens, in Alloy, West Virginia.

Anxious to provide its subsidiary with cheap electricity, Union Carbide founded, in 1927, a new company, the New Kanawha Power Co., with an eye to building a thirty thousand–horsepower hydropower station at Hawk's Nest, West Virginia, on the New and the Kanawha rivers. The project would involve the digging of a thiry-two-foot-diameter tunnel between Gauley Bridge and Hawk's Nest to bring water from New River to the plant, a distance of three miles. Construction was assigned to contractors Dennis and Rinehart and not supposed to last more than four years from the actual start date.

This project was amended twice.

On the one hand, US law prohibits the construction of tunnels involving a navigable waterway without the permission of the Federal Power Commission, which has strict rules about work conditions and methods. Seeking to avoid the extra cost this kind of inspection would unfailingly incur, the New Kanawha Power Co. decided to dispense with permits and get the best of the Federal Power Commission; they counted on procedural delays but even more on speed of construction. The four-year period was cut in half.

On the other hand, a committee of engineers and geologists sent to Gauley Bridge had established that for over 1.9 miles, the projected tunnel would pass through virtually pure deposits of silica. Following this discovery, the New Kanawha Power Co. decided to widen the tunnel from thirty-two to almost forty-six feet in diameter to harvest the silica, which would then be delivered to Electro Metallurgical for the manufacture of special steels.

And that's it for the dollars.

As for silica, it is an oxygen-containing silica compound (SiO_2), a mineral found most frequently in the earth's crust. Sand, quartz, sandstone, and flint are more or less pure varieties of silica, and it is also contained in the ores of gold, silver, lead, copper, and zinc.

Now let us abandon the mineralogist's point of view for the doctor's. Silica dust causes an illness whose effects have been recognized since antiquity. (Hippocrates describes certain symptoms, and Pliny the Elder in his *Natural History* recommends the use of what, today, we call a mask to prevent the inhalation of dust.) But the history of the illness designated as silicosis has only been described in the last thirty years, particularly by Australian, South African, and American scholars.

Silicosis is caused by the deposits of silica dust in the lungs of a person who inhales it. This dust has no immediate irritant effect, and for this reason the lungs and airways tend not to expel it as they do other foreign bodies. And introduced into the body this way, the infinitesimal particles of silica begin to dissolve, and because they are a poison, the lungs protect themselves by coating them in lymphatic tissue. It forms a series of nodules that multiply and gradually bond together, blocking the lymph nodes, then the blood vessels that supply the lungs, and finally the airways. The patient breathes with increasing difficulty, has chest pain, loses a great deal of weight, is unable to perform the same amount of work as he did in the past, and soon the slightest physical effort leaves him breathless, he eventually dies of suffocation, unless he succumbs to tuberculosis or pneumonia first, for his lungs are so damaged by silica dust that he has a weakened resistance to germs. It is possible to stop the progress of silicosis if it is caught in time, but we can never restore the patient's natural vigor. The illness tends to develop very slowly: the three stages of silicosis, as described in medical literature, often take several years to develop.

This consummate work-related disease, though almost incurable, can be easily prevented. For this, it is mandatory in mines, tunnels, quarries, and other places where the presence of silica has been reported to provide perfect ventilation, replace dry drilling with water drilling, give employees masks and extremely short workdays.

That's it for silica.

We have said that the history of the Gauley Bridge tunnel included a third element: men. We're getting to that.

There was no lack of labor force in West Virginia, where numerous coal mines shut down starting in 1930, resulting in a high rate of unemployment. The inhabitants of the surrounding communities, Gauley Bridge, Gamoca, Vanetta, etc., were not about to say no to this unexpected source of livelihood. However, most workers were recruited from other areas. Agents from Rinehart and Dennis traveled the United States singing the praises of the construction that was about to begin: easy, high wages, safe. Miners liked the idea of going underground with no risk of firedamp; Blacks willingly abandoned the plantations of cotton, tobacco, and poverty; the unemployed had nothing to lose. Men begin to flood into Gauley Bridge.

They came from Pennsylvania and Ohio, Maryland and Delaware, but mostly from the South: Florida and Alabama, Georgia and Virginia, and the Carolinas. Two thousand men, primarily Blacks, were hired to drill the tunnel. The worksite was opened in 1930.

ARGUMENT

Rinehart and Dennis had set up camps—separate camps for Whites and Blacks, naturally. They consisted of box-like hovels of ten by sixteen feet: four walls, a floor, a roof, a door, and a skylight. Ten or so people to a hut were housed in the white camp, twenty to thirty in the black camp. Some workers brought their families; men, women, and children all slept together. They had to buy bedclothes, a stove for the winter or do without. The only furniture was old dynamite boxes.

The rent was set at fifty cents a week per person. They took shack rent from anyone, even for workers who slept under the stars.

These were not the only expenses. Though the company had not provided stoves, it sold coal. Each man had to pay fifty cents per week, whether they used fuel or not, and regardless of the number of people in the hut. He even had to make a weekly payment to the company doctor: fifty cents for Whites, seventy-five cents for Blacks. One worker, George Houston, said later: "I sent in a call for the doctor for four weeks and he never came, and I was still paying for him."

The salary was first set at fifty cents an hour, fell rapidly to forty, thirty, and finally twenty-five cents. Laborers kept pouring in; if you weren't happy, all you had to do was leave. The workday was officially ten hours: in truth it was two hours longer, hours that were not paid. At shift change, each man received a check for the amount of five dollars, which was lowered to $2.50. It wasn't a real check, payable at any bank, but a voucher that could only be cashed at the company canteen. For this operation, workers were charged 10 percent of the check. They could have waited until the end of the week and exchanged their vouchers without a service charge, but provisions were bought at the company store, which did not accept credit, or payment with vouchers, so workers were forced to pay the daily 10 percent.

Still, the men had a bit of pocket money and one of the guards, called McCloud, had opened a "club" in the black camp where they drank and played hard. On each game of dice or cards, McCloud levied a duty of twenty-five cents per head. This money reverted to the company. Late at night, McCloud roamed the hills with a baton and two revolvers, hunting down anyone who had the gall to go play elsewhere and hauling them back to the "club" with kicks.

The same McCloud was responsible for waking the workers in their shacks. The local authorities had appointed him sheriff on the recommendation of the New Kanawha Power Co.; armed and vested with police powers, he made his morning rounds. "We couldn't fight back," says one of the workers, George Robinson. "If we didn't want to go with him, he hit us with his club. If we'd resisted, we'd have been shot. We had no choice but to obey. If a Black was too sick to work, there was only one thing to do: hide before McCloud arrived." The ill had to work like all the others.

In the tunnel, the work never stopped except on Sundays. The teams changed every twelve hours, and for all the time they were underground, they were not entitled to a moment's rest. Sixteen mechanical drills were run without stopping, six wet, ten dry. If a worker took a break, even just to replace a drill bit, a foreman immediately ordered him back to work. When the boreholes were deep enough, they were loaded with dynamite, everyone scattered, and an explosion tore through the rock. The echoes of the detonation were still rumbling through the gallery when the men rushed back, pursued by the foremen's cries and blows.

The drills were run on two gasoline-fueled motors at the very bottom of the tunnel. They burned forty gallons of fuel every twelve hours, filling the men's lungs to bursting with carbon monoxide. More than once, asphyxiated workers had to be carried up for fresh air; twenty-eight men lost consciousness in a single night. Foremen called them soft and told the others to step up the pace.

Rocks frequently collapsed on workers; one day, a driller and his co-worker were killed on the spot. There were other accidents but the foremen assured everyone that all was well and told them they had to hurry.

When, by chance, inspectors from the Bureau of Mines came by the tunnel, lookouts posted outside warned the supervisors, who stopped the dry drilling and pulled the motors up to the gallery entrance. The inspectors left, and work resumed as usual.

The scarce light bulbs dangling from the walls could not penetrate the clouds of dust that bathed the tunnel. The men could not see much farther than fifteen feet ahead. They tripped over the instruments and jumped aside when a wagon veered toward them. The white dust got thicker with the drilling and explosions, coating the men's faces and hands and clothing, it coagulated in eyebrows, filled nostrils, coated the water that no one could stop themselves from drinking. As the day went on and the pace stepped up, the workers breathed more heavily, lining their lungs with dust. When they came back up, no one could tell the Blacks from the Whites: both were covered in a layer of fine pale dust: silica dust.

Workers headed for the camps and as they didn't want to dirty their shacks, they undressed as they walked and beat their overalls against the trees. Groves of trees around the houses had turned white, and not even the rain could wash them clean.

They could have stuck to water drilling, but that would have taken about three times longer than dry drilling: the company had no time to spare. They could have waited, if only half an hour, after each explosion, but the company had no time to spare. Electric motors could have replaced gasoline engines, the ventilation pipe could have been repaired, the workday shortened, men given masks: the company had no money to spare.

Masks were cheap: $2.50 each. A thousand dollars at most to protect the men. But when a salesman came around selling them, Kies, a Rinehart and Dennis employee, said to him: "I wouldn't give $2.50 for all the niggers on the job."

A few months after work began, the men started to feel sick. They went to the company doctors, who gave them black pills. Leo Grey, a worker, said: "My head, stomach, and side began to hurt, I went to Dr. Mitchell, but all I got was little black devils. If a rock fell on one of us they would have just given us those little pills."

The men grew thin, dark shadows formed under their eyes, they breathed with difficulty. The Blacks had spent their lives on plantations and were unaware of work-related illness. But they wanted to know the truth. They asked the company doctors, who sometimes diagnosed asthma or pneumonia or high blood pressure. One day Dr. Mitchell told the men they were suffering from "tunnelitis," which does not even exist. Rinehart and Dennis and the New Kanawha Power Co., forbade doctors to call it by name, silicosis.

Yet there was no doubt about it. The company knew the soil around Gauley Bridge contained 99.4 percent pure silica, all they'd thought about was increasing the diameter of the tunnel. The fact is, as a general rule, the symptoms of silicosis do not start to appear for several years, and management told themselves the work would be long completed by then, and the workers dispersed all over of the country, before they started to choke. But there was too much dust in the gallery, too much silica in the dust. Whereas it usually takes years, several months had been enough. The same Kies had once said to Hawkins, the site supervisor: "I knew they were going to kill these niggers in the next five years, but I didn't think they would kill them so quickly."

Because the Blacks began dying. Whites too. They crashed to the ground in the camps, in the tunnel, under the rocks, and did not get up again. The company physicians talked about a "pneumonia epidemic." The police scoured the shacks and chased out the men who were too sick to work. They left with great effort, clinging to silica-bleached trees to catch their breath. New workers were hired.

Rinehart and Dennis had drawn up a contract with the H. C. White funeral home. White had agreed to bury the dead for fifty dollars per head, well below the usual fee. In exchange, the contractors had guaranteed him a large volume of business.

White took the corpses to Summerville, about forty miles from Gauley Bridge, and buried them in a field next to his mother's farm. The field, slightly curved with good sun exposure, was plowed and seeded with corn. In the summer they harvested the corn. The thick yellow stalks marked the place where 169 workers lay rotting in the overalls they wore at the moment of death. A woman whose husband had died at four in the morning went to the funeral parlor at seven to dress the body: she learned that the burial had already taken place. They had to act quickly, prevent investigation, essentially impeding any attempt to perform autopsies: laying bare the lungs of the dead would have revealed the truth.

Mrs. Charles Jones lived in the hamlet of Gamoca near Gauley

Bridge. Her husband; her three sons, Shirley, Cecil, and Owen; her brother-in-law; and Jeffrey, a boy that the family had taken in, all worked in the tunnel. Shirley was only eighteen. One day he came home gasping. He said:

"Mother, I'm awful short-winded."

"I think that dust is making you sick," said Mrs. Jones, and she kept him home.

After a few days, the foreman Anders paid her a visit.

"You're imagining stupid things," he said. "I've been working the tunnels for thirty years. It won't do him no harm."

And Shirley returned to work with the others. The six men came out of the tunnels covered in white dust; when they stepped out of their clothes, the floor was white, too. The boys coughed, lost weight. Mrs. Jones went to see a doctor, who talked to her about X-rays and money. She stood on the highway and asked motorists for donations. She begged so much that she was able to take her sons to be X-rayed at the Charleston hospital. The doctors put a name to the disease: silicosis. Shirley, who knew nothing about it, because his mother had concealed the truth, said:

"Mother, after I'm dead, I want you to have them open me up and see if I didn't die from the dust. Take the compensation money from the boss, because you won't have anything to live on once we're all dead."

Shirley died in June 1932, Cecil in September, and the oldest boy, Owen, a year later. Their friend Jeffrey died next, and then the brother-in-law. Only Charles Jones, the father, was not dead, just dying.

The mother had her youngest son "opened up," as he had requested, and so, thanks to Shirley Jones, murdered in his twentieth year, tunnel workers learned the truth. It was not pneumonia, or asthma, or "tunnelitis," but silicosis that killed Raymond Jackson and Henry Palf, Clev and Oscar Anders, Frank Dickson and Frank Lynch, Wall the supervisor and Pitch the foreman. None had even reached fifty. All were white. As for the Blacks, we do not know their names or the number of dead. An employee of Rinehart and Dennis, whom a curious person had asked if the company made a record of the dead, said:

"What's the point, there's plenty of niggers to go around."

That's when agents from the law firms descended on the region. Each sang the praises of his boss and dangled magic numbers before the reddened eyes of the silica workers. Three hundred sick men agreed to take the company to court.

The trial took place in the spring of 1933. One after the other, witnesses for the defense appeared before the jury. O. M. Jones, chief engineer of the New Kanawha Power Co., said "the air was as clear as it is in this courtroom, except on foggy days." The chief inspector of works, Charles Waugh, said: "In all my thirty-five years on the job, I have never seen better working conditions." The foreman Gilmore came forth to say, "there was no dust in that tunnel." The driller W. Cunningham swore they "drilled with water." Since then Waugh, Gilmore, and Cunningham have died. Dead of silicosis. Only Jones the engineer survived: he had never entered the tunnel without a mask.

Each evening, cars sent by Rinehart and Dennis took the jurors home. By law, the jury's decision must be unanimous. In this case, it was a hung jury; two jurors refused to consider the matter. There would have to be a retrial. So the company asked the workers' lawyers to settle. It was ready to pay a sum of $130,000 in exchange for the transfer of files. The lawyers hesitated: they were supposed to receive $30,000 in fees. The company offered them $20,000. And so, paid by their clients and their adversaries, the lawyers reached a compromise. They gave each victim a sum they had set themselves and refused to provide any explanation. All anyone knew was that Whites received more than Blacks. The life of a worker was assessed at $500, $300, $200. Lindsey Jones's widow received $185.85.

"I don't understand," she asked, "why the eighty-five cents?"

Some Blacks received only eighty dollars.

Work on the tunnel was long since finished. Five hundred

workers died at the site, every one of the twenty-six foremen died too. Over a thousand men were scattered throughout the United States; for a while, they wrote to complain about their health to their friends who'd kept on living at Gauley Bridge; then one day, there were no more letters.

A few hundred workers still lived in the tunnel area. The company burned the shacks they'd lived in, had them arrested for "trespassing on private property." These men could not leave for lack of money, they could not work for lack of breath; they could barely even move. One of them, George Robison, says: "It gets worse every day. Sometimes at night, I have to get up to catch my breath. If I stayed lying on my back, I think I would die."

The Charles Jones family: the sick father, the mother, and six grandchildren had bought a small farm and a cow with the money they received from the company for the death of the three older sons. Now they lived on unemployment benefits, two dollars a week. Relief wanted to cancel these: the family fed their cow and fed themselves. The Relief people said they must have hidden resources. Mrs. Jones explained that one week she bought fodder for the animal, and the next week flour for the children. The unemployment office was located almost twenty miles from Gauley Bridge. Mrs. Jones and other survivors made the journey there and back by foot.

In the summer of 1934, there were only ninety-one people left in the hamlet of Vanetta: fourteen children, thirty-four women, forty-three men. Only fifteen men could still work; they provided for all the others. All but one had silicosis. They were employed in the construction of a road twenty miles from Vanetta, and they walked to and from work. The people in the village had only one meal a day: beans and cornbread. Nobody had seen milk for two years.

In 1935, all that was left of Vanetta were a few dying people. One of them, George Robison, testified later before a commission of inquiry. Here are the questions and answers:

"What effect does the disease have on Blacks?"

"It affects only their breathing. When you have silicosis, you lose weight. I have two friends in Vanetta who will probably be dead by the time I get home. I have another friend, Johnson, who I think will die soon."

"Are they afraid or do they want to die?"

"They have to breathe a little faster."

"Do they seem afraid of dying? Or does their suffering make them prefer death?"

"No, sir, they do not want to die. They want to keep living as long as they can."

"But they know that their days are numbered?"

"Yes, sir, they know it."

They were the only ones who knew it until December 1935. The country had not even heard the name Gauley Bridge, and would not have heard of it if a salesman visiting the new tunnel had not alerted his friend, the editor of a left-wing newspaper. The mainstream press spoke of the case reluctantly. The House of Representatives called for an investigation. Mr. Faulconer and Mr. Perkins, respectively president and vice-president of Rinehart and Dennis, refused to go to Washington to testify, stating that they had no knowledge of any deaths from silicosis contracted on the tunnel operations at Gauley Bridge.

THE MORAL OF THE STORY

The work was completed long ago, Rinehart and Dennis launched new sites. The New Kanawha Power Co. had ceased to exist: on the completion of the hydroelectric power plant, the company was immediately acquired by the Electro Metallurgical Co. That company was taken to court by the Federal Power Commission for failing to obtain the necessary permits for the construction of a tunnel involving a navigable waterway, but it has retained the services of Mr. Newton D. Baker, former Secretary of War, one of the most influential business lawyers in America: the trial will go on for a long time. As for Union Carbide & Carbon Co., the first quarter of 1936 showed the highest net profit in company history: $7,502,393. The Morgan and Mellon families are in good health.

And that's it for the dollars.

The yards of Electro Metallurgical Co. are heaped high with silica rock so pure it can be used without refining. This raw material that cost them nothing, a by-product of the tunneling operation, is used in the manufacture of special steels.

And that's it for the silica.

In a cornfield in Summerville, West Virginia, the fourth crop has been harvested. All around Gauley Bridge, earth was amply repaid with cadavers for the silica the men extracted, so in the end, the dead, too, were just a by-product of tunnel construction. There are new crosses in cemeteries in Pennsylvania and Ohio, Maryland and Delaware, but especially the southern states: Florida and Alabama, Georgia and Virginia, and the Carolinas. The last survivors of the two thousand tunnel builders are waiting their turn. They have lost half their body weight, move with great difficulty, they hardly breathe. At the bottom of the mine or the corner of a street, in a hospital bed or a cotton field, down to the last man they will strangle to death, and if we think of opening their chests, their lungs will appear compacted, petrified blocks of tumor and silica: Gauley Bridge tunnel silica.

That's it for the men.

Now tell me if anyone in the world has shown more interest in mankind and the problems of the individual than the American businessman?

CONVENTIONAL AMERICA

III. ART

This ad in a New York newspaper caught my eye.

> ### BUREAU OF GHOST WRITERS
>
> Experienced writers at your service.
> Articles, reports, important statements,
> speeches, *very special* letters,
> literary assistance, drafting and research.
> *We write, YOU sign.*

I knew that what they call a "nègre"* in France is called a "ghost-writer" in the United States. I went to inquire in person.

Number 17 East 49th Street looks like all the other buildings in New York: a choice of elevators, an apparent absence of stairs, a tenant directory. However, this directory has something unusual about it. Among the inevitable Sullivans and Clarks, I see this: *Ideas Unlimited, Inc.*, which leads me to expect other revelations, like *Genius, Anon. Co.* for example. But under "G," I see only *Ghost Writers Bureau.* I go up to the tenth floor.

On the frosted-glass door, the managers' names: Henry F. Woods, Fred E. Baer.

---

* "Nigger" in French.

Mr. Baer is short with a big nose and gray hair. He is flattered by my interest in his company but not unduly: he is aware of its value.

"Was the office your idea?"

Mr. Baer smiles modestly.

"It was in the spring of 1933," he said, "just before President Roosevelt was elected. Times were bad, going to hell in a hand-basket. I thought back to my days in journalism before the war: since the armistice, I'd been writing advertising copy. You know what I mean? Well! I remembered the days when businessmen would make no statements to the press at all. The word was mum, and if they told you anything, they insisted it could never be made public. I told myself: business is bad, very bad, and businessmen, who were chatty in the boom years, will clam up again. What'll happen to me, a copywriter, if they clam up? Then I thought: display advertisements, publicity editorials, what are these? 'The manager of the X factories told us . . .' etc. Three quarters of it is done by ghostwriters. That's how I got my idea. We published our first ad in February 1933, just before the big crash. We're still small-scale, of course, but moving up, there's a market out there: New York's a big city, seven million inhabitants. A little mine to tap for starters."

"Where do you begin?"

"We've got a wide range. On the same day we got visits from a diner waitress who was speaking to her union, and a very rich man who wanted to give an address at his club, one of the classiest in New York. We provided both the speech and the address."

"What kind of subjects do you handle?"

"Well! Articles on business for businessmen, studies on medicine for professional journals that physicians ask us to write. The guys know their trade, but it's too much bother to go to the library and do the research. We take care of it for them."

"What are you asked to do most often?"

"We do a lot of articles for magazines published by industries and companies. You know, customer magazines that are supposedly written by managers. They don't feel sure of themselves, so they come to us. We do a lot of work for clubs: speeches, reports, presentations. We're asked to write toasts for singles' dinners. Reports on trusts too, not full reports, but preambles and conclusions. The customer only has to add in the numbers; as for eloquence, that's our stock in trade. We also write book summaries for members of ladies' clubs: that way they can avoid reading, which can be tiring. Sometimes we write academic dissertations. Off the record, we don't much like that kind of work, but since there are people out there who are going to do it anyway, why refuse?"

"Do you have a lot of people working for you?"

"About a hundred and twenty on file. When an order comes in, we go into the files and pull out the ghost best suited for the job. The hundred and twenty people I just mentioned are specialists: one in agriculture, another in chemicals or porcelain, and so on. We need specialists," Mr. Baer concludes firmly.

"How do you recruit?"

"Almost entirely through our ads. Every week, three or four people come in to apply. Mostly young, novice writers. There's no doubt some have talent, but what can I tell you, the only thing they know how to do is write."

"How do you pay them?"

"By the job, of course. When we agree on a price with the customer, we calculate how much we can offer the ghost. It's never a percentage of the fee. Sometimes it's less, sometimes more. We know how difficult it is to write and we try to be fair with the ghosts," says Mr. Baer.

"Suppose someone asks you to write an article on Chinese art in the tenth century."

"I go into my files."

"And if you can't find a specialist?"

"I try to find one outside of the hundred and twenty on file. You want to push the example farther? Let's say there's no such specialist in New York. Well, I make a deal with a person who's used to working in libraries, they collect the documentation and we write the article. I should add that the research is generally done by women, whereas 70 percent of our employees are men. As are 99 percent of our clients."

"And how many are we talking?"

"Twenty a week, give or take."

"Do they pay up front?"

"Depends. If it's a businessman, someone with references, he pays on delivery. Otherwise, we ask for a third up front. That way, we're sure he'll be back. Otherwise we might never see him again."

Mr. Baer smiles wryly.

"Do you have a fee?"

"You're looking at somewhere between one and a half to six cents a word. It depends on the kind of work they're asking for. If research is required, we ask for more. If it's a simple welcome speech or a few flourishes over a fresh grave, we ask the minimum."

"What's the average price?"

"Apart from large orders, forty and fifty dollars. That's not a lot for a businessman, but for a private individual, of course . . . Invoices for five dollars are not uncommon. We're often asked to write letters. Those are five dollars apiece."

I remember from the ad: "*very special* letters." Who could imagine a suitor so naïve or a blackmailer so reckless?

"What kind of letters?"

"Almost always job applications. You know, it's a delicate thing, and you need to know the right turns of phrase. Sometimes very wealthy people come to see us. The other day there was a big company director looking for a job in the West."

"Do you ever get complaints?"

"It happens. We take the manuscript back for review. We can't accept money for a service that doesn't satisfy the customer. Every client has a right to be satisfied."

"Has anyone ever congratulated you?"

Mr. Baer smiles bitterly.

"Never. Everyone who comes to us is embarrassed, as if they were committing a shameful act. Most of the time, they don't even tell us what they're planning to use their order for. When they arrive for the first meeting, they don't know how to begin. We have to put them at ease. And once the work has been delivered they vanish."

A short silence.

"But they come back when they need us again."

"No one ever asks you to do fiction?"

"Oh, yes! Usually that kind of client just promises to share his possible royalties. Of course, we refuse this kind of transaction straight off. So one day a very rich man asked me over to say he had an idea for a novel. I introduced him to a famous writer. In the end, it turned out the gentleman intended to set aside a percentage of his future sales to pay us with. You can't do business that way."

Mr. Baer smiles philosophically.

"All men think they can write," he says. "But they can't. (There is a touch of rancor in his voice and a great deal of resignation.) "There's that question of talent."

He falls silent, but quickly the honest businessman returns to banish the ghost of the sixteen-year-old boy who probably once composed verse and dreamt of glory.

"In the manuscripts we deliver," he says with composure, "we can guarantee spelling, rhetotic, and punctuation, but decline all responsibility as to the merits of the book itself."

NOTEBOOK

APRIL 1936

April 5. It's happened! Last night my neighbors, who have a radio set, invited friends over, probably to make the most of the news. When the speaker announced the death of Hauptmann, alleged kidnapper of the Lindbergh baby, a woman began to applaud.

The drama had gone on for four years, the child's corpse become a mere pretext. Republicans and Democrats struggled for political control of the State of New Jersey. The Democrats had relied on Hauptmann's guilt, the Republicans on his innocence. It was essential to make the convict talk.

The gangster William Zeid was to be executed the same night as the kidnapper. It was decided that the executioner would perform Zeid's final grooming in the presence of the German carpenter. Four minutes were to elapse between the two executions. In the interval, Hauptmann would talk.

The plan was changed at the last moment. Hauptmann would die on April 1. The guards came to shave his head, slit his pant leg down one side to insert the electrode. He still remained silent. Then they told him he had another forty-eight hours to live. With a shaved head and split pants.

In the United States, cashed checks are returned to the people who write them. Autograph collectors flooded the Hauptmann cell with checks for a dollar to get his signature on the back.

Agents for the film company to whom Bette Davis was under contract phoned the actress from Hollywood:

"Mrs. Hauptmann is currently in Trenton. We want you to go there immediately, stay with her during her husband's execution and convey your impressions to journalists."

Bette Davis refused.

Hearst, owner of a newspaper syndicate, made a fortune on the case. He had signed an agreement with Mrs. Hauptmann, who had given him exclusive rights to her "impressions." A reporter kept track of the woman's every movement for almost two years.

The night of the execution, Anna Hauptmann was in a hotel room in Trenton. The whole world knew she was a widow except for her. Two Hearst reporters rushed to tell her the news. At the same moment a photographer was taking her picture. She wanted to be alone, but the reporters would not let her out of their sight. Other journalists hovered in the hallway, in front of the closed door. They heard Anna Hauptmann shout to the Hearst men:

"Go away! Do you think I'm some kind of animal? Go away, for God's sake!"

They did not leave. She had to lock herself into the bathroom to cry.

Drawn by the shouting, the public flooded into the corridor. Two women got down on the floor by the door to hear more clearly.

The widow, who wanted to return to New York to be with her son, had to fight her way through the rubberneckers. In the street, a crowd of photographers lit the way with explosions of magnesium. One of them shouted: "Anna, over here!" to get a full-face photo.

She returned to New York, locked herself in her room.

In the room above, Hearst reporters lay watching through a hole they had drilled in the floor.

April 6. An editorial in the *The Daily News* read:

". . . it was impossible to provide our readers with a photo of Hauptmann's death, a photo we and our audience both wanted.

All the newspapers sent their top men to attend the execution and report on it in full detail. Yesterday, *The Times* gave the story close to three columns, the *Herald Tribune* five columns, the *American* six and a half. Unable to get photos, we sent an illustrator. His sketch of the final moment adorned the front pages of most of our yesterday's editions and is reproduced on the following page of this issue."

And, speaking out against the ban on photographing executions, the paper concludes:

"The most popular image ever obtained was that of Ruth Snyder in the electric chair. It is the image that most visitors to our building want to see first. We've got two on display, one on the first floor and one on the seventh."

April 7. In Omaha, a young man of twenty-two was sentenced to a house of correction. He had told the judge:

"I went to high school and for two years tried to find work. I spent some time in an office, I worked in a gas station, I even tried to write. I was unable to earn my living, find a stable job. I had studied philosophy and English literature; I planned to teach or write. But there were no jobs for me. I traveled through the Midwest in search of a position. My parents had given me $1,200 to help me get settled. I was full of zeal, frugal, determined. After two years, I realized that my parents had made a bad investment. There was no place for me in the Depression world.

"At least I was able to repay my people. I dismissed the idea of suicide: I was afraid that if I killed myself, my mother wouldn't get the $1,500 of my life insurance policy. I decided to commit a crime with the firm intent of getting myself killed."

On his fourth try, Linden was arrested, having failed to die. The judge who sentenced him said:

"I fear that you have adopted the atheist and communist viewpoint that all in life is vanity."

April 7. Today, in Washington, Mrs. Lawrence Roberts, wife of the former Under Secretary of State for Economic Affairs, held a reception to celebrate the eighth birthday of her horse, Saint-Jean-Baptiste. In attendance were Mrs. Alice Roosevelt Longworth, cousin of the president, and Mrs. W. Morgan, wife of the Secretary of the Democratic National Committee. The father of the lady of the house made a special visit from New York to attend the festivities. One of Washington's leading orchestras was on hand to play "Happy Birthday."

April 8. 918 Los Angeles residents have become ministers by correspondence. All they needed to do was write to a certain address and send money with the letter. Ten dollars got them ordained to the ministry, fifteen dollars the distinction of Doctor of Divine Science, and twice that amount, consecration to the office of bishop.

April 9. A *Daily Mirror* editorial discusses the war against criminals. "For reasons of economy and efficiency, if possible they should be placed in a small cell hooked up to the exhaust pipe of a small car. That way, we'd get rid of them like rats, economically, for less than half a cent per capita. It would be true and effective justice that would deter future criminals."

"That's the night shelter," says Michael Gold.

We are out walking in New York.

"And over there," he says, "they give out free meals. These streets are full of cripples. See them leaning against the walls, sitting on the ground?"

I look and I see.

"Jesus!" he exclaims. "That's what they do all day. Too poor to take the subway, too weak to hobble through the city. In the morning, they shoo them out of the shelter. They wait for mealtime. In winter they wait in the snow, in summer with the sun beating down. At night they go back to the shelter."

We've passed Bellevue Hospital, an undertaker's, the morgue. We pass a limping man. Mike talks to him: he hasn't been around for a while and asks what's been happening. Nothing has changed, except that they are in the process of expanding the night shelter.

"I know every inch of New York," Gold says. "I've lived in Latin America, I've visited Paris and Moscow, but it's New York I know best. Sometimes I even feel I've had enough. There isn't a city that's harder on the people who live there."

We cross Little Italy, a kingdom of oranges, and chillies, of sheaves of spaghetti and peppers in all the colors of the House of Savoy. Overhead trains make the tenements on both sides of the avenue tremble. We get into one of the antique wooden subway cars. The local train jerks along on the third level. Through open windows, you can see red bedspreads and pillows, plants in tin cans that Sicilian or Calabrian peasants will water tonight when they come home from their shoe repair stands; men in shirtsleeves, noses buried in newspapers. The Italian headlines are replaced by titles in Hebrew: Little Italy is behind us, melted into the ghetto.

All these streets, the hordes of kids, the garbage belong to Jews without money. They have changed since Michael Gold's childhood, but so very little.

Two kids lie flat out on the manhole cover: Are they looking for the bottom of the ocean? A little girl gazes dreamily at the paper flowers a street vendor is selling: Has no one ever told her about the country? An old peasant woman, Hungarian or Romanian, is out for a breath of air, on the sidewalk beneath a Chinese parasol. Hebrew characters line the signs and the display windows.

I've been here before on the pages of *Jews Without Money*, Gold's best book. I recognize Orchard Street, where the market is held. On either side of the narrow street, handcarts cluster in the shade of huge orange umbrellas emblazoned with a pawnbroker's address, name and traditional three-ball logo. Leaning out in the windows, chins on elbows, the locals see only the usurer's invitation and the double rows of bric-a-brac. In one cart, a top hat, three tennis racquets, an old cushion, a still life, a copper pot, a pair of riding chaps. A few books scattered in a pile of rusty locks: *An Observer in the Philippines*, *Code of Etiquette*, *Equine Diseases*, the Bible. A taxi driver gets out of his car to buy a canary in a cage. A man as bald as the melons he sells adjusts his skullcap. Gypsies sweep the sidewalk with their skirts patterned with flowers and fronds. A peddler sells a stain-removal liquid. "Three cents a bottle," he cries, "three cents! Wrap it for you? Too much paper, no money!" A blind man passes, playing the guitar; he moves in a straight line, with a certainty that only a blind man or a surveyor possesses. Some only sell one item: oranges, birds, or corsets. But most peddle everything: mismatched clothes, samovars without lids, car cushions, cucumbers, neckties, American flags, baby carriage wheels, bronze horses, cameras, candlesticks, old suitcases, skeletons of umbrellas. And, amidst the complicated din of voices, a mishmash of biblical curses, American slang, jeers, insults, haggling, jokes, and lamentations, a Jew all in black gazes lovingly at a pathetic violin; there must be a son in the family, who knows? So many great musicians started this way; it would spell the end of misery, and music is such a beautiful thing.

When Mike was very small, a firecracker had exploded next to his head while he was sleeping in the street. To calm the child's nerves, his parents had invited a healer to their home.

"The old lady sent my mother to the Orchard Street market to buy a glass that I had to carry that very night to the East River. Jesus! I had to drink water from the river and throw the glass in, while chanting *koom, toom, soom*. I did.

We walk along Delancey Street where he was born, Hester Street, where he played Cowboys and Indians and waited for the Messiah to arrive in the form of Buffalo Bill, and Chrystie Street where his mother lived for years.

"This country is hell for writers," he says suddenly. "I envy you: you can be a writer in France. Here we have to apologize for it: here they only respect people who make money."

I think of the words his father told him: "In this country, you're better off dead than poor." I think of the secret society that Mike founded with his friends in childhood, "The Avengers of Chrystie Street."

We are coming up to the Bowery.

"This is where I sold my first newspaper," he says. "Later I drove a horse and buggy. Jesus, was I proud!"

A beggar sleeping under a sign: "Before selling your old gold, check our prices."

"I'll write a novel about the unemployed," says Mike.

THE PARADOX OF THE
GANGSTER

. . . the type of criminal which I call an organized
criminal, a criminal who is in the business of crime,
who has organized it as a business for the purpose
of making money, or as we commonly call him,
"the gangster."

Harry S. Toy, Prosecuting Attorney,
Wayne County, Detroit (Michigan).

"William Randolph Hearst was not yet making half a million dollars
a year, but already enjoying tremendous success from launching
papers in San Francisco and New York, and decided to create one
in Chicago, eventually *The Examiner*. At that time, there was only
one major daily in that city, the *Tribune*, with editor Joseph Patterson. Let us picture, for a moment, the map of that city: a chessboard. The *Tribune* had newsstands at every intersection, on the
right-hand side, that is, next to the flow of traffic, just before the
cross street, at places where motorists and pedestrians naturally
stop so are most strategic for buying papers. Hearst could only set
up shop on the opposite corners, where business was virtually nonexistent. First, he suggested sharing newsstands with the *Tribune*.
The idea fell flat. Then he decided to build new ones next to Patter-

son's. They were run by boys of thirteen or fourteen. The *Tribune* vendors, who were no older, took umbrage. Daily battles ensued.

"The *Examiner* hired a Mossy Enright, who was not a gangster for the simple reason that the word did not yet exist. He was nicknamed Mossy because he always wore a three-week-old beard. His job was simple: to make a daily round of Chicago *Examiner* vendors, inquiring whether they'd been beaten up that day by their neighbors and competitors, and if they had, Mossy was then required to treat the perpetrators in kind, which was easy enough, considering that he was an adult and they were kids. Might as well leave them for dead on site.

"Next, the *Tribune* availed itself of the services of a Moe Annenberg, charged with a mission similar but opposite to Enright's, if I may say so. As of that day, two punitive campaigns were carried out daily, with victims on both sides.

"Enright and Annenberg didn't take long to form gangs around themselves whose members spent their time respectively in the basements of the *Tribune* and the *Examiner,* headquarters for the circulation of these newspapers.

"At the time, I worked at the *Examiner.* Every Saturday I got my pay: two twenty-dollar bills. None of my fellow writers were flush enough to break my bills, so I took to ambling down to the basement, where Mossy himself, or one of his henchmen, were delighted to give me change for my banknotes. That's how I got to know Enright, and Dion O'Bannion, prior to his motion picture fame, and other regular employees, paid weekly, in the circulation department.

"Little by little, the *Examiner* made a place for itself in Chicago, and management wanted to get rid of Enright and his band. But Mossy refused. "I'm an employee of this paper," he said, "and I'm not leaving." Relative calm prevailed for a time, interrupted by nocturnal skirmishes between the two gangs. One day a guy called Charley in circulation disappeared; later it was learned he'd been killed by the rival gang. Or the police picked a John Doe off the street, bullet-riddled and carrying a *Tribune* or *Examiner* card: the editors hastened to publish a note saying that the man had been fired three days earlier.

"Up until 1910, cooking, in Chicago, was done by gas. Electricity was still too expensive to be competitive. In the cream of Chicago society, one would occasionally meet well-appointed gentlemen, directors of the Gas House. Starting in 1910, other well-appointed gentlemen were spotted in this *beau monde*: these were the power-company directors. The cost price of electricity having decreased, the race was on.

"Gas appealed to the *Tribune* gang. Electricity turned to the Hearsts for support. The fighting resumed with renewed vigor.

"Maintaining a gang involves considerable expense. The newspaper administrations were no longer around to bankroll them. Enright told himself that he had to find a stable source of income for the bit players in his gang. As the Chicago mayor could refuse the Hearst paper nothing, Mossy set his sights on road maintenance. This had the dual advantage of paying employees from the municipal purse while clothing them in a white uniform that was such a familiar sight that wearers were guaranteed a kind of anonymity. And so Enright's subordinates became street cleaners. Of course, everyone in Chicago knew that the guys busily sweeping the sidewalks were gangsters, but there was nothing to do about it.

"That is, the people could do nothing about it. Fortunately, Moe Annenberg was keeping an eye on things. His gang hunted down the road workers. Too late Mossy realized that the anonymous white uniform made easy targets. There were casualties, and Enright had to find some other way.

"And now you know how gangsterism took hold in Chicago. Don't think for a minute that after creating the gangs, the newspapers never called their protégés back. Remember the Dempsey-Carpentier boxing match in 1921 in Atlantic City? The *Tribune* had made some fancy calculations to determine whether a photo of the boxers taken in the first thirty seconds of the match, transported by special plane to a locale about 125 miles from Chicago, transferred to a locomotive with a lab car and developed on the way, could appear in the six a.m. edition.

"The *Examiner* learns of the plan three days before the match. It's too late to do what the *Tribune* is doing. They have to act quickly. Hearst's newspaper gets in touch with a half-crazy aviator, who agrees to bring a picture of the fight directly to Chicago. Only, the aerodrome is too far from the printer's, and the only way of getting a negative there in time for the morning issue is to land in Grant Park, right in the middle of the city. Now, in this park, it is forbidden to drop even a piece of paper, to say nothing of a plane. The editor of the *Examiner* phones the mayor to announce his decision. The mayor has no choice but to accept, which he does, not without informing the *Tribune*. The *Tribune* mobilizes its gang with orders to invade Grant Park, and if the pilot succeeds in landing, to seize the picture at any cost and destroy it. Of course the *Examiner* is wise to the plot, and dispatches its own gang to the scene on the double to protect the precious negative. The editor of the *Tribune*, always in the know, phones the police chief and orders him to withdraw his men from Grant Park for the night. The official conveys the order.

"The big day arrives. Two planes take off from Atlantic City. The *Tribune* plane entrusts its cargo to the staff of the special train. The *Examiner*'s sits on the grass in Grant Park. Fighting, a shootout, victims. Both negatives reach their destination. A few hours later, Chicago readers of the first edition of the two dailies can admire photos of the biggest fight of the century. A black square with two white blotches: Carpentier and Dempsey.

"Thirty years have passed since the war of the *Tribune* and the *Examiner*. William Randolph Hearst runs forty-odd newspapers and earns half a million dollars a year. Mossy Enright was murdered. One of his henchman escaped death by being sent to Alcatraz for evasion of taxes required by the State on smuggled alcohol, white slavery and his other sources of income: this boy we called Al you probably know better by the name of Al Capone. Dion O'Bannion fell in the struggle for the supremacy of beer: a flower enthusiast, this gentle man with a score of murders on his conscience was shot in his florist shop, holding a bouquet of lilacs: you must know the story, Hollywood ate it right up. As for Moe Annenberg, he's head of circulation for a major New York newspaper, he's a big shot."

I heard this story from a friend glutted with anecdotes from thirty years of journalism. To me, it seemed a bit far-fetched at the time: I'd just arrived and was completely ignorant of certain facets of American life. Later, my friend's story was confirmed by various sources. Details may have differed, the essentials hardly ever. That is what got me interested in gangsters, which I had until then, quite wrongly, filed away among accessories of Conventional America.

Is it a big problem? Is it happening as we speak?

> According to the testimony of Senator Copeland* in 1933, the cost of crime and the fight against it in the United States was at least $13 billion a year, a little over a quarter of the national income.
>
> At the end of Prohibition, there was a robbery every four minutes, a murder every three-quarters of an hour. In 1935, in Chicago alone, there were on average thirty hold-ups a day, and more than ten thousand crimes committed in the first quarter of 1936.
>
> During the winter of 1935–36, the newspapers in New York revealed the existence of many rackets, involving the dairy industry, artichokes, newspapers, truck transport, etc.

So the problem is considerable and the army of crime immense. What is it made of?

---

* Senator Copeland chaired a Senate committee that undertook, in 1933 and 1934, a survey of crime in the United States. The investigations came to no practical conclusions but generated hundreds of invaluable testimonies. The minutes of the Committee's work was published in Washington under the title *Investigation of So-called "Rackets."* It is a thousand pages long, and it's where I got most of the testimonies we will read farther on.

Gangsters' biographies inform us that they mostly come from poor big-city neighborhoods. The larger the urban center, the higher the percentage of crime. A civil servant working for the New York courts said: "The governors of prisons and reformatories indicate that the proportion of craftsmen and skilled workers among prisoners is remarkably low. Criminals are mostly people who have received no professional training." In addition, 1934 federal statistics show that more than half of offenders arrested that year were under thirty (15 percent were not yet twenty).

Let us note that the criminal comes from a poor background, that he belongs more precisely to the lumpen proletariat, that he starts very young. We know where this potential army of crime grows up. Let us observe him from his beginnings.

In the populous districts of large cities, when kids do not throw themselves into baseball, they play gangsters. They cluster at the entrances of movie theaters, eyeing pictures of "public enemies" and millionaires. They scrounge for newspapers with daily comic strips in which both lawbreakers and police get raked over the coals. They read the headlines in the evening rags: "AIR POLICE GIVE CHASE TO AIR SMUGGLERS." "GUNMEN KILL TWO, WOUND FOUR, GET AWAY WITH $27,000."

Influence of the movies, press, games? A timeworn explanation, but insufficient. Millions of poor Whites have played Redskins without scalping anyone later in life.

The answer must lie elsewhere. Following the indirect example, the direct. Professor Frederic M. Thrasher, of New York University, writes:

". . . each city block has its stories of men who went to prison and boys from this or that New York neighborhood proudly boast that their block supplied more tenants for Sing Sing than any other part of the city . . . Too often, boys witness the triumphs of local gangsters, whose resplendent Packards and Lincolns establish the neighborhood standard of success. This teenage hero-worship translates into practice; they measure success not in the idealistic terms set down in history textbooks, but in material, tangible assets and manifestations of the very real power the criminal and his political allies have at their disposal."

A more serious line of reasoning, but insufficient. The example of the upstart gangster encourages a tendency for crime without making it out to be etched in stone. Let us remember that the average criminal starts very young and has no work skills. Let us take note of some more general information:

even during the years of "prosperity," a considerable part of the population had incomes below the bare minimum;

child labor is widespread in the United States. It was reduced to some extent by the codes of the NRA*; since their abolition, it is back again, in spite of the Depression, due to the cheapness of child labor;

nevertheless, hundreds of thousands of teenagers who've grown to adulthood in the last six years have never had the opportunity to work, or even learn a trade.**

If society allows children to work (in other words obliges them to do so), the choice, for them, is no longer between school and play, on the one hand, and work on the other, but between one kind of occupation and another. In addition, unemployment and its consequences—enforced idleness, giving up the pleasures and necessities of life—can lead certain people to a life of crime.

Could the reserve army of crime be a division of the reserve army of labor?

Objection: unemployment, poverty, etc., exist in countries other than the United States. How is it that a young American more readily chooses a career in crime than a European of the same age?

---

* National Rifle Association. (Editor's note)

** During the winter of 1935–36, the New York City Board of Charities conducted a survey of the economic situation of young men and women between sixteen and twenty-five. It turned out that of one hundred adolescents, eleven are unable or unwilling to work, twenty are at school, thirty-six have a job, and thirty-three are unemployed. The number of these unemployed in New York is 390,000.

Could it be that the atmosphere of the United States predisposes him to making such a choice?

What attitudes, when they become widespread, lead to making the Law inoperative?

Contempt for lawfulness.

A habit of violence.

The worship of money.

I have encountered these three elements, singly or combined, at every step in America. I have cited many examples in this book. Here are two more.

> John D. Rockefeller, in his early days as a major oil producer, made a secret agreement with rail companies to give him a discount. Other oil companies paid full price, and the difference between the latter rate and the price Rockefeller paid was handed over to him by the railways, so Rockefeller earned a few dollars on each tank shipped by his competitors.

> Andrew W. Mellon, when he was Secretary of the US Treasury, consented to discounts and repayments of amounts paid to the IRS as income tax. The companies in which Mellon held shares recovered $14 million and the financier himself, $400,000.
>
> More recently, the IRS filed a lawsuit against the former Secretary, accusing him of fraud to the tune of $3 million.

Regarding the habit of violence, I could limit myself to citing the same two names next to a list of their companies where workers were killed by private guards. I quote, nonetheless, from among recent cases:

> *The Crempa case.* The Public Service Corporation, which controls the production and sales of electricity in New

Jersey, wanted to build a new line through the land of many smallholders. One of these, Thomas Crempa, refused to settle. The discussions went on for years. Finally, on September 26, 1935, sheriffs surrounded the Crempa home and ordered its occupants out. When the farmer and his wife appeared at the doors, hands up, the police opened fire, killing Sophie Crempa and wounding her husband. Crempa was prosecuted and convicted.

The Schoemaker case. Time: November 30, 1935. Place: Tampa, Florida. Police officers burst into a private home where a small group of men, most of them socialists, are drafting the statutes of an association they've just founded, to be called the Modern Democrats. The police push three of the assistants into cars, drive them out of the city, strip, beat, tar and feather them and abandon them half dead. One of the victims, J. Schoemaker, dies from being tortured.

I will dispense with providing examples of money worship and conclude that, indeed, the American climate is favorable to the hatching of criminals.

I anticipate an objection: the parallel between the dealings of financiers and those of gangsters is an abstraction; a criminal does not concern himself with moral alibis. I reply that, 1) the imitation can be unconscious, and indeed, I've just mentioned climate, and 2), that it is often conscious.

Examples:

Dr. Kirchwey, former Warden of Sing Sing prison said:
    "One day I was talking with a group of inmates about very stringent draft bills pending in the House of Representatives. One of the men said: 'It won't make any difference to us, our chances won't be reduced. This is our

game now (his game was armed robbery), it's ten times less dangerous than Wall Street.' 'Yes,' another prisoner said, and ten times more honest.'"

Testimony of Albert W. Johnson, Judge at the Court of Lewisburg (Pennsylvania):
"The racketeer, the highwayman, seems to have no conscience or feel any remorse. He believes he's doing what a lot of other people do. *Senator Copeland*: He thinks he's no worse than some financial magnate? *Judge Johnson*: That's exactly what he thinks."

Finally, these words from Commissioner Mulrooney, of the New York Police Department:
"Today's criminal—I mean the young hardened criminal—is convinced that the law of the land is the dollar."

A Rockefeller, a Mellon thought so too. What's so surprising if a greenhorn, possessed of the same thirst for money, but living at a time when all the so-called lawful sources of profit have dried up or been appropriated by others, seeks to broaden his elders' range of experience?

I am tempted to conclude that the gangster is a businessman operating in areas that sometimes do and sometimes do not coincide with those controlled by businessmen approved by the powers-that-be, and who *continuously* employs methods to which the latter type of businessmen only resorts in more or less exceptional circumstances.

This hypothesis, if correct, provides a better explanation than most for the flourishing of crime in the United States. To be fully convinced of it, I must consider two issues: is the gangster a businessman? Is crime an industry?

First of all, I observe that the gangster has many employees whose occupations are often perfectly normal in themselves: the distilling of alcohol, the management of cafes and clubs, etc.* I also note that all major gangsters keep their accounts in order, have checking accounts, rent safety-deposit boxes, pay their income taxes unless they are trying to evade them, in which case the Law comes after them, which tends to prove that the State implicitly recognizes the commercial nature of their occupations. I note again, without making a point of it, that criminals often draw attention to themselves through displays of charity: in Chicago, you hear all sorts of stories about Al Capone distributing toys to poor children, etc.

How does a gangster proceed? He begins by rounding up all the support he needs to run his business. In other words, he behaves like any other businessman except for the fact that right from the beginning, the latter has the advantage in a society shaped by and for his class, while the gangster has to work to acquire the services of this preexisting machine.

And so:

the gangster Torrio will be backed by former boxers and ace gunmen, not unlike Manville, heir to "King Asbestos," who spends his time replacing bodyguards with guard dogs and police dogs with private police;

the said Torrio will be represented by the protégé of the head of the Democratic Party in Chicago, just as Electro Metallurgical Co., taken to court by the government, will hire in their defense Newton D. Baker, Secretary of War under President Wilson;

the bootlegger Jack Zuta will have a list of Chicago police officers tucked in his safe, and beside each name the amount of money he is paid, just as in Harlan County (Kentucky)

---

* Bloody incidents occur only when a competitor intervenes. They are relatively rare compared to the volume of transactions, considering, for example, that around 1927, Al Capone alone controlled nearly twenty thousand depots and bars that he had to constantly supply with liquor.

police salaries will be paid not by the authorities but by mining management;

in Cicero, a suburb of Chicago, Al Capone will arrange for the election of his mayor and chief of police in the same way that Wall Street will have its representative, Herbert Hoover, named president of the United States.

I observe that the very practice of the profession of crime establishes monetary relations between two worlds that the law is supposed to separate. A series of services required and rendered on both sides leads to an increasingly tight collaboration, and eventually to the forming of an organization whose every cog is essential to the functioning of all the others, and to the machine as a whole.

Examples:

Gangsters and police.
A government inquiry into the activities of the Genna brothers, Chicago bootleggers, brought to light the following: "The Company is run with the consent, approval and protection of the police . . . Each month, four hundred policemen in uniform line up to be paid, along with a significant number of civil servants wearing their badges. To avoid all fraud, a messenger of the Maxwell Street Police Station provides the names and numbers of officers on duty, and these men do not receive their pay until they have signed an attendance sheet."

Gangsters and magistrates.
A letter from a Chicago judge to gangster Mops Volpe:
"Dear Mops, thanks for your help on election day. You took care of the polling in the best possible way. I wouldn't have been able to do as well without you. Thank you, old boy. Hope to see you soon."

Gangsters and politicians.

Testimony of Judge Lyle, Chicago Municipal Court:

"I went into the 27th district whose president was one Garrison, a member of my own party. I had just issued twenty-eight arrest warrants, including one for Dago Lawrence Mangano, a well-known gangster. Arriving at the meeting, I received a frosty reception. Mr. Garrison took me aside and told me that I could not speak that evening. "Why?" I asked, "this is a regular meeting of my party. I'm on the electoral list." He replied: "Well, you just signed a warrant for Dago Lawrence, and he's my right-hand man."

General findings.

Testimony of District Attorney George Z. Medalie, New York:

"In almost all cities, the racketeer, the gangster, the gangs are key elements in the machine for controlling town councils. I'm not referring specifically to a political party, because both parties,* when in power, resort to exactly the same practices."

Testimony of Frederick Kernochan, president of the Court of Special Sessions in New York:

"I know myself that many of these men (gang leaders) pay money to the political parties or to the party they think should win, and that the money creates obligations for the district leader. *Senator Copeland*: Do they often give money to both parties? *Judge Kernochan*: I think they would if they doubted the outcome of the election."**

Finally, here are the words of J. Edgar Hoover, head of the FBI, which was engaged in the war against gangsters at the national level:

---

* Democrats and Republicans.

** For the senatorial election of 1926 in Illinois, the banker Samuel Insull paid $125,000 to the Republican candidate and $15,000 to the Democratic candidate. This is common practice.

"In this country we have allowed an organization to form that extends from small-time dealers and neighborhood politicians to the powers controlling large cities, and that are often more influential than the courts, the police, and the district attorneys."

I observe that you can be a gangster in a country that has laws, police, and judges, just as it is possible for three companies to control 66 percent of the chemical industry in this same country though there is an anti-trust law in effect.

And so, in his relations with the State machine, the gangster goes about his profession like any other businessman. What is the nature of this profession? Before answering, I want to know if the crime industry has evolved in the United States, and if so, in what direction?

I'll take the most famous example, Chicago.

Around 1910, there were, in that city, a public drinking establishment for every three hundred inhabitants and over one thousand houses of prostitution. Procurers were plentiful and knew each other and worked together on occasion. "Often they belong to political organizations and exchange shady work at the polls for protection from men in power for their 'wives.' The police close their eyes to the state of things: they're paid off to know nothing."* The future "public enemies" are dedicated to newspaper circulation and introducing the use of gas or electricity. The big gangs have not yet formed. Chicago is in its cottage-industry era of crime.

Then comes the mass-production era, which takes place after the war and the beginning of Prohibition. Many bootleggers and their little gangs work on reduced territories. Competition is not yet serious; each has his own customers and would not think of taking over his neighbors'.

---

* *The Social Evil in Chicago, Study of exisiting conditions with the recommendations by the Vice Commission of Chicago*, Chicago, 1911.

In 1920, Torrio appears on the scene, and shortly thereafter Al Capone. Gangs become fewer and more powerful, competition is more intense. Chicago is divided into zones. Bombs and machine guns enter the picture. The little guys disappear or are eliminated. The struggle is narrowed down to two or three gangs vying for a monopoly on alcohol. In 1926, Al Capone attempts to form a cartel of bootleggers who divvy up the city and its outlying areas. The alliance does not last long and the shooting begins again. Finally, Capone gets rid of the competition: he controls almost all of the drinking services and outlets, as well as the suppliers in Florida and Canada, hundreds of gambling dens and brothels, an entire township, Cicero.

Is Chicago, at this final stage, an exception?

I refer you to other examples.

Attorney Harry S. Toy recalls:

"There were two gangs in Detroit, the Scarlet gang and so-called Sicilian gang, and other groups who joined forces with them or became part of them in order to perpetuate the organized trade of crime. They extorted from illicit businesses, managed the smuggling of alcohol, the sale of narcotics, and every kind of racket in existence; they invented new rackets, attacked legitimate trade and made it pay protection money . . . Statistics show that in 1929 and 1930, Detroit was the city where the most murders were committed in America: 18.6 for every 100,000 inhabitants as compared to just over 12 for every 100,000 in Chicago."

World Telegram, May 20, 1936:

"Federal prosecutor Thomas J. Morrissey revealed today that stocks and bonds stolen by the majority of American criminals were sent to Denver to be cashed. Police are looking for one Sam Webber, head of a New York group, who bought back stocks for 30 percent of their value.

On April 15, Webber wrote to R. W. Blackett in Denver with a list of securities he had in his possession. On May 5, Webber flew to Denver with shares valued at $27,000. They had been stolen from banks from Boston to Iowa and the Midwest. R. W. Blackett, entrusted with the task of re-selling and arrested with the securities in his possession, is the former president of the Denver Stock Exchange."

In May 1936, the Supreme Court of New York judged the gangster Luciano and his accomplices. They were accused of controlling most of the city's brothels for the past two years. The gang was based on the model of a holding company, with four independent trusts managed by several common administrators. Luciano made the girls pay him weekly dues that he would use to pay their bail if they were arrested. Furthermore, he decided to demote the "madames" to the status of regular employees, managing the brothels on behalf of the trust in exchange for a fixed salary.*

One need only compare Luciano's business practices with those long-ago days in Chicago, when pimps made ends meet by exploiting a girl and earning a few bucks on election day, to assess how concentrated and rationalized the crime industry has become since the beginning of the century.

Crime *industry*? I still have only circumstantial evidence. To go any further, I again must ask myself: What is the nature of this industry, and first, what are its main subdivisions?

Stealing, of which I have provided examples.

Kidnapping. Some believe that the abduction of humans is common in America. This erroneous impression arose in large part as a result of the Lindbergh-Hauptmann affair. More often than not,

---

* See: chain stores.

both kidnappers and abducted are members of rival gangs and kidnapping is just another form of competition, like the use of firearms.*

These two types of crime are relatively nonlucrative and needlessly dangerous. Two hundred and eighty-five bank robberies, in four States and over three years, brought in little more than $1 million. The sixteen top kidnappings, including that of Lindbergh's son, resulted in profits of just over $1 million but also in fifty-two death sentences and imprisonments. On the other hand, long before the war, prostitution brought in over $15 million a year in the city of Chicago alone. It is logical to assume that gangsters will increasingly avoid direct robbery, good for the isolated petty criminal but increasingly anachronistic in times when a rational capitalizing on vice is so very lucrative, whether through alcohol smuggling during Prohibition, or at all times, through prostitution, gambling, narcotics, lotteries, slot machines, etc.

However, these businesses are not fundamentally different from the food industry, for example, except that they are considered illicit. If tomorrow prostitution were legalized in the United States, almost nothing would change in existing conditions, except that normal economic development, from cottage industry to monopoly, would be made easier and quicker. The same goes for alcohol since the Eighteenth Amendment to the Constitution was revoked. In the spring of 1936, New York wholesale liquor merchants went to war. It was never known whether a monopolistic trust was trying to eliminate independents or if two competing companies were angling for control of the market. In any case, in the space of a few hours, retail prices fell by 20 to 50 percent. Scenes from Prohibition were replayed, as when strangers posted at the entrance to a wine store forced the driver of a delivery truck to turn back.

And so, the shift from an outlaw trade—or a trade under outlaw

---

* "Most people who were abducted were materially interested in a racket and were themselves racketeers and gamblers." Testimony of W. Shoemaker, chief of detectives of the Chicago Police Department.

protection (that is, the modification of that law)—pushed the so-called criminal element into the so-called business world.

What remains to be examined is the gangster's main occupation, which, since the end of Prohibition, has proved most costly for the American people: the rackets.

The origin of the word is obscure. It seems that at the end of the last century, some New York clubs held big dances called rackets. Ticket sales were the main source of income for these organizations, people who refused to buy them got themselves in trouble. Later, the name of these big dances was applied to the method of ticket distribution. Then the word had an unexpected stroke of luck. Today when someone inquires what you do for a living, they frequently ask: "What's your racket?"

As for the current meaning of the word, we need only mention the following incident. One day, the Crime Prevention Bureau of New York learns that in the schoolyard, two twelve-year-old boys have been extorting two cents a week from younger children to defend them against the "big kids." Replace the protected youngsters with manufacturers and merchants, and the protectors with gangsters, multiply the two pennies by $10,000 or a $100,000, and there you have a racket.

Examples:

A. J. Smith, secretary of the Jurors Association, County of New York, says:

"An anonymous company was formed in Albany. It had a president and administrators who hired a general manager, who along with other employees visited the furriers and told them: 'We are asking you to join our association. You will pay a percentage of your sales.' If you answered: 'And what will I get in return?' they said, 'We will protect you against all movements forming among your workers. If your customers do not pay, we will do our best to collect the money for you. We have two conditions: you will deliver your goods to no one except the members of our association and you will use our trucking service. If you do not join our organization, let us draw your attention to what happened in Connecticut.' If I remember correctly, the incident to which they referred was the blowing up of the shop front of a fur workshop. And they continued: 'We would also like to refresh your memory about certain events in New Jersey where a fire broke out. And also remind you of the stink bombs of Thirtieth and Fortieth streets . . .'"

Steve Summer, secretary of the Chicago Dairy Workers Union, recalls:

"They (the gangsters) arrived at our offices and told us politely: 'We're getting in on this, and you're getting out.' And well, that's what happened. They told us, very up-front, that after Prohibition, the milk business looked pretty good to them. They offered us a $100,000 to withdraw and let them take over. We told them it was out of the question. Finally, we said, 'Okay, if it's a fight you want, that's what you'll get.' Things degenerated. We had to fortify our offices. Now they're all armored with steel."

One could believe that racketeers are criminals who use blackmail, threats, and terrorist acts to extort money from bosses and workers.

If that were so, the victims would eventually rise up against the evildoers who exploit them. If American Justice is having such great difficulty convicting racketeers of their crimes, it is because they are almost never denounced by their vicitms and prosecution witnesses are virtually nonexistent. Appeals to civic-mindedness from those with the authority to do so, guaranteed secrecy—nothing worked. There has to be something to explain this unanimous silence: a motive more powerful than the terror inspired by racketeers. On this last point, I refer you to the following concordant testimonies.

"The racket flourishes in the branches of trade where competition is particularly fierce. Some businessmen will tell you they agreed to pay dues to racketeers, because the arrangement is profitable; in doing so, they improve their position in relation to their competitors."*

"This crime has a double aspect. On the one hand, it exists only for the purposes of extortion. On the other hand, the criminal forms an association with a person who otherwise has a normal commercial activity and in exchange for cash, gives the client priority treatment by pursuing and boycotting its competitors."**

"In trade associations sworn to the rackets, as they exist today, the bosses pay protection to gangsters, generally backed by attorneys; in exchange, they are protected against the violence of criminals and competition from people who might seek to engage in the same branch of trade. For this reason, it is impossible to make the businessman decide to testify against his protectors."***

Now it will come as no surprise that the Senate commission of inquiry was able to enumerate over one hundred and fifty different rackets. In the city of Chicago, the following industries were subject to racketeers: dry cleaners, soft drinks, construction, trucking, street paving, garbage removal, coal selling, entertainment, fish shops, meat, poultry, vegetables, fruit, and milk.

The rackets have prospered, especially since the Depression, because of increasingly severe competition between capitalists. Added to the "normal" means of competition, which have become inadequate—rebates and secret discounts, credit, bonuses, etc., are the racketeer's bomb that shatters the neighbor's storefront, the

---

* Testimony of Police Chief Whalen of New York.

** Testimony of Judge E. Hammer of the Supreme Court of the State of New York.

*** Testimony of Dr. Ettinger, author of *The Problem of Crime*.

veer of the steering wheel that sends the vehicle of the independent milkman into the water, compliments of the milk trust.

The war on gangsterism is doomed to failure: it never attacks the root cause, but its consequences; at most, its indirect causes.

Some believe that educating youth and eliminating the bad places where they spend their time would deal a crippling blow to gangsterism. This overlooks the facts of the matter, for if at the bottom of the heap, there are poor adolescents pushing their way into crime, at the top, individuals are being recruited to perform functions that correspond to social necessities. Threats and preaching are ineffectual; the arrest of Public Enemy No. 1, announced at regular intervals, is nothing but a paper transaction, with no. 2 moving up to first place, no. 3 becoming no. 2, etc.

In short, the success of the gangster in a profit- and competition-based economic system is due to a small number of reasons, some related to the conditions of historical development in the United States, but whose determining cause is that American capitalism has reached its peak.

Clausewitz said, "War is nothing but the continuation of state policy by other means."

I offer this definition: gangsterism is the crime industry in the era of monopoly, and its largest branch, racketeering, is nothing but the continuation of capitalist competition by other means.

NOTEBOOK

APRIL 1936 (CONTINUED)

Walking in New York

Around Tenth Avenue, the area they call Hell's Kitchen.

A boy of four years aims a tiny wooden gun at a two-and-a-half-year-old girl and pulls the trigger, while she, with an angelic and lightly sensual smile, puts the barrel against her belly.

Columbus Circle. Between the statue of Christopher Columbus on his column and Broadway, a Jew in a skullcap talks about God to a crowd of onlookers. A sign proclaims him the Wandering Jew, who preaches every Monday and Wednesday at three p.m.

Broadway. Shirts for sale, cars for sale, women for sale, gods for sale. Behind a display window dappled with butterflies: "Sale on pens," a young man, puffy-faced and poorly shaven draws the same line over and over with a pen he's chosen from the stack in front of him: "Special Day. Come in and buy me."

Union Square. Standing near a shoeshine boy who sports a red straw pith helmet, a hawker sells music. Gaunt face. A huge eye-tooth emerges from the gash of his mouth when he speaks.

It's noon. The crowd sweeps by without stopping. The man shouts, opening his toothless mouth:

"You've got things to do, you're in a hurry, you don't stop."

And suddenly, with a triumphant laugh:

"When I'm rich, I'll bury you all!"

April 12. Two black robbers were whipped in a Georgetown, Delaware, prison. The judge added the following to his verdict: "We want to dissuade your kind of people from wanting to come here."

April 12. A destitute man died at Harlem Hospital. It was discovered by chance that the man was George Dickinson, one of the most renowned journalists in New York, circa 1900.

April 13. Ten days ago, near Huntsville, Alabama, the corpse of a murdered white girl was found. The crowd traveled all around the countryside, looking for the murderers and settled on four black boys, the eldest twenty-four and the youngest seventeen. When police arrived on the scene, the lynchers had already wrapped wire nooses around the Blacks' necks.

Today the four young men were released from the prison; there was no semblance of evidence against them except the color of their skin.

Spent the afternoon with Waldo Frank.* I'm the one who's read his books, and he's the one who asks first:

"What do you think of the United States?"

Later, he will answer:

"Of course, the United States is the flower of capitalism. We're a funny people. At the very worst of the Depression, the average American did not realize it was anything more than bad luck, individual incompetence. The social-thinking minority has increased

---

* Waldo Frank (1889–1967). Prolific writer and historian. (French editor's note.)

but remains a minority. The majority of Americans don't think. Between the newspapers, radio, and moving pictures, you'd have to be an intellectual athlete to be able to think. In America, the act of thinking requires a special effort of which few people are capable and which appeals to only a few. The media of entertainment and information create a habit of "superficiality." Moreover, intellectuals don't think either.

I talk about children, who seemed to me more mature than in Europe.

"Our children," he says, "live the same lives as their parents: they read the same papers, listen to the same radio shows. American kids know the Hauptmann case inside out. But as for their intellectual and emotional development, they fall behind little Europeans. The truth is not that our children are more mature, it's that our adults are more childish. Most Americans never reach adulthood.

"It is difficult and dangerous to generalize. America is one of the hardest countries to understand. We ourselves have yet to assimilate our traditions. Everything changes too quickly in the United States. It is good, to an extent, that immigration has been curtailed: that way we can arrive at crystallization more quickly. Until now, American tradition has remained an idea. It will not materialize until we've had a social revolution."

I talk to him about his book, *The Rediscovery of America*.

"Yes," he says. "We really are a funny people. Our fascism—if we ever have one, which is not at all certain—will be a very special kind. It will quote the Constitution to support its actions, in fact, it will be based on the Constitution. It will be a constitutional and parliamentary fascism. As for an Italian- or German-style fascism, I don't think so. It would be possible in small towns and the countryside, but in big cities, no. Our fascists won't wear brown shirts: they'll stick to their starched ones. We'll have a fascism with formal clothes."

"No violence?"

"Oh, no, the practice of fascism is the same everywhere. We

have a long tradition of violence and contempt for the law. It is an essentially American paradox: a worship of the Constitution that goes hand in hand with a total lack of respect for the law. The current state of civilization favors this trend: we have a huge mass of unemployed who gradually degenerate toward fascism. Violence is widespread among us: just look at the number of private police, bodyguards, thugs. That's how it's always been in the United States, but today, what with unemployment, the reserve army of henchmen knows no limits. We are faced with corrupt human material. Which performs the same tasks as our marines in Cuba and Nicaragua, and for the same masters. All, of course, outside the Law and the Constitution."

He interrupts himself to answer his own questions:

"And despite it all, our fascism would be extremely respectable. It has to be: we have a multitude of people who firmly believe in Jefferson and Lincoln. Hence the need to camouflage fascism with extreme care. Unlike countries such as Italy and Germany, we have a true democratic tradition."

"What does the average American know about Lincoln?"

"Above all that he was extremely honest—honest Abe." Just like Washington, the poor boy, born in a log cabin, he made his way to the presidency of the United States. Until recent years, social classes in the United States were extremely fluid. The current generation is probably the first we could say that possesses class consciousness. Until recently, on one hand, we had immigration and on the other emigration to the West. I'm not so old and yet I remember the days when the government distributed land in the west. Today there is nothing left to distribute, and immigration has ended. For the first time in history, we are becoming a people.

"But the ideology of the past is still very strong. In general, men are more sensitive to ideas than to reality. I mean that the average man faced with a reality that runs counter to his ideas, will tend to adhere to the latter at the expense of the former. The existence of classes is a reality, but what still prevails is the idea of the poor boy who goes on to become President of the United States. It's part of American mythology, like measuring a man's value by the size of his fortune. Mellon has a $100 million, X has only $1 million, therefore Mellon is a hundred times more valuable than X. This mentality is dying out. Do not forget that we are latecomers. And crystallization is inevitable."

THE NEW BUSINESS
WORLD

PINKERTON, PRIVATE DETECTIVE

There was a time when little booklets with tantalizing covers were sold for the price of a piece of candy. Kids who'd got past the age of barley sugar devoured these dime novels in which Nat Pinkerton, famous American detective, punished criminals and came to the rescue of the widow and the orphan.

On January 10, 1937, Americans tuning in to their radio sets would have heard a program on "men who rarely appear on the front page of the newspapers, but whose daily work, necessary, interesting, and often fascinating, amply contributes to making America a better place to live." The following dialogue would come in:

"Tell me, sir, what is the general activity of a Pinkerton detective?"

"They help the business world serve the public better, guard and protect valuables, and collaborate with the police in the search for criminals."

"The Pinkerton archives must be full of fascinating cases?"

"We've hunted down many notorious criminals!"

After this introduction, a case would be reproduced, and the speaker conclude:

"This is only a page from the book of Pinkerton, the captivating story of a war that never ends: the war that the Law has waged on crime and criminals."

A pause, then:

"This program has been brought to you by Realsilk, creator of made-to-order hosiery for women and the finest socks for men."

At the time this program was aired, Realsilk was a Pinkerton client, but the audience was unaware of this and could not suspect that the great detective drew 60 percent of its profits—more than $1 million a year—by ratting on the labor force.

For Pinkerton does exist, Pinkerton National Detective Agency, Anon. Co., headquartered in New York, near Wall Street, Robert Pinkerton, director, owner, and principal shareholder along with two elderly ladies, his aunts: "eighty-five years of history, four generations of the same family—a major fixture in the business world."

And indeed, Pinkerton has nearly 1,300 employees whose sole business is labor spying. Of these, over 350 are members of 91 different unions: there is not a union, no matter how small, where Pinkerton does not maintain informers, whose dues they pay. Approximately 100 occupy management positions. Information they provide is consolidated, compared and classified. A blacklist of several thousand names is continually updated, including all names of labor movement activists. At the agency headquarters, which subscribes to dozens of publications, a library of several hundred volumes even contains the *Communist Manifesto*.

Pinkerton is discreet. Each agent is identified by a number or initials used to sign reports, which are sent to a post-office box rented under a false name. The informer often does not even know for whom he is working: the detective who has hired him claims to have done so on behalf of a shareholders' group, an insurance company, or even a charitable organization interested in the operational health of the plant and the well-being of workers. He is paid in cash and in person. He never goes to the agency. In correspondence and accounting records, the nature of his work is filed under: theft, sabotage, extremist activities, public opinion, general situation. Often the name Pinkerton does not even appear on the bill, replaced by the name of some employee. The client's name is coded. Reports and statements are sent to managers or owners of the business in question, preferably to their home address and marked "Confidential."

From The Stork, the most sought-after restaurant in New York, to Alaska gold, Shell Petroleum, Libby's canned foods, Colt revolvers, and Firestone tires, Pinkerton has an excellent clientele. "Our three guiding principles are: hire the worker and give him work, pay him well for what he does, and treat him as you'd want to be treated yourself." Those are the words of Alfred Marshall, Chevrolet's chief of staff, a.k.a. MHUPO in the *Pinkerton Code*.

On the date of January 22, 1936, the Agency's order book reads:
   "Account: MDABY.
   "Nature of work: public opinion.
   "Reports and Invoices: address to Pegwood."
   Pegwood is secret agent Peterson, MDABY refers to General Motors, "public opinion" to informing.
   Immediately, Pinkerton sets up an office in Detroit where information supplied by all informants is consolidated: General Motors has over sixty factories, 230,000 workers. The door shingle reads: "William Smith, sales representative." In addition, the agency rents a room next door to the office of the autoworkers' union, whose phone they wiretap as well its president's private line. Informers are even sent to General Motors' suppliers. They report everything: Mr. X vacated his position in the workshop two minutes before the siren, Mr. Y talked to his neighbor, Mr. Z said "a union is a good thing." William Smith, sales representative, transmits the information to MDABY. The culprits are fined, fired, terrorized. "The work secretly conducted among employees on behalf of employers is in the best interests of both," proclaims the Pinkerton agency's *Declaration of Principles*.

Activists who visit cities where General Motors have factories are followed day and night. At all public meetings, Pinkerton men record the speeches in shorthand and take down the names of the workers who attend: Agent OC takes down the lecture of the great American sociologist Professor Ross in Milwaukee; Agent AH attends debates organized by a group of ministers from Detroit. "We strive for honesty when it comes to espionage," said the Chevrolet chief of staff, a.k.a. MHUPO.

Pinkerton has fifty-two informants in the automobile workers' union. They attend all meetings, even the most secret, participate in all the conferences. In Atlanta, an agent steals the archives of the local Chevrolet union. At the Norwood union center, another grass* has all the documents copied, and steals the funds. At the Lansing factory, all five union leaders are informers: as it happens, there are no other members. In Flint, where there are several factories and where, in 1934, there were 26,000 union members, in 1936, only 120 remained: of the thirteen leaders, five are informants. The remaining union members meet at each other's homes: in the basement, in the evening, lights off. "The Pinkerton Agency," we read in the *Declaration of Principles*, "recognizes the need for unions and means them no harm."

When a strike breaks out at the Chevrolet factory in Toledo, Pinkerton sends its men into occupied buildings and picket lines. The government sends in Mr. McGrady, former Deputy Secretary of State for Labor, to mediate the conflict. Throughout his stay, he is shadowed by two Pinkerton employees. A room next door to McGrady's is rented at the hotel, and the same agents listen, ears glued to the wall, to any discussions he may have with strikers' representatives.

Twice a week, and even every day at certain times, William Smith, sales representative, withdraws behind closed doors with

---

* Informer.

Andersen, head of General Motors' "relations with personnel." They review all the MDABY factories. Management is made aware of the workers' every action, their material and moral situations, their plans. As one of the informers so aptly said of the man who chairs the autoworkers' union, "the only thing we didn't know was the number of times he went to the bathroom."

Pinkerton is not alone. In the United States there are 220 agencies like it, employing over one hundred thousand men. It is estimated that American industry pays them nearly $100 million a year, which is the total amount received in annual unemployment benefits by some 350,000 four-person families in the city of New York.

G-265

"My name is Virgil Mazza, I live in New York, and I'm a shoemaker by trade.

"This happened in 1933. I read a classified ad in the *New York American* for a shoemaker who knew how to read and write. So I wrote the paper, and after three days I received a letter telling me to go to the General Motors building and ask for a Mr. Allen. So I went, I went up to the office of the International Auxiliary Co., and Mr. Allen asked me where I had worked before. I told him that at the moment, I was unemployed but had worked in several companies.

"I thought at first that the agency was looking for a shoemaker, but the truth is, bosses in the shoe business never ask if you can read and write, the only thing that interests them is if you can make shoes. So I told Mr. Allen it all seemed a bit fishy.

"'No,' he said, 'it's a good job, but the boss pays so well, he's looking for men who can meet the standard.'

"'Well,' I said, 'if we have to meet the standard, that's fine by me, but I want a letter.'

"'Come back in two days,' he went, 'or better, just wait and we'll send you the letter.'

"'But,' I went, 'listen, Mr. Allen, I can't wait two days because if I don't find a job this afternoon, tomorrow will be too late, because I'm broke. My landlord wants to throw me out, I have to pay the rent.'

"'Don't worry,' said Mr. Allen. 'How much do you need?'

"'Five dollars.'

"He gave me the money and said: 'If we don't find you work in two days, come back and we'll give you some money.' 'This isn't scab work?' I asked, and Mr. Allen said no.

"They ended up asking me back and gave me work. 'Where?' I asked, and Mr. Allen said: 'Well, it's a good company. The best we have in New York. It's Miller's.'—'But that's a prison,' I went.—'What do you mean "prison"?'—'I mean we call Miller's a prison because it's a real Sing Sing. All that's missing is an electric chair.'—'All you have to do,' said Mr. Allen 'is go over there. You deliver this letter to Mr. Squire, the general manager.'

"So I went to see this Mr. Squire, he opened the letter and called the foreman, and the foreman brought carpenters, and they bolted down my tools to the table.

"When I returned to the office of International Auxiliary Co., they told me: 'Sit down and write what you might call a letter or report. Tell us how you were treated. What the workers said. What the foreman told you. Who you met going to the company and who you met coming back here.'

"I did my best to write what they told me to. Then Mr. Allen said, 'Now you should have a union card. Go to the Hides and Skins union at the corner of Fourteenth and Fifth, and ask for a card. We'll give you your membership fee and pay your dues.'

"I still didn't understand what they wanted from me. 'Okay,' I said, 'fine.' And he said: 'The head of the union is called Biedencapp. He's a Communist. Make friends with him because he's very smart, and your boss, Mr. Miller, is very interested in him.'

"I went to a meeting and listened to Biedencapp make a speech, but in truth, he didn't talk about communism. He simply said that workers could join unions of their choice, just like Roosevelt was saying at the time. After the meeting, I met this Biedencapp. When he found out I worked for Miller, he told me: 'Make sure no one from Miller sees you here, because they're all spies. Miller sends informers here. You could lose your job tomorrow.'—'Don't worry,' I said, 'I know how to look out for number one.'

"Mr. Allen told me to write a report on the meeting and send it to them. So that night, when I went home to write it, I saw that it was what you might call spying, and I couldn't finish the report.

"The next day after work I went back to Mr. Allen and I said, 'Listen, Mr. Allen, I see now that it's grassing, and I will not do it.'—'Come now,' he said, 'you don't have to be afraid. This is what you might call counter-espionage, what you might call journalism. So don't let it scare you.'

"Maybe a shoemaker can become a journalist overnight, but I don't really see how. So I told Mr. Allen: 'I'm leaving right now. Count me out. I'll give back the five dollars I owe you.'—'Last week you signed a contract with us,' he said, 'you can't just leave.'

"He tried to persuade me and I told him: 'Let me think about it.'

"So I went home, and I thought it over, and I saw the fifteen hundred workers at Miller who were killing themselves for a few bucks a week, and I saw how I'd suffered myself and I said, 'I'll take this job to help the workers. When I'm finished, I'll tell them the truth.' I decided to be a grass to teach myself all about grassing, and so I kept on writing reports.

"Whenever I went to the office, Mr. Allen told me:

"'Call first, because sometimes we get other visits, and we don't like our visitors to meet.' The truth is, they don't use real names but just initials and numbers, for instance, they gave me the number G-265. So I'd call them and just say: 'G-265,' and Mr. Allen answered: 'Okay, come up in five minutes.'

"I go up one day, and Mr. Allen says, 'You know, Mike Miller, one of the Miller brothers, is complaining because you don't get the right information. You accuse the foremen and not the workers.

And you say nothing about Communists, but the place is full of them.'—'Tell me, Mr. Allen,' I answer, 'I've talked to friends, and some are Communists, but they don't talk about communism in the shop. The only thing they say is that they don't earn enough. I don't earn enough myself, but I'm not a Communist.'

"So he goes, 'Just say the workers are dissatisfied with their salaries, and leave it at that.'

"Mr. Miller was very interested in Communists. He even told me: 'Let your hair grow and muss it up when you go to meetings, you'll look like a Communist and make the workers like you.'

"And one day Mr. Allen said: 'We want you to talk about communism in the union, because they're all extremists. Read communist literature and learn their politics. Join the Communist Party.'—'You want me to join the Communists,' I said, 'when I'm a practicing Catholic?'

"In August 1933, the union decided a general strike. They knew that Miller was the most tight-fisted and decided to start with smaller companies. On August 18, the union declared the strike at Laval, Laprasto and other places, and close to hundred percent walked off the job, but at Miller's, there was no way.

"The strike had lasted three weeks, and there were nearly seven thousand strikers. They went to the union and they said: 'What's going on? We're on strike, and at Miller's, they're still working.' The union bosses said a big demonstration had to be organized in front of the factory and then the Miller workers would strike.

"They set the event for Monday morning. Mike Miller knew and told me to inform him of the date and exact time. I had to send him a report because he had his own spies on site. He got the scabs ready, and the police and detectives. There were nearly two hundred officers on site and I warned the union. At the last moment, the event was rescheduled to Friday, which was payday.

"And so the demonstration happened, I made my report, and Mr. Allen said: 'Keep in touch, call us every two or three hours because right now it's important. Be the first on picket lines and try to get yourself arrested. It's good to be arrested right away.'—'Why?' I asked.—'Because it'll convince the workers you're a good striker and they'll listen to you.'

"In a few days we had nine hundred strikers at Miller's, and Mr. Miller called the agency office and said: 'Listen, send Mazza over.' I go to see him, and he comes out and says, 'I'm sorry, Mr. Mazza, I can't see you at home, I got painters in the apartment. We'll go talk in a restaurant.'

"We go to the restaurant, he orders my breakfast, and it's him who pays. 'Listen,' he says, 'you know these Communists, they're very smart. Last year, I had a strike, and they had these signs with the name of the Hides and Skins union written on them. But this time, the signs just read: "Miller workers on strike." I can't tell which union they belong to and file a complaint to prevent them picketing. But I saw the judge, he's a friend. All we need is the name of the union. You have your union card,' Mr. Miller tells me, 'and tomorrow morning if we can prove that one of the picketers is on strike and has a union card in his pocket, we will get a judgment against Hides and Skins.' 'Okay,' I say, 'that's easy enough.'

"The next morning I go to the picket line, but beforehand I talk to one of the organizers. 'Here,' I say, 'take my card, because if they arrest us today and find the card, they can file a complaint against the union.' I tell him the truth, he gathers everybody together and says, 'Guys, give me your cards.' And he collects them all.

"And just then Mr. Miller comes out of the factory and comes toward the picket line, and beckons to me. 'What's your name?'—'Mazza,' I say.—'Do you work for me?'

"Like he's never seen me. I say, 'Yes, of course.'— 'Are you with the Hides and Skins?'—'No,' I say.—'Do you have a union card in your pocket?'—'No,' I say. He gives me a dirty look but doesn't open his mouth again.

"At my agency, they tell me Mr. Miller wants to see me again. I go find him and he says:

"'Listen, do you work for me or those Bolsheviks?'—'Why?' I

ask.—'Because of the union card that should've been in your pocket.'—'Let me explain,' I say. 'The organizer took our cards, and I couldn't say no.'—'If that's how it is,' Miller says, 'then that's okay. Keep doing your job.'

"When the strike was over, Mr. Allen wrote me to stop sending reports because the client had unsubscribed. 'Go back and be a shoemaker,' was what he said. And I went. Mr. Squire, the director wasn't there, Mr. Miller neither, and I went to find the foreman. 'What do you want?' he told me. 'You're a Communist. Get the hell out of here.'

"And soon after, I left International Auxiliary. I'd learned all I wanted to know. When they turfed me out of Miller's, they told me, 'Look, we'll find you another job.'—'Well,' I says, 'you can stick it where the sun don't shine.'

"I signed up at the unemployment office, and was out of work until two weeks ago."

FOR LAW AND PUBLIC ORDER

Three companies share the same clientele: Federal Laboratories, Chemicals Corporation of Lake Erie, and the youngest competitor, Manville. All three offer the same items: emetic and tear gas, gas masks, truncheons. Each has its specialties. Federal Laboratories: armored cars, armored shields, "Jumbo" gas bombs, and the famous Thompson Sub Machine guns, the ones you see in all the gangster movies. Lake Erie: the pocket gas grenade, the "bouncing" grenade that discharges gas three times and moves a few yards each time; the "Green stripe" grenade that releases an invisible gas, "which makes it all the more effective and terrifying." Manville makes the gas pen, the gas machine gun, and the automatic revolver that shoots gas-filled paper capsules.

The merchandise has its advantages and drawbacks. The Lake Erie truncheons are not as good as Federal Laboratories', according to the California rep of the former. He writes, "Here, the police, when hitting a man on the head, are not satisfied unless he falls to the ground with a skull fracture. Our clubs are too light. If you decide to manufacture heavier ones, let me know." On the other hand, the company's gas weapons are the best. Lake Erie writes: "The items we recommend for controlling a large number of violent rioters are the most aggressive and conclusive of any produced in this country." As for Manville, it makes much of its gas-filled paper capsules: "very humane," because they make it possible to avoid the kind of injuries caused by the metal casings of grenades. The new weapon was even filmed for the news, and people could see for themselves that no one had suffered: it is true that on this occasion, the capsules were filled with flour.

Metal-coated or paper-frilled, the gas is what counts: CN (chloroacetophenone), or tear gas, and DM (diphenylaminechlorarsine) gas or emetic gas. The former, according to Lake Erie, "causes almost insurmountable pain in the eyes, nose and throat." The latter provokes "violent nausea and vomiting, a feeling of suffocation as if several people were sitting on your thorax, and severe pain in the chest and head." Neither is fatal.

And why all the equipment?

"For law and public order," proclaims Federal Laboratories in their letterhead. Manville clarifies: "Our equipment was used to break the strike at Ohio Rubber Co., at the Toledo gearbox plant, etc. In each case, it was used by detective agencies hired to defend the factory." "We're surrounded by strikes, but they're too peaceful for my taste," wrote one Lake Erie salesman, and another confided: "I hope the strike will break out and be very, very bad: we need the money." "I'm still waiting for a good juicy strike. Those damn things don't happen often enough for my liking," complained the Federal Laboratories' California agent. His manager consoled him: "Labor disputes are spreading across the country. I feel it's going to be a good year for all of us."

To sell the equipment, you have to advertise. And Federal Laboratories gives their customers a free brochure, *Crimes and Social Disorder of the Reds*, and publishes a newsletter that proclaims, "the class struggle has become more clearly and sharply defined; sales far exceeded $1 million in the first half of the year."

Also technical advertising. Lake Erie writes that the "Green Stripe" grenade, whose metal casing explodes into a thousand pieces, "should not be thrown into the crowd, *unless severe treatment is essential.*" As for the knockout gas, "once the rioters have been brought under control, they will not ask for a new dose as long as the memory of the first one remains." That means a danger of reduced sales. And Federal Laboratories writes their agents: "Do not forget to tell your customers that when they use the gas, use a lot. Experience has shown that if police try to disperse a crowd with too little gas, it is not very successful. We cannot expect to overwhelm a combative crowd with a pair of grenades or bombs. You have to give them gas, a full ration of gas."

At each company headquarters, management has the newspapers read, articles on strikes clipped and often sent by telegram, FYI, to inform representatives who in the meantime must remain aware of their local situation. "It is important for us," writes Federal Laboratories, "to know we can count on you to monitor strikes very closely. We have to stay up late and be up at dawn to catch the prospective customer at the psychological moment where he may need to place an order."

It is sometimes necessary to instruct the police in how to handle the equipment or at other times bribe a sheriff, or write to the mayor of a community where a strike has just been broken to congratulate him for "having expertly employed tear gas and known the human effect it has on the crowd." They must keep track of the police and industrialists' conventions and meetings, and provide them with demonstrations. If it is a sheriffs' meeting, one agent is enough. But it is the Lake Erie vice-president himself who goes to Pittsburgh on July 7, 1936, and performs tests in the presence of management for "several steelworks interested in the use of tear gas in the impending struggle between unions and the steel industry."

All this is expensive, but customers will remember what they've been told at the psychological moment that night when Carnegie Steel orders thirty revolvers for immediate delivery, or the day Omaha orders a special plane, loaded with gas bombs, "to test their emetic effect on the masses."

Gas may well be the most humane way of dealing with workers, but employers do not like to buy it openly. They have invoices sent without letterhead for "merchandise as ordered," usually delivered after hours and preferably to the home of the plant manager or his right-hand man. The most common method is to place the order through the police or the municipality. The order books are full of entries such as: "Delivery to El Secundo police, invoice Standard Oil," "Delivery to Flint police, invoice to Manufacturers Association of Flint (equipment for Chevrolet plant but management does not want this known)."

Once the conflict is settled with machine guns or gas grenades, the supplier tries to obtain a written statement from the customer for use in dealings with future buyers. Representatives must report to management on the equipment's performance and provide photos. "I returned to San Francisco," writes the Federal Laboratories agent, "to learn that riots had broken out in Eureka again, a man was killed and many others wounded. I phoned the police chief, who informed me our equipment had functioned satisfactorily." The Eureka death will get them new orders and maybe even oust Lake Erie, their most dangerous competitor.

Albeit interesting, the demonstrations for select groups of industrialists do not hold a candle to those performed on human material. In this respect, the great strike of San Francisco in 1934, in which nearly eighty workers were killed, proved particularly favorable to the task.

The situation was very tense in California, "full of gas" in the words of McCarty, the Lake Erie rep, backed by the municipality of San Francisco, while his competitor, Roush of Federal Laboratories, enjoyed police support. As long as the situation remained calm, both sides were content to consolidate their respective positions. But one day the strike broke out.

Roush had a police car at his disposal, McCarty the airplane of "a rich and patriotic friend" who acted as pilot. No chance of sleeping. At night there were orders to be sent by telegraph or telephone, and by day, demonstrations to be performed.

"I haven't seen the Fox-Movietone News yet," McCarty wrote later. "Apparently, it shows the Federal Labs rep in the middle of the street, aiming at a crowd three hundred feet away, and he appears to be driving back fifteen hundred to two thousand people. Actually, he arrived at the very last moment, when we had already driven back the crowd and firing had ceased. When the Movietone car drove up at this very moment, of course, the Federal Labs rep roared into the street and posed, shooting at people. He launched dozens of bombs without rhyme or reason, and I saw strikers pick them up to throw them back. So I did the same, urging reporters and police to observe a real bomb in action. It landed at the edge of the crowd, a man stooped to pick it up, but it exploded in his face. I asked a doctor friend at the hospital and learned there was a guy being treated for serious injuries caused by a bomb: no doubt about it, that's our man."

The version provided by Roush, the Federal Labs representative, is different. He writes: "The first riot started early in the morning, and we attacked with grenades. My competitor was there too in an official car, but it stayed around the corner. I started in with long-range shells and believe me they solved the problem. Since then, every riot has ended in victory for us. It was very interesting and at the same time instructive. Next week I'll get photos of the riot. I might mention that during one of the riots, I shot a long-range projectile into a group, a shell hitting one man and causing a fracture of the skull, from which he has since died. As he was a Communist, I have no feeling in the matter and regret that I did not get more."

Superfluous regrets. Roush had sold $30,000 in equipment, while McCarty had barely exceeded $16,000. However, one must go to great lengths to sell gas, and competition is ruthless.

But there is one exception to the rule: when it comes to justifying the use of the merchandise, "We sell gases as a humane way of protecting property and human life," said a manager for Federal Laboratories. The vice-president of Lake Erie Chemical similarly reflects: "I believe that I not only improve industry, but that I improve society."

THE HOLE

C. M. Kuhl, a.k.a. the Redhead, was a railroad worker and a soldier. In 1921, he set himself up in business. He worked simultaneously for Central Industrial Service, whose main line of business was spying in factories, and for its affiliate, Central Service, whose specialty was strikebreaking. He learned the trade in Cincinnati and made his debut in February 1922 in Yorkville during the Wheeling Steelworks strike.

In 1926, he signed onto the Railway Audit & Inspection Co., a large-scale agency with offices in twelve cities, providing industries with informers, scabs, gas, and machine guns alike.

On behalf of Railway Audit, during the Ohio Edison strike, Kuhl undertook to replace the ninety company electricians with a hundred-odd men recruited in New York and Chicago. He performed similar tasks, usually with success, until the spring of 1929, in Pittsburgh, when Dairy Freedom truckers walked off the job and had been tough enough to frighten scabs away: even the twenty-five gangsters dispatched from Chicago to restore order fled in terror.

Being a strikebreaker is a trade. When a representative phoned the office to place an order, you had to get your hands on a scab. These men had rallying points: in New York, at the corner of Forty-Second Street and Broadway; in Chicago, around Randolph Street; in Philadelphia, around the Reading Depot. They all knew but distrusted each other, their employers, and the police. All they believed in was money, and did not believe in that either until it was in their hands. Most had been in prison for reasons unrelated to their trade, like their most senior member Sam Cohen, who for twenty years worked for all the agencies and was at all the strikes except the ones that broke out while he was inside: he'd served sixteen sentences, armed robbery mostly, and disappeared from view for nearly ten years; his broken nose and two scars were as familiar to scab recruiters as to the guards at Sing Sing.

Strikebreakers arrived at the office, were made to sign contracts that released the agency of all liability, and were given railway tickets to the cities where their services were required. Railway Audit & Inspection Co. was not as rich as its competitor, Bergoff Pearl, who once sent four hundred scabs from New York to Milwaukee by plane.

When it came to big orders, Kuhl-the-Redhead accompanied the men and stayed along with them. So it was that in July 1929, he and a few other Railway Audit employees went to New Orleans, where tram workers had gone on strike.

Fifty thousand motormen, conductors, and guards had been recruited in Buffalo, New York, and elsewhere, some directly and others through ads. They slept and ate in the five transport company depots, which paid all their expenses and paid Railway Audit's costs, plus 25 percent. The higher the bills, the greater the profits: it was in the company's interest to prolong the conflict and from the first day, two or three workers were killed.

Kuhl worked for Railway Audit until 1931. That year, he went to the National Trusts Service, which specialized in labor spying. At first, business was not good. Five representatives spent all their time visiting manufacturers. When a strike was foreseen, they were given an order without hesitation. But if things were calm, they had to speak the language of insurance agents:

"Do not wait for trouble to break out to find out what is happening in your plant. Prevention is better than cure."

Gradually, business expanded. A branch office by the name of Affiliated Trusts Service provided strikebreakers. It serviced the customers of several large factories with a personnel of three hundred informers. Most were trained by Kuhl-the-Redhead himself.

There was Agent 503, George Camm, secretary of the Youngstown Steelworkers Union, Frank Timlin, Agent 59, who performed the same duties within the Molders Union, along with his daughter, Dorothy, Agent 98. Number 104, Glen Fiske, was responsible for wiretaps and dictaphones. William Lewis, 505, was a politician and member of the reactionary Crusaders; he earned over ten dollars per report. Nemenyi got fifty dollars, but he only reported on trade union conferences, which he attended via connections and his press card. Number 84 was a woman, Mrs. Hazel Strothers, who after spying in six different plants wrote reports on a seventh, where her husband was employed: he told her anything she wanted to know; unaware of what was going on, he did not mistrust her. Their son Robert knew everything, though; he went by the number 84 X.

And then there was 311, the lawyer C. Murphy, and A2, E. C. Vermillion, who would later become secretary of the Manufacturers Association Cleveland, and J. P. South, who mixed up his agent number, 520, with others he had worn in prison in Georgia and Pennsylvania, and Reverend Bunch, a Leavittsburg priest.

These men and women sometimes worked inside factories and sometimes outside. Some spied in unions, others acted as "missionaries," which involved visiting local shopkeepers during strikes to get them up-in-arms against strikers, but most of all to visit strikers' homes to talk to their wives, mothers, and daughters and try by all means to demoralize them.

Kuhl-the-Redhead trained agents, paid them, and when a customer complained about not getting enough value for his money, he told the agents: "Put a bit of juice in your reports. If you want to keep this job, use your imagination."

It was he who hooked the informers: hooking is a technical term.

It is not easy to plant an informer in a factory; his sudden appearance may incur the mistrust of other employees: the American worker has learned to be wary. It is often necessary to recruit someone already working on the premises.

First you had to find workers whose peer trust and union duties made them good candidates: factory management often provided a list of these. It was a point in their favor if they were married. If they were poor, even better. Family obligations, number of children, and state of health—as bad as possible—were all taken into account. Once the candidate had been identified, Kuhl would go see him and offer money in exchange for information, without explaining what it was about. He would say he represented a bank or an insurance company who had invested money in the company.

"They're more interested in managers and foremen other than you guys," he'd say.

If the worker lets himself be hooked, Kuhl taught him to write reports. The first details he asked for, about production yield and quality, were gradually replaced by descriptions of union activities. And if the man twigged to what he was being asked to do and wanted out, there were receipts bearing his signature, and threats to expose him to his comrades.

Three-quarters of the agents of the National Trusts Service agents were workers that had been hooked.

Unions grew more powerful, strikes more frequent, and business more prosperous. Kuhl worked for steel mills and taxi companies, dairies and power plants, automobile factories, and laundries. He knew all the ins and outs, he had trained a generation of spies, he earned a lot of money; he could have struck out on his own.

Then one fine day—July 1935—C. M. Kuhl, known to American strike agitators and breakers by his nickname, The Redhead, felt that he was in over his head. He could not explain it as well as he'd have liked, but told himself his job was pretty abhorant. And he pulled out of the business, never to return again.

THE STRIKE THAT NEVER HAPPENED

West Point Manufacturing Company, headquartered in West Point, Georgia, has five cotton mills, located in the city of Lanett and four surrounding villages. Five thousand workers in all, about half of them in Lanett. These plants, built between 1894 and 1915, have never seen a day of strike: their staff is not unionized.

In the summer of 1934, the Federation of Labor decides to launch a campaign in the southern United States, where textile workers often earn no more than five cents an hour. West Point Co. reacts.

It contacts Eugene Ivey, agent for the Railway Audit & Inspection Co. In July, Earl Hemphill, specialist in union matters, arrives in Lanett, makes inquiries. He writes: "They feel that textils give them more greef then all the others put toggether, because textil bosses are used to explotting werkers however they want for allmost no money and macking big prophits."

Earl Hemphill doesn't know how to spell, but writes his reports, signing them #3550, and sends them to the office of Railway Audit & Inspection Co., which, after all, has not hired him to be a grammar teacher.

He contacts all those who support the workers' cause. He has come, he says, to organize the factory workers. He visits their homes, has them sign membership forms, encourages them to meet at each other's houses. He works tirelessly, and in the evening, he writes a report chock-full of names and addresses. At the end of July he gets his first payment: eight dollars per day, plus a dollar for expenses.

The Federation of Labor calls the textile industry strike for Saturday, September 2 at 11:30 p.m. On Sunday, factories in the region are closed as usual; on Monday, contrary to routine, they remain closed.

The staff of the West Point Co. is not unionized, the bad blood has been removed thanks to Earl Hemphill, there never was a strike; on Monday, it's business as usual.

But there is reason to fear the example of unionizing might spread. The president of West Point Co. puts in another call to Eugene Ivey, who is also the agent for Federal Laboratories. He wants to know how to obtain machine guns immediately.

Ivey explains that a new law has instigated a series of formalities for individuals wishing to acquire firearms. It's long and sometimes compromising. Therefore it is preferable to make the purchase through a police officer.

On September 6, John Davidson, West Point city councilor, orders Police Commissioner Boyd to sign a telegram. It is an order for four machine guns and the necessary ammunition. To be shipped by air immediately. Confirmation will follow. Two days later, Davidson and Boyd go to the station, where they meet Jennings, assistant manager of the Lanett plant. The Commissioner signs a receipt and takes delivery of several parcels, the invoice reading: "Sold to the city of West Point (to be delivered to the chief of police) . . . ," etc. Without looking at it Boyd gives the invoice to Jennings, hands him the parcels, and leaves.

Jennings returns to the factory with four Thompson .45-caliber automatic machine guns, capable of firing one hundred rounds per minute, and twelve chargers.

The textile strike has lasted nearly a week, but at Lanett the employees are still working. Are four machine guns enough? Management borrows three more from a neighboring mining company; it doesn't need them at the moment because it's unlikely the miners will strike. Four plus three, that's seven machine guns, seven hundred rounds a minute—but is that enough?

The city of Lanett, whose police officers can be counted on the fingers of one hand but whose city councilors include the son of the president of West Point Co., rounds up a few hundred emergency officers for backup. The sheriff of the county where the factories are located immediately invests a few hundred citizens with police powers. These men, employees of West Point Co. almost without exception, are now double employees: the company will pay their salary as police officers. There are 729 of them, all bearing firearms.

They are numerous but poorly trained. This time, Pennsylvania Department of Labor and Industry provides what is required. After a hasty journey across the United States, seven guardsmen arrive in Lanett.

Jennings meets with them in the manager's office, along with the county sheriff, the mayor and the police commissioner. Machine guns are assigned to the envoys from the Department of Labor and Industry.

While the latter take up position at the city limits, a certain number of Lanett personalities publish an appeal.

"Believing ourselves more fortunate than most communities due to the magnificent spirit of understanding and help our industry leaders have demonstrated, we feel duty-bound to express our viewpoint at this critical moment.

"We would be very vexed if the staff of the West Point Co. went on strike. In fact, if that happened, we would be forced to suspend our activities until normal conditions are restored."

This call is signed by the innkeeper, the mechanic, the hairdresser, two councilors, and the Institute of Modernist Beauty. Among others who threaten to suspend their professional activities are a doctor, teachers, and the two local pastors.

The doctor is a factory employee, the teachers live in company-owned houses, as do the chief of police and the two pastors, who receive $600 each per annum from West Point Co.

Bales of cotton are blocking the main road between Fairfax and Lanett. The bridge over the nearby river is impassable. All passing cars are ordered to stop, their occupants searched. If they do not stop, a burst of machine gun fire shreds their tires. Armed men patrol the countryside. The county is under siege. But it would be unwise to complain, especially in writing. The West Point postmaster reads all letters and writes summaries he hands over to factory management.

The general textile strike has now been over for two weeks. The workers of Lanett work as they have for forty years. West Point Co. pays the bills. Nearly $27,000 to the police and sheriff for extra staff salaries. $1,869.38 to Railway Audit for the reports of Earl Hemphill. $1,233.85 to Labor and Industry for the guards. $1,002 to Federal Laboratories for machine guns. $75 to the Mayor of Lanett, $25 to the police commissioner. All recorded as profits and losses.

Lanett now has a new police chief. His predecessor is in prison. During a fight, he killed a policeman.

NOTEBOOK

APRIL 1936 (END)

The New York Anti-Vivisection Society decided to give its semi-annual reward—a statuette—to a Brooklyn police officer who saved the life of a wounded wild duck by dabbing antiseptic solution onto the wound.

April 17. Former journalist Max Schulz committed suicide in a small New Jersey town. He left a note saying, "our economic system, which throws a man in the garbage when he's over fifty, gives you no reason to keep on living." Schulz was fifty-one years old.

April 20. A great event yesterday afternoon at Saint Mark's Church in the Bowery. A large brown curtain separated the altar from the nave. It rose on six young women, barefoot and white-robed, who performed a dance symbolizing the Annunciation. The nave was in total darkness while four spotlights, red and blue, illuminated the dancers. The altar was enveloped in thick clouds of incense.

For lack of funds, the schools of Jefferson County, Alabama, close their doors end of April, a month before the summer holidays.

An improved electric chair has just been installed in the Chicago prison. Instead of fastening the straps around the body of the condemned, the executioner will now simply have to lower a lever. Instead of forty seconds, the preparations will take no more than ten.

Most American universities are private establishments, funded by legacies and donations; three-quarters of their administrators are bankers, businessmen, and lawyers. Dr. McGrath, University of Buffalo, from whom I borrow this information, adds: "A small group of financiers and businessmen has taken control of higher education in America."

April 27. In Chicago, two boys of nineteen who murdered a doctor have each been sentenced to 199 years in prison. The *Daily Mirror* wrote:

"A sentence of 199 years for murder seems cruelly long, but remember, many religions, maybe yours included, teach us that for crimes less serious than murder, sinners are imprisoned for all eternity. In comparison, 199 years is a short time."

At last! The National Institute of Social Sciences has decided to award its annual Gold Medal Award to JP Morgan, the largest American bank, "for introducing high ethical standards to the business world and maintaining the honor and the credit of our country."

A manufacturer of creamed corn publishes entire full-page color ads showing Melvin Purvis, "America's No. 1 G-man," relaying his feats to children, advising them to try the product and join his "Young G-Men club." "Boys and girls, I'll send you a free official Junior G-Man badge. To be secret Young G-Men, all you need to do is sign up. I'll send you a big and fascinating book that will teach you tricks of the trade, confidential codes, invisible writing, self-defense and other secret information that only a G-Man knows."

A competitor, a cream of wheat manufacturer, has enlisted the aid of Tom Mix. "Boys and girls, this revolver is a beaut', an exact replica of my special automatic. Act quickly! Be the first in your neighborhood to have one." Pictures show the famous actor, his revolver, scenes from his life, and the silhouette of a naked man wearing a sombrero, his body covered with red circles and black crosses. "Tom Mix's wounds. Crosses are fractures, circles gunshot wounds." A detailed list follows. "Note: Scars from twenty-two stab wounds not shown."

April 28.

Read in the *New York Evening Journal*:

"A newspaper should be interesting. It should also give you the bare facts. Crime is interesting as well as important. In our country and in this day and age, it would be difficult to find a subject more interesting and more important."

Ads

In a jewelry store window:

"Win her love with a quality diamond."

In a hairdresser's window:

"We specialize in physiognomic haircuts."

Caption in a laxative ad:

"Fired . . . because of constipation."

Poster for a funeral home:

"A dignified burial for only $150. As cheap as you want and impressive as necessary."

In a grocery store:

"Extraordinary! Modern chickens! Grown under ultraviolet light in an air-conditioned room and scientifically fed. The orchids of the poultry world."

In a bookstore:

"The greatest novel ever written about a 'love triangle': *Anna Karenina*."

An agency:

"Who is the Einstein of advertising?"

CONVENTIONAL AMERICA

IV. LOVE

"LEARN TO DANCE"

In upper Manhattan, billboards and neon signs urge you to learn the art of dance. To be a social success, you have to know how to dance: you have to be a good dancer to find a woman, friends, a job.

You go up to the second floor. You leave your hat in the cloakroom on the right; at the box office on the left you buy a book of tickets, six tickets for a dollar. On each ticket, you read:

THE RAINBOW GARDENS
Dancing
Every night
From 8:30 p.m. to 3 a.m.
Good for 2 INSTRUCTIONAL DANCES

So for a dollar, just a dollar, you are entitled to twelve dances.

Above the door the inscription: "Ye who enter here, abandon all worries." If Dante was not lying, this is the gate of heaven.

The big room is dimly lit. Chinese lanterns hanging from the ceiling provide frugal lighting for the wooden counter, in the back the dance floor surrounded by a walkway, and a black jazz band in the corner.

By the bars on either side of the dance floor, men and women stand facing each other. Mostly young men. The worn out tie, creased collar, tight jacket betray the petty office worker, sales clerk, errand boy. There are no rich boys here, and definitely no workers. Women, some young, some pretty, all made up, wearing evening dresses slit to mid-thigh.

They dance.

Watch the heads, heads only. Mouths are closed: nobody talks, nobody smiles. Jaws unnoticeably move around balls of chewing gum. The dancers vacantly gaze at the jazz band, the bar, and as a last resort, their partners. The dance is slow and couples move with majestic indifference. Sometimes a man reddens, closes his eyes, grits his teeth; a vein bulges on his forehead: he looks as if he is suffocating. The crisis is short-lived. The immobile dancing goes on.

The movement is happening lower down, at hip level. Rumps poured into white satin or black velvet roll frantically right and left, up and down. What man, even old and worn out, could resist that belly pressed against him, that thigh continuously sliding in and out between his?

And indeed, nobody resists. Along the wall, men sprawl on benches, dog-tired, slumped over, emptied of their substance. Some are sleeping. Others look straight in front of them with a dull expression. These men are not rich, and cannot return any time soon to spend a dollar on "instruction dances." Must make the pleasure last, make the twelve dances last several hours to climax effectively. The men recover their strength.

Others, leaning on the copper bar, slide their eyes over the swaying female buttocks. With a solemn and critical air, they gauge, size up: they make their choices.

In this place, the notions of *service* and *efficiency* are put into practice. What is this really about? Men suffer from a buildup of semen in their genitals. They have no relations in the desert of New York, they do not dare get close to a girl because they are scared to death of getting her pregnant or of being blackmailed; they are not rich enough to get married, or even to go to a brothel where, in any case, they might catch something.

However, a few simple movements are enough to bring relief. Many take care of it themselves, alone. But their satisfaction will be multiplied by ten with a bit of female help (incidentally, the word "help" in the US has this specific meaning when a woman says: Shall I help you?). It seems absurd from a mechanical point of view, but that is how it is.

It's a matter of women "helping" men in the shortest possible time, for a very low price, and with no risk for men of contracting a disease or for women of becoming pregnant.

And so, the Rainbow Gardens were born.

The triumph of *service* and *efficiency*. There are no private rooms. At the end of the evening, no man ever takes a dancer home: what would be the point? The bar serves only beer and non-alcoholic drinks. There are no curtains or partitions: everything can be seen. And everything is absolutely aboveboard. A kiss is never exchanged. Arms are never lowered. Pants remain buttoned. Nothing behind their backs, nothing up their sleeves.

The music stops. It's show time, mandatory in all American institutions. A black woman performs an acrobatic dance. An old woman clinging to a microphone sings a sentimental ballad. Then a magician walks onto the dance floor. Every movement he makes points to the ham and the failure. His routines are like so many wrinkles on an old jacket. He unfastens knots without touching them, separates metal rings that seemed inextricably tangled, pulls a string of colored scarves out of a battered top hat. The orchestra plays quietly in the background.

"You don't like our show?" says a female voice beside me.

The girl continues:

"Do you want to dance with me later? My name is Rosita."

She is silenced by a drum roll. With a slow and solemn movement, the magician reaches in his hat and the Stars and Stripes unfurls. A smattering of applause.

I ask Rosita:

"How many of you work here?"

"Sixty-five."

"Every night?"

"Six times a week."

"How many hours?"

"Six and a half. And two hours more on Saturdays."

"And you earn?"

"The boss pays us eight cents a ticket. It's the luck of the draw."

"How much do you earn on average?"

"Around thirty-five dollars a week."

I calculate:

"That makes around 900 dances, 150 a night. Isn't that tiring?"

"Oh! The dancing isn't what's most tiring. It's standing around until you're asked."

I calculate again. Rosita is not the prettiest dancer, nor is she the ugliest; her comrades must earn about the same as she does. Nine hundred dances correspond to seventy-five books of tickets. Assuming each customer buys just one per evening, it means that nearly five thousand men come to get helped at *The Rainbow Gardens* every week.

On the floor, the dancing has started again. The benches are empty. Near a window, a sign proclaims: "Dance is your ticket to a rewarding social life."

"Are you leaving already?" Rosita asks. "Where are you going?"

"Bad places." And she simply replies:

"But this is the worst place in the city."

ON HUMAN DIGNITY

To Lillian

I

The street begins in a cemetery and plunges into the water! A street as short as its name: Wall Street.

The cemetery is old; no vacancies. Around the black Trinity Church, the dead crush down on each other like Stock Exchange brokers on panic day. All around, skyscrapers stand guard.

A dozen buildings to the left, as many to the right. Where the street starts, a florist displays only gardenias and orchids. What a fine investment for a banker in love.

I go down to the first corner. To my right: the gray Stock Exchange building. Facing it, a solid block of a building with extremely thick walls, the only one on the street not identified at the entrance. To my left: on the steps of the Treasury building, the statue of Washington. I stop, draw an imaginary triangle between the monument, the Stock Exchange and the Morgan house, and behold the United States of America.

The triangle gives way under the pressure of a vendor's tray and row upon row of poor-quality black and brown shoelaces. The tray hangs around the neck of a thin, stooped man slowly approaching. Gray plaid jacket, gray-striped pants, face of uniform gray: skin, stubble, lips. A nondescript man from head to toe, and worn-out except for his laces, not the ones in his shoes, but the ones on the tray. Holding onto his cane, he moves along muttering:

"Five cents a pair, five cents a pair."

I follow him.

Around us, the cash collectors, briefcase in hand, make the daily rounds of the banks. The Western Union telegraph operators zigzag from door to door. Police amble by, playing dowser with their batons. A multitude of isolated individuals move from place to place by the shortest route. This torrent that surges into and out of one skyscraper has the precise logic of inputs and outputs in accounting.

The man with the vendor's tray makes his way down the Street with slow, short steps—it's called "the Street" the way they called Rockefeller "John D."—turns into New Street, sits on a hydrant facing the Irving Trust (capital: $70 million) and rests. He continues in the same direction, past the shelter offered by the corner of a building's door, where a poor woman wearing a flowered hat sells razor blades, turns into Exchange Place, then Broad Street, passes three shoeshiners, whom he greets. At the entrance to the Brooklyn Trust Co., across from the Chase Bank, both controlled by Rockefeller, he sells his first pair of laces. He walks along the Stock Exchange, arrives at Wall Street and begins his circuit again.

In front of the Washington statue, I catch up with him.

"How's business?"

He looks around.

"I'm almost blind," he says timidly, and then, "Not good."

"What are you selling?"

"Shoelaces." He brightens up. "I have something else too," he says. "It's new."

He rummages in his pockets and pulls out a tiny rubber pouch, blue, yellow, and orange.

He brings it up to his mouth and puffs out his cheeks. He blows with all his might, grows pale with the effort, gulps some air and blows again. Between his gray lips, the bag swells, grows taut and round, hiding the man's chin, nose and cheeks. I recognize Europe, the Atlantic, the entire Earth daubed in bright paint on the rubber sphere now bobbing over the tray of laces. Over the North Pole, two eyes look at me with hope, and in a voice half-pleading, half-ironic says:

"Five cents. It is not expensive, the world for five cents."

Standing in my imaginary triangle, under the watchful eyes of guards armed with revolvers and the indifferent gaze of Washington, I acquire the world. It deflates immediately and I ask:

"Have you always worked in this area?"

"Oh, yes. I've been on Wall Street for forty years."

"Forty years selling shoelaces?"

"Oh, no!"

He looks angry. We walk a ways in silence. I ask:

"And what did you do before? I mean, when you started out?"

"I was a telegraph operator for Western Union."

"Well paid?"

"A few dollars a week. But life didn't cost much. This was 1900. I was sixteen."

We turn onto Broad Street. He sits on the fire hydrant, the same one, and quietly continues to speak.

With a few friends his age, he had formed a small group to play the stock market. Everyone played then, he says, and everyone made money. When they had gathered enough money, the group sent it to a stockbroker whose typist one of them knew, and she gave him a tip: she read the boss's correspondence. Western Union was going up.

"I bought five shares, and we played for a rise," he says.

He gets up, and we move on.

Each week they grew a little richer. He'd decided to stop as soon as he had earned $2,000 to set himself up in business: a shoe shop to start with, and later a shoe factory.

He smiles at the poor woman with the flowery hat. I wait, ask:

"And then?"

"You must know. The panic of 1901. The collapse began on a Tuesday. On Thursday, the stockbroker sold our shares because of the deficit."

"What caused the panic?"

"The row between John D. and old man Morgan."

"And who won?"

"Morgan, I think."

"You mean he ruined Rockefeller?"

Shocked:

"Oh no! No one ruins John D."

"But he ruined you?"

"Me? He didn't even know me."

One of the shoeshiners calls out to him:

"How are you, John?"

"Fine," he says, and we move on.

"So," I say, "You lost everything?"

"Even my job at Western Union."

"So, unemployment?"

"No, sir!"

Again I sense that he's angry. He explains that three days later, he was hired as an errand boy by the stockbroker who had sold his shares. He could have found a better paid job, but, he says, he didn't want to leave the Street. Those were the golden days: good harvests, good business, and high morale. He still regrets not having played the market again, even if he'd had to borrow. He believes he would not have lost all those years. But he was young and liked going out with friends.

"I even got married, almost," he says with astonishment.

He stops and looks around. We are in front of Chase Bank, where he found a customer earlier.

"Five cents a pair," he mumbles. "Five cents a pair."

It's lunchtime, and the mob employees are surging along close to the walls, some headed for the docks, others to go rest in the cemetery, newspapers in hand, open to the financial pages. In thirty minutes, they'll go back to their offices, abandoning the dirty sheets of newsprint, and fat pigeons will waddle over to peck at stock quotations.

Nobody needs shoelaces.

In 1907, John tells me, there was another panic, and his boss fired him. He was twenty-two years old, and for the second time out on the street.

"On the Street, on the Street," he says with irritation.

And what a street! I should know that here, there's always something for anyone who wants and likes to work. Because he had not played, John had a bit of money put aside. He came upon a classified ad: a bank was looking for a young man, hardworking, intelligent, and ambitious. He copied the addresses on envelopes, glued the stamps on.

Thrown from a thirtieth floor, a roll of paper tape crashes at our feet. John stoops to pick it up.

"That's ticker tape," he says, "you know, from the machine that prints the Stock Exchange quotations."

He gently runs the white tape through his fingers. The morning's transactions are marked upon it. He looks up to locate the window the roll fell from. Thousands of windows, all alike, confront his eyes.

I interrupt his thoughts:

"Did you stay at the bank a long time?"

"Ten years."

"And then?"

"The war. Yes, sir, the war."

He had set aside $600, found a shoemaker's workshop for sale. Every month, he went to see the boss, inspected the premises and the tools, taught himself the trade. The war came and ruined everything. As if he needed a vacation! When he got back, it was too late. The workshop no longer existed. The bank didn't need him anymore. He looked for work and eventually found it.

"Where?"

"Around here."

"But where?"

"The docks," he says, after a pause.

From where he unloaded cargo, he could see the skyscrapers of the Street. He went back sometimes, to the point where the gulls from the port meet the cemetery pigeons. Then things sorted themselves out: he got work as a barber's assistant.

"Close to here," he says.

We pass in front of the Stock Exchange. A sandwich-board man comes toward us: a slice of old flesh between two slices of cardboard reading, "We buy old gold."

"It was prosperity," says John.

Customers didn't haggle over tips. Some confided information that the barber's assistants resold. One day a customer told him about a wonderful invention: a machine that manufactured shoe polish for almost nothing. It only cost $250. The customer knew John and trusted him: he agreed to one hundred dollars cash and three dollars a week for a year. John moved the machine to a basement, ordered tins with his name on them. During the week, he worked at the barber's and on Sundays he made polish. On each box, he earned two cents. Selling two hundred boxes a day to start with, he would have made twenty-five dollars profit per week. That was in October 1929.

"The biggest Wall Street crash," he says with a touch of pride.

I want to know the causes, but he only shrugs: as if the causes mattered.

From his pedestal, Washington appears to contemplate the House of Morgan. In reality, his head is slightly turned to the right: his eyes are fixed on the entrance of the Stock Exchange. John looks in the same direction.

"A Thursday," he says. "At the barber shop, we figured something was up: not a single customer all morning."

The Street was packed with people. There was talk of panic

inside the Stock Exchange, two suicides. For the first time, the offices stayed open all night. Stockbrokers rented entire floors in neighboring hotels so their employees could rest for two or three hours. There must be fifty thousand people working on Wall Street. Soon the hotels put up signs: "Standing Room Only." Curious onlookers passed through on special buses. Everyone who played the stock market was there. They stayed glued to the tickers for hours. The men swore, the women wept. That lasted over Friday and Saturday and Sunday the offices stayed open. People did not say anything. The following Tuesday, John D. announced that he would keep buying in. The next day, the barbershop was overrun with customers with week-old beards. Shortly after, it closed; the boss had lost everything in the crash.

We've been walking in circles for hours. We had lunch at a counter, a sandwich and a glass of milk. A shoeshine boy stopped me to ask if I planned to earn my living by photographing passersby with my camera, and told me that on the Street it would be hard, very hard. My feet are sore.

At the age of forty-five, John found himself without money, without work, with his tins of shoe polish that were drying out and nobody wanted. He still owed sixty dollars on the machine. He had to give it back.

After the Pearl Street elevated railroad, the Street widens and becomes plebian. The houses, low-roofed and dilapidated, are full of eateries. Bums settle on the sidewalks and stop passersby to ask for cigarettes. The streets of the port smell of roasted coffee and cocoa. Brick houses daubed with red, ocher, and black, grimy and squalid, are tenanted by vague semblances of offices and invisible residents. Suddenly on the horizon, through the carcasses of fire escapes, we see a three-masted schooner deploy its triple set of sails.

Litter, oil stains on the surface of the river. This is the sewer, the end of the town, where an old wooden building stands, flanked by a veranda, the municipal refuge.

In 1929, this is where John came for food. He slept anywhere he could. He looked for work.

"And did you find any?"

He gestures toward his tray:

"This."

Begging is forbidden by law, you must have pretexts to beg, and if you want to hold out your hand, you must have razor blades, pencils or shoelaces in the other. Instead of asking whether the crowd on the Street is given to charity, I ask:

"How much do you earn?"

"Fifty cents a day, a dollar. No more." He has a flash of insight. "People don't like to buy from the poor," he says. "John D. never bought laces from me."

He smiles faintly, brightens:

"Now I have these balloons. If I sell ten a day along with laces, I can put twenty-five cents aside."

We're back at our meeting point. The day is drawing to a close. I take my balloon and blow into it. Continents and seas bloom on its surface, and the world, inflated with Wall Street air, gently sways between my fingertips.

"The world for five cents," mumbles John. "The world for five cents."

The crowd passes without a glance in our direction. Soon on Wall Street, there will only be the dead in the cemetery. Between my fingers, the seas and continents pucker and shrivel. All I have in the palm of my hand is an empty rubber pouch, ridiculous and futile.

"Goodbye, John D.," I say.

He studies me, surprised.

"My name is John," he says. "Just John."

II

I'm mad at Cheyenne, madder than hell. What was the point of driving nonstop from Chicago, crossing the Mississippi at sunset and the Missouri the next day at dawn, keeping the interviews short with Tom Sawyer, and Uncle Sam, and the waitress with the blue uniform and slow smile at the "Trucker's Oasis"? What was the point of watching all the corn in the world fleet by the window while playing back in my head the best memories of my fifteenth year, to end up here?

Tom Sawyer approached me on the shores of the Mississippi—it couldn't happen any other way, a gray felt cap pulled low over his blue eyes, cheeky and naïve; he'd talked about politics, the flooded river, school, the newspapers he sold after class, and then he left to go meet Huckleberry Finn. Uncle Sam was very old, clean-shaven, wearing overalls, lost with his gas station somewhere between the corn and the stars. I had rushed them, and the waitress too, who was better than all of us put together, and now I'll never find them again.

Cheyenne, nicknamed Hell-on-Wheels, theater of the bloody war between cowherds and shepherds, capital of the Far West, the Wild West, the scenery where we all played cowboys and Indians and gold diggers. I had vaguely expected saloons where you enter on horseback, a revolver in each hand, gold sold by weight, rivers of alcohol, and singers emerging from foamy yards of lace. I found neon-lit signs, chirping radios, gas stations, tourist trinkets, a garrison, and prostitutes without literature. In storefronts, a range of wide-brimmed hats, silk shirts, riding chaps, high-heeled boots, all bearing the label of the great cowboy outfitter, Levi-Strauss.

A man dressed by Levi-Strauss from head to toe sat on the front porch of a house. He was reading. I leaned down to see the title of the book. *Spicy Western Stories*.

The other man, a craftsman, was sitting in the back of a junk shop. Moccasins, beaded belts, dolls were heaped on tables, eagle feather headdresses hung from the ceiling. There were enough of them to clothe an entire Fenimore Cooper novel. But the man was wearing a khaki shirt, black pants, big shoes trod down at the heels.

My first cowboy and my first Indian. Well worth it. I left

Cheyenne in the morning, disappointed and disgusted, to land right back in the Wyoming scenery: sand; tufts of grass, purple, gray, white, yellow, olive green; huge telegraph poles in the shape of crosses; the Union Pacific rails, with interminable freight trains full of coal, cattle, minerals, oil tanks, the white cold storage wagons of United Fruit. On the roofs of the cars loomed the shadows of hobos, standing or sitting. The desert steppe was devoid of hazards. Neither trappers nor Redskins. Only big billboards planted in the undergrowth showing the silhouette of a cowboy taking aim. And underneath:

LEARN TO SHOOT
PROTECT YOUR HOME
THE "DEAD ON TARGET" REVOLVER
PROVIDES THE MEANS

Under one of these signs stood an old man. Dark suit and cap: a city man. No luggage, not even a bundle, as if he'd stepped out for a breath of air. The nearest village was a hundred miles away. The man waved his arm. I stopped the car.

His suit was well-worn, with holes, but clean. Behind his white metal-rimmed glasses, the man had blue eyes, somewhat childlike, surrounded by a network of tiny wrinkles that gave him an ironic expression. Around the neck and temples, abrasions as if he had shaved with an old razor blade or cold water. He sat on the bench and immediately presented his typesetters' union card. A Czech name: Novak.

"I'm behind on my payments," he said, smiling, "eighteen months behind."

Thirty-two years ago, he left Prague and his parents to emigrate to the United States. He went back to Europe only once, in 1917, for the war. After the armistice, he returned to his linotype; his eyes were failing, he could no longer typeset by hand. He has been unemployed for three years.

"I'm forty-nine," he said, "Too old. I'll never have a steady job again."

He grinned, pleased with himself. Everything was perfectly normal. He had passed the age of work and reached the age of begging.

At the moment, he was coming from Texas by way of Colorado and heading for Utah. The day before, in Laramie, a Chinese man had given him two sandwiches. A Chinaman! He was amazed. The Chinese never give anything away, he said. The event was worth telling. In fact, everything was.

Since he'd stopped working, he'd traveled through all the states of the Union, except for two. He knew all the American cities, all: Corpus Christi, Olympia, Tallahassee.

I asked: "And New Orleans?"

"Too many mosquitoes down there, but I stayed the night in a hotel."

"And Miami?"

"I worked there for three weeks running."

"And St. Louis?"

"Get this. A St. Louis girl, Czech—pretty too—married a Black. The other Czechs ran her out of town. I like the Blacks. They always give you something and they don't hide what they think. If they don't like you, they'll tell you. Mexicans will never say."

He traveled with a map on which he'd marked all the cities of at least three thousand people where he was sure to find a printing company and a local paper. Once he got to a place, he went around to all the printers and asked for work. If there wasn't any, he asked the typos for a little money.

Besides, he wasn't choosy about work. He washed dishes, repaired machinery, brought in the crops, he did anything in exchange for a roof or a meal, and if possible, a few pennies. He even begged, cheerfully and with dignity. If there was absolutely nothing he could do, he knocked on the doors of religious missions: the sisters sometimes gave out food.

"There is also the Salvation Army," he said, "Salvation, ha! The Salvation Army. All they give you is beans, and sometimes not even that. In a small town in Colorado, I went there to ask for some soup and they called the police to run me out of town. It happens often. You arrive in a place, and the judge or the police give you fifteen minutes to clear off."

Rabbits and other animals were strewn over the asphalt, run over by cars; some were intact, as if sleeping, others unrecognizable, completely crushed into the asphalt.

"I never refuse a job, no matter what it is," Novak said. "I even worked in the borax mines in Southern California, in the Mojave Desert near Death Valley. The nearest town was almost two hundred miles away. We were well paid, and very, very well fed."

He described the food in detail, meal by meal.

"It's unhealthy work, first your lips dry up and crack, then you get food poisoning. No one stays more than six weeks, in spite of the pay and the fare. Then there's the boredom. The only entertainment is a gas station nine miles away. Can't buy gasoline, even for ten bucks a can, but for two you can get yourself a nice piece of tail."

He accepted a cigarette.

"Well, look at this, custom-made," he said. He must have been used to roll-your-owns. He inhaled the smoke with care, smiled, and continued talking.

In the summer, he went to the Dakotas to bring in the crops. The farmers were nice, they paid you well, let you sleep in the barn and gave you plenty to eat, even a huge amount: again Novak listed all the dishes, from morning coffee to dinner. But farmers only hired Catholics.

"That is," he said, "you just have to say you're Catholic. I don't care. If it's for work, I am whatever you want me to be."

When winter began, he left and wandered through the Dakotas. In the West, people were more hospitable than in the East and more understanding than Southerners.

"In Kansas, they once sentenced me for vagrancy for ninety days, on top of the fine. We have no money, and the judges know it. They make you pay the fine in kind. I spent three months picking cotton for nothing. In Texas, they treat you like a hobo too. Here, they understand that you're looking for work.

But in the West, there are other drawbacks: climate and distances.

"Beware of Wyoming," Novak said gravely. "Here it starts to freeze and snow all of a sudden, you get caught out on the road and you freeze to death."

Before us the horizon grew even wider, the desert, pink and purple, stretched as far as the eye could see, and, all at the same time, we saw blue sky, white clouds, gray clouds, dark clouds, rainbows, three-forked lightning and ten different torrential rainstorms that blacked out the sun five or six miles apart.

I asked:

"Do you ever get stuck at the side of the road?"

"No," says Novak. "If people see you're clean and clean-shaven they let you ride. I'm always clean."

He reached into his right inside jacket pocket and took out a pouch containing a comb and a safety razor, and from the left pocket a piece of soap and a little mirror. In his right side pocket, he had a shaving brush.

"I shave every day," he said.

"Where?"

"Along the tracks, where the locomotives go to fill up."

"And how do you wash your clothes?"

"When I've made a little money, I'll spend a night at the hotel and wash my clothes. They stay clean for four to five weeks. But I wash my collar and cuffs more often: those are what people see and judge you by."

"Do you also hop freight trains?"

"No. Never. If you do, your suit gets dirty. It has to stay clean if you want to apply for work."

I gave Novak a few dimes and told him the truth: the car wasn't mine, I had very little money, just enough to get to San Francisco, but when I was sixteen, I too was a typo in a ridiculous provincial printer's where all the typesetting was done by hand, the letters were worn, and the kid who put the letters back in the cases always put them in the wrong slot, we'd swear and say he did it on purpose. Novak shook my hand without saying anything while I jabbered away. A little later, he told me that with the money I'd given him, he would be able to buy ground coffee for a month. "It's easy to find boiling water for nothing and it's cheaper than going to a tavern." I realized that my outpouring had in no way spoiled our relations.

But I still hadn't quite run through my stock of naïveté. I could be forgiven: it was the first time I'd met a man who possessed nothing but his body and something to cover it with. I asked him if he had ever been married.

"Jesus, no," he said. "I do not drink spirits, beer only, I smoke but do not chew, and I never play cards or dice. Years ago, I was engaged to a Chicago girl, and after two weeks, she accused me of smoking. I broke up with her."

"Do you have family in the United States?"

"No, nobody."

"Friends?"

"You know how it is: you have friends if you have money."

"Never any women?"

"If I've got twenty-five cents to spend."

"Often?"

"No."

"Are you hungry?"

"Pardon me?"

"Are you hungry now?"

"Well, I ate the Chinaman's sandwiches yesterday."

"And since then?"

"Nothing."

"And where do you sleep?"

"It depends. Mostly outside."

"Tonight?"

"Yes. Outside."

"You only have one shirt?"

"Of course."

"And when you wash it, what do you do?"

"I wait for it to dry."

"Does it take long?"

"In summer, no."

"You're forty-nine?"

"Yes."

He had answered all my questions and understood what I was getting at. But he preferred to stick to the facts. We passed through a mining village he knew, of course. In the middle of the road, an emaciated dog devoured a piece of mule dung.

"Probably a vagrant, like me," said Novak.

He laughed for the first time: that would teach me to ask stupid questions.

A Levi-Strauss van was coming toward us, filled with wide-brimmed hats, silk shirts and men in boots with Louis XV heels.

I asked Novak, "You've never tried being a cowboy?"

"A cowboy?" he repeated. "No. It's hard work, dirty and badly paid. Why bother?"

"This is a big country," I said, "wild, barely colonized. Have you ever thought of digging for gold? They're still doing it in California, aren't they?" I tactfully inquired.

"Oh, yes," said Novak. "There are companies that dredge the riverbeds with big modern machines. But at my age, no chance I'd be hired as a miner."

"And aren't there any more prospectors?"

"Oh, yes! Day after tomorrow, when you get to California, you'll be sure to meet a few between Reno and Sacramento. If you see a man and a mule with a bag across its back, you'll know what they're doing. They go up into the mountains, along the streams, with a shovel and sieve, and they wash the gold sand. They don't know how to do it: it isn't their job. Sometimes they're rich people, city people on vacation, having fun. Or they're unemployed city people who got their benefits turned down. I'm in the summer so many come that some counties put up signs at the foot of mountain trails saying there hasn't been gold there for years. They come anyway. Work from morning to night, and with a bit of luck, you can earn fifty cents a day, a dollar at most. Thank God, it hasn't come to that for me yet."

Night had fallen. In the flat desert around us, nothing to reflect the dazzle of the headlights but rodent eyes and empty tin cans. Soon we would leave Wyoming to cross into Utah and the Mormons, whose rigorous charity is not to be trusted, in Novak's opinion. He got out at Green River to go look for a print works. I saw him peering through his glasses to read their signs. His pockets bulged with toiletry items: all that he owned in the world.

III

Tom Mooney sits behind the wooden partition in the visiting room of the San Quentin Prison, on the Pacific, my trek across the continent has come to an end. The room is a sober harmony of beige and pale green. On one wall, a black plaque with gold lettering indicates that visitors are forbidden to give prisoners anything, or to receive anything from them; that visits should not be unduly prolonged and that it is forbidden to smoke. Above the plaque, a clock counts out the seconds, minutes, hours, and months, but neglects the years. For twenty-two years, the life of Tom Mooney has been regulated by the San Quentin clock.

An organizer of three big strikes in San Francisco, he was accused of throwing a bomb into a patriotic demonstration, arrested, tried, convicted. The case of Tom Mooney is one of the cases of the century, like Sacco and Vanzetti's. The hands went on making their way around the dial, witnesses eventually confessed their testimonies were false, tick-tock went on; former jurors, former judges ended up admitting that the man they believed guilty was innocent: the pendulum swung.

The partition that separates us is nearly five feet high. To see and hear each other, prisoners and visitors must stretch up their necks and bend their heads forward. A double row of slightly tilted heads on outstretched necks adorns the pale green partition. On one side, wives, children, relatives, friends. On the other, gangsters, murderers, counterfeiters: gray jackets, gray or blue pants, and black five-digit numbers across the back.

Tom Mooney's once-abundant and black hair is thinning and gray. He is of medium height, broad-shouldered, burly. A thin mouth opens over white teeth. Bushy brows overshadow eyes that are clear and calm.

You have no choice but to look the person opposite in the eyes. The eyes are shifty, the voices fleeting: in this room, only the clock does not whisper, and the only discernible movement is that of the pendulum. My neighbors—a couple who, in the waiting room argued and wept at length—exchange pleasant smiles with their host and discuss the weather. "A clear hot day." The window behind Mooney's shoulders overlooks San Francisco Bay: fine black and white steamboats, white and gray gulls, and the refinery tanks of Standard Oil; what people call a glorious day. His back, with the number 31921 stamped between the shoulder blades, turned toward this twenty-two-year-old landscape, Tom Mooney looks me in the eye and says:

"From when I was a kid in school, I loved geography and dreamed of traveling. Later I left the city of Holyoke, Massachusetts, where I lived with my parents and went to Europe."

He describes in detail his peregrinations from Scotland to Italy and stops to talk about the cities he visited: Paris and Antwerp, Vienna and Budapest. Then the European tour ends.

"In Rotterdam, where I was supposed to take the boat back

to America," Mooney says, "I met an American in a museum, a socialist, and we talked. I was not yet aware of anything, but already had what was necessary inside myself. I owe a lot to that man."

He sets off again right away.

"Back in New York," he says, "I started looking for work. In 1907, there was a panic in the stock market, and unemployment was widespread. Thousands of journeymen wandered across the country in search of a livelihood. I did what they did: I jumped freight trains, I went to New Orleans and from there to Houston, Texas, but still no work. Then I crossed the border into Mexico. I saw how Mexican workers lived. The best-paid workers ate meat once a week and the others, never. They walked barefoot with cracks in the soles so deep you could have pushed a finger inside them. I left again and in Stockton, California, I finally got a place as a molder. All that way to find work. But at least I'd been around."

Outside, the flowerbeds are impeccable, the paths carefully groomed; the palm trees sway and preen, and the Star-Spangled Banner at the top of the flagpole is pristine. His back turned on the picture-postcard scenery, Mooney says:

"There are six thousand of us in San Quentin: an entire city. Mostly young. Locked up for all sorts of crimes: theft, murder, rape, counterfeiting—everything, as long as the sentence is at least a year. Locked up for union activities as well. Here, they don't make a distinction between political prisoners and common criminals. I'm considered a murderer sentenced to life for the murders he committed. Like the others, I'm allowed to write a letter a day, a two-page letter. I do mine on the typewriter. I have one I brought with me. It's an old prisoner too, twenty-two years in jail."

He stops suddenly, asks:

"Do you know Michael Gold?"

I say:

"He's a friend."

"Ten years ago or so, Mike wrote a poem saying how every night at midnight, Tom Mooney walks past the guards, leaves the prison and goes wherever men are struggling."

He looks at me as if I doubted Gold's words, says:

"It's true. I'm not here. I've never been here. I'm in Spain and China, India and Brazil, everywhere in the world where people suffer and struggle. Some Spanish comrades came to see me not long ago and I told them: 'Don't think that I'm far from your country. I'm there on the front lines, fighting shoulder to shoulder with you.'"

He seems to consider himself from a distance.

"I remember Sacco and Vanzetti," he says. "I lived through their trial as if it were my own. Especially the last three hours before the execution. I felt as if I were sharing their cells. They were murdered at one minute past noon, and I could see everything: the electric chair, the executioner and the two men. You know, Vanzetti said one day: 'When I get out of prison, I will devote my life to getting Tom Mooney free.' *He* said that."

He looks embarrassed, explains in the way of an apology:

"I've never considered myself a personal case. I saw all the political implications. I was chosen at a time when anyone might have been chosen—you, for example. The struggle for my release is beyond me. Dreyfus spent only a few years in prison, and yet he found a Zola to write *J'accuse*."

He barely raised himself from his chair. At his feet, a double row of prisoners and visitors, wardens, the room, the watchtowers, the prison, the country.

"I accuse," says Tom Mooney, and he repeats in French, "*J'accuse*."

NOTEBOOK

MAY 1936

May 1. The day before yesterday, Fred Wilson lost his job. Yesterday his baby died. Today Wilson told reporters:

"We don't have a dime. But the child was insured. We will get the twenty-five-dollar premium, which I've promised to the undertaker. A lady gave us a free plot in the cemetery. And friends have lent us a car to take the coffin there. I won't have to worry about my wife, anymore. You know, she was very sick, but police told us that now she'd get medicine. All these men and women were so good to us. Until our baby died, I didn't know there were so many good people in the world."

All New Yorkers can have their fingerprints taken by the police. To entice the public, the police announced it has collected the prints of 126 people who believe in reincarnation and want to be able to prove their existence after they are dead.

May 3. The State of New Jersey has eliminated unemployment benefits. Now, each community must come to the rescue of its own unemployed.

In the *Sunday News*, a reader wrote about the matter:

"I am fed up with paying taxes right, left, and center. Just because a man has a few dollars in the bank, does he have to give it to the

225

poor? I came to this country and made my way to the top. Let the poor do the same or CROAK. My door is not open to beggars and vagrants. They work or they croak."

Signed: "One who is enchanted."

May 4. On April 10, police arrested a black farmer in Georgia, Lint Shaw, accused of wanting to rape a white woman. The man defended himself with a knife; the officers wounded him with three bullets and arrested him. Immediately the crowd attacked the prison, armed with axes and metal rods. An elderly judge yelled at the lynchers and they withdrew. The next day, the local sheriff said: "Now everything is fine, unless something happens. The crowd has promised me to do nothing until tonight. They talk as if they'll come for the Black later, when it'll be hard to recognize them."

Shaw was moved from prison to prison. He was to stand trial on the morning of April 28. The night before, at midnight, a dozen cars stopped outside the detention center. About forty people entered the cell and dragged the Black out.

He was found at dawn, hanging from a pinetree, his body riddled with bullets.

That makes one.

April 29, this time in Arkansas, Willie Kees, a simple-minded young Black, was led away by ten masked men. He was discovered two hours later, his hands tied behind his back, shot three times.

That makes two.

Today, May 4, John Rushin, a black laborer on a Georgia plantation, had an argument with a white man, killed him, and fled. More than two hundred people with police dogs on leashes found him in no time. He was killed on the spot.

That makes three. In one week.

May 4. The Society for the Protection of Animals just finished building in Chicago a refuge for homeless cats and dogs. The home, which cost $100,000, includes a kitchen with an electric refrigerator, a bathroom, and dog pens with glass doors. The building has a garden around it.

The only people who live on Wall Street are the dead. They do not speculate, they have inalienable property: by the walls of Trinity Church, a few square feet of the most valuable land in the world. Every yard of this rocky soil, which not even the most destitute farmer would want, for nothing grows there but old bones, is worth more than an entire American village.

It is half past twelve. At the foot of the Washington statue, a crowd mills around two speakers. One, a proud and insolent old man, is shouting in the shadow of the Stars and Stripes:

"Do you want to burn the Bible and the churches? That's what Moscow wants. But what does God say?"

He points to the upper floors of the Stock Exchange.

"He said, 'Look for high wages.' Never before have the wages been higher, never the working hours so short."

Thirty feet away, a union activist for office workers tells anyone listening:

"You need an organization because you are even more exploited than factory workers. When I think a stenographer receives eight, ten, or twelve dollars a week! Is that why you went to school and your parents denied themselves?"

May 5. From *New York Herald Tribune*:

"Paul Rother, fifty, of Jersey City, spent three years without continuous employment. He made ends meet by doing odd jobs.

"Yesterday he was hired to unload freight cars for the Merchants' Refrigerating Co. It was a prospect for steady employment. He'd been working ten minutes when he keeled over. A doctor said that Rother had died of an embolism, apparently brought on by emotion. The widow confirmed that her husband had been 'terribly excited' to learn that he'd been hired."

An obliging friend takes me to the Bankers Club on the thirty-eighth floor of the Equitable Building. I recall only the washrooms, their mellow magnificence.

Then we go to the Stock Exchange. From the balcony, the room resembles a train station where temperamental travelers clamor for information around kiosks arranged in the shape of a double-horseshoe. On the wall, numbers light up on a huge board and brokers run for telephones connected by direct wire to their offices. In two opposite corners, letters and numbers slide diagonally on an illuminated transparency: all transactions appear. They are simultaneously recorded and transmitted across the country.

May 12. The director of the Lafayette School in Georgia ordered Betty Jo Wallace, eleven, to come to class wearing a dress and not overalls. The child's mother said: "Since the day she was born, Betty Jo has had a total of six dresses. I put one on her on Sundays. Other days, she wears overalls."

A hero.
From *Liberty*, May 16:
"Among the many candidates running for election this year, we come upon the unique figure of Judge John H. Lyle, Chicago. He is fifty-three, but boxes almost every day. He runs easily four or five miles a day. He shaves with a safety razor in each hand. The operation lasts about thirty seconds. Four hours of sleep are enough for him, he says. He has never smoked or chewed. He has never drunk alcohol. He is five feet ten and a half inches and weighs 167 pounds naked."

Stock prices are rough-and-ready. Otherwise, I'd write them up another way.

The steel mills are buoyant: Tennessee Coal, Iron & Railroad Co. is on strike, private company guards sweep the factory access roads with machine gun fire, five men have already been wounded.

Marble is caving in: the quarry workers in Proctor, Vermont, are on strike; at the hospital, a striker seriously injured by scabs, whispers: "I've worked, worked, worked thirty-seven years to keep my people from starving. I've never fought. I've never been in prison. And now, I think, I'm thinking of a lot of things." Technically, the position of blue chips is healthy. In Detroit, a Motor Products Corporation foreman killed striker Carl Swanson. In Washington State, the private police of Standard Oil killed Shelby Daffron, striker. Rish Fister and Henry Witt, both black, are killed in front of the mines of Republic Steel. Lead holds firm.

THE BEGINNING AND END OF THE AMERICAN REVOLUTION

To Harry

The first thing I see through the window of the train taking me to Boston is a huge sign looming over the tracks:

PURITAN ICE CREAM

Puritan ice cream, Puritan ice cream, it's time to close my suitcase again, I've arrived.

What do I know about Boston, the most aristocratic city in the United States, where people affect an English accent and a handful of families play court to two tribes, noble among nobles, Puritan among Puritans, the Lowells who deign to speak only to Cabots, and the Cabots who speak only to God?

Boston, cradle of the American Revolution, home of Samuel Adams, John Hancock, and Paul Revere, a city that jettisoned in its bay two boatloads of precious leaves the British Crown wished to force upon it, a city that treated the English gentlemen to the most famous "tea party" in history, and waged the first battles of independence, the first struggles to free the black slaves.

Boston, the cradle of American civilization, home of the Latin School, the first public school, Harvard, the first university, the *Newsletter*, the country's first gazette, birthplace or home of Emerson and Edgar Allan Poe, Hawthorne and Thoreau, Whittier and Channing, Louisa May Alcott and Longfellow.

What has become of the American Revolution and American civilization in the place of their birth, in the year nineteen hundred and thirty-six?

I have a friend in Boston, Professor Henry W. L. Dana. I could not dream of a better guide. His family has been actively involved in the country's history since its beginnings. Everything about him bodes well, right down to his first and middle names: Wadsworth, after his ancestor the General, a comrade of Washington, and Longfellow, after his grandfather, author of *Evangeline*.

Dana and I follow the same itinerary of events that occurred one and a half centuries ago.

First stop, the heart of the city, State Street, site of the Boston Massacre. Houses, shops, cars, commemorative plaques. I buy a postcard: British soldiers in red and yellow fire a salvo at Americans dressed in green. In the middle, a black man, the only one who has neither coat, wig, nor tricorn is dying, club in hand. March 5, 1770. The Black was named Crispus Attucks, the first casualty of the Revolution.

Next, the old cemetery where massacre victims, relatives of Benjamin Franklin, Paul Revere, lie beneath stones with the inscriptions half washed away. The sky over the graves is a huge neon sign and is called Chevrolet.

We jump ahead five years, years of smuggling and rising customs duties, debates in the London Parliament, and heated discussions in the homes of patriotic Boston merchants, the closing of the port by the British fleet and blockade of the garrison by the neighboring population, and then the night of April 18, 1775, when General Gage, learning the insurgents had stockpiled weapons and ammunition in Concord, about twenty miles from Boston, decided to send out soldiers to seize and destroy.

That night, while the men of the Tenth Regiment were preparing to leave under the command of Colonel Francis Smith, the engraver Paul Revere, a citizen of Boston, crossed the Charles River and made the midnight ride he repeats year after year in every American school.

He followed this road past the Ford assembly plant and the blocks of slums, up the concrete pavement that leads into Lexington. He arrived in the middle of the night, and entering the little street to the right, knocked at the door of the house where patriot leaders Samuel Adams and John Hancock were sleeping. The house is locked, but through the windows we can see a canopy bed, black furniture, copper plates. Outside, a commemorative plaque.

In the early hours of the morning, when Colonel Smith arrived on the lawn in Lexington, he was met by a thin line of Minutemen, so called because they had to be ready in just a minute, the sharpshooters and partisans of the American Revolution. A stone marks the spot where they took their positions that night, engraved with the words of their leader: "Stand your ground, don't fire unless fired upon, but if they mean to have a war, let it begin here." And indeed it is here that the war began, on this lawn, lined with little wooden houses and a profusion of plaques, some providing directions and distances, others dates and events.

Under a pyramid in the middle of the lawn are buried the Lexington fighters "who fell on this field, the first victims to the sword of British tyranny and oppression, on the morning of the ever-memorable Nineteenth of April, A.D. 1775."

At the end of the Common, a house; a plaque commemorates a wounded Minuteman, who dragged himself here and died at his wife's feet.

We return to Concord.

There, the Patriots had stockpiled swords, brush hooks, cartridge paper, flares, scrap metal, cannonballs, rifles, musket balls, and also molasses, salt fish, and oat and wheat flours: enough for a revolution.

A tree-lined driveway, a sign, an obelisk, the bridge over the Concord, and, on the other side, the statue of a Minuteman.

The sign reads: "On the morning of April Nineteenth, 1775, while the British held this bridge, the Minute-Men and militia of Concord and neighboring towns gathered on the hill across the river. There the Concord adjutant, Joseph Hosmer, challenged, 'Will you let them burn the town down?' There the Lincoln captain, William Smith, offered to dislodge the British, the Lincoln captain, Isaac Davis, said, 'I haven't a man that's afraid to go!'" and the Concord colonel, James Barrett, ordered the attack on the regulars. The column was led by Major John Buttrick, marching from his own farm. His aide was Lt. Colonel John Robinson of Westford. The Minute-Men of Concord, Acton, Lincoln, and Bedford followed. After them came the militia. At the British volley Isaac Davis fell. Buttrick cried, 'Fire, fellow-soldiers, for God's sake fire!' and he fired first."

The obelisk says, "Here, on the Nineteenth of April, 1775, was made the first forcible resistance to British aggression. On the opposite bank stood the American Militia. Here stood the invading army, and on this spot the first of the enemy fell in the War of the Revolution which gave Independence to these United States."

"I like to imagine this place as our American Cathedral," says Henry Dana. "The center of the green is the nave, the sides are the aisles, and the trees are the pillars. They all lead up to the obelisk, which represents the choir. The open space in front of the monument is the transept, and there, on the left, are the graves of the British soldiers killed at Concord, as in old churches, they were buried on the spot. Then, there's the bridge, and finally, the Minuteman statue: the altar of our cathedral."

Near the final resting place of Colonel Smith's men, an old man wearing a cap stands by a bench, surrounded by watercolor paintings: the bridge, the obelisk, the statue, the green, skillfully executed and conventional. He speaks without being prompted; he must have said the same things to thousands of visitors.

"I'm Howard Melvin," he says, "I am the great-grandson of one of the Minutemen who fought here. I will be eighty-one next month; since the shoemaker died, I am the oldest inhabitant of Concord. I was born in Concord, April 19, 1855, a nice date for an inhabitant of this country, isn't it?"

He smiles mischievously.

"My wife, who was not from Concord, never understood why they fired the cannon every April 19. 'They don't do it just for you?' she'd say. 'Oh, yes!' I told her."

He laughs for the thousandth time.

"I do these watercolors you see here, and I do them without glasses. I learned painting from the sister of Louisa Alcott, she was a true artist and gave me real lessons. I also sell pieces of wood from the old Concord Bridge, real pieces from the bridge they've replaced with this concrete one because visitors carried off pieces for souvenirs. I also knew Emerson, but not as well as I knew Hawthorne. I usually saw him go by around sunset, Hawthorne, out for a walk. He gave me pencils when I was a schoolboy. I sold three of them to teachers and I still have some at home. I saw soldiers returning from the Civil War and I remember the Cuban expedition."

He no doubt embellishes his memories, but he probably did know the people he is talking about. He is part of the landscape and part of history, this old man who gets his Concord Bridge splinters from the nearby woods and buys his Hawthorne's pencils from the village store, which is a testament to the youth of the American Revolution. And the Melvins are an old Concord family. There are several in the town cemetery.

The cemetery is vast and indolent. The graves climb the hills, far apart or crowded together depending on how hilly the spot is, and cluster around the roots of the trees. On one of the hills, next to a path, sleep forty years of American civilization: a block of stone, an erected stele, an anonymous plaque—Emerson, Hawthorne, Thoreau. A few steps away, the country rambles on, wild and deserted.

Beyond Concord is the solitude of the forest. Little white birches sparkle among the fir trees. A small lake in a basin is covered with a thin layer of lusterless ice. The trees grow down to the edge of the water. All sounds are muted, as if wrapped in cotton wool. There are a multitude of Indian legends about this lake: it is said that it has no bottom, like all lakes that inspire legends. In a cove, hidden from view, the house where Thoreau lived.

We retrace our steps on the path lined with houses where the people buried in the Concord cemetery once toiled to fill the future libraries of America. Emerson's white house. Farther along, the beige house, where, at the very top behind soundproofed walls, Hawthorne wrote undisturbed by noise and visitors. And then the brown house of Louisa May Alcott. All three have green shutters, and all the shutters are closed.

This is the road Colonel Smith and his men took to return to Boston. Paul Revere alone had watched them go; the whole country witnessed their retreat. Farmers armed with shotguns came out of the forest and aimed at the Englishmen, whose uniforms were redder than squirrel's pelts. Through Lexington, Arlington, Charlestown, the regulars fled to Boston, the American Revolution close on their heels.

At sunset, Dana's old car enters Cambridge, whence the British once left for Concord. The shadows lengthen across the road and the houses with black clapboard cladding.

We walk around Harvard University and go into the Faculty Club. In the dining room, serious gentlemen talk in low voices; at the restroom sink, the hairbrushes have acquired through contact with so many heads full of knowledge, a treasure trove of silver hair.

Dana lives in his grandfather Longfellow's house. For ten months it was the home of the commander of the insurgent army, General George Washington. It was here that he read *Common Sense*, the famous pamphlet by Thomas Paine, it was here that he saw the need for independence. Insofar as Washington is "the father of this country," it is in this house that the United States was born.

It was here, too, that Longfellow settled in 1837, the trace of his presence added to that of Washington before him. Both lived in the same rooms, both played host to the revolutionaries of their times, from the great American Benjamin Franklin to the great Hungarian Lajos Kossuth.

Of the writer, there remain busts and manuscripts, paintings and cupboards packed with books: Chateaubriand and Victor Hugo, Dante and Tasso, Schiller and Goethe, a cupboard for each language, a cupboard for each literature. Of the man of action remain a bullet and a bayonet.

From this day trip through the history of the United States, I bring back a few postcards and the memory of commemorative plaques, funerary monuments, dusty volumes, closed shutters, and two cemeteries.

It is time to inspect Boston, 1936. What has become of the descendants of the patriots, the Minutemen who inscribed in the US Constitution the inalienable right of all to "life, liberty and the pursuit of happiness"? What have the great families of Boston become? In what church do the Cabots speak to God? Has the Puritan ice melted?

Quick, the phonebook. I locate names. There are two Longfellows, four Hawthornes, thirty-nine Cabots, forty-four Lowells.

"Look for Irish names," says Dana, "you'll understand."

Suddenly, a deluge. 778 O'Briens, 1,097 Murphys, 1,331 Sullivans. There are more John J. Sullivans than Lowells, more Mary Murphys than Cabots. There is nothing left for the latter to do but talk with the Lord.

"I remember the early days of Irish immigration," says Dana. "Mostly servants. Calvin's hand had come down on Geneva, then Edinburgh, then Boston. The English and Puritan population despised these Catholic Celts. Forty years ago, it was quite common to say, 'Hit him, he's Irish.' And classified ads read 'Irish abstain.' But they kept coming, in greater numbers. They elected their man

Curley to the mayor's office; now he's governor of Massachusetts. Cardinal O'Connell's residence is near the city limits, just as you leave town, opposite the Catholic University. The oppressors have changed but not the oppression. In Boston, "amoral" and revolutionary plays are prohibited, on stage we hunt down swear words and on the streets we hunt down Reds."

After the telephone book, newspaper ads. Not serial advertising that is the same from New York to San Francisco, but the local variety, unique.

Here it is from Filene's department stores: "Who were your ancestors? A heraldry expert is permanently on hand with a comprehensive library of books on the Anglo-Saxon shield. A family tree of relatives abroad is included, when available, with the coats of arms. Authenticity guaranteed."

And in the Heraldic section of the *Boston Transcript*: "Are you looking for a revolutionary ancestor?"

The revolutionary ancestors I know. It's the descendants I'm looking for.

"Go to a concert," says Dana. "Go to Trinity Church. Go to the Church of Christian Science. Go to the Capitol. Go to the Opera."

I go to a concert of the Boston Symphony Orchestra. I think I'm the only person without a season's ticket, and another friend has to give up his seat. I've never seen so many chignons so white they are transparent, or slightly rust-tinged like very old fabric, and darting ear trumpets: could it be that only the deaf in Boston listen to music? I open the program and read: "This concert will end at 4:28 on Friday afternoon, and 10:13 on Saturday night." The ear-trumpeted chignons won't have to wait for their drivers.

I go to Trinity Church on Sunday morning. Hundreds of cars parked in front wait for the service to end. Inside, the dry wind of prayers chewed by thin lips bends indifferent heads forward.

I go to the Mother Church of Christian Science. The walls are covered with the words of the apostles: Mark, Luke, Matthew,

John, and Mary Baker Eddy.* Gentlemen in uniform: black jacket, striped pants, detachable collars with bent corners, smiles pinned to their lips, pointing the way. Lowing organs. A smiling man in tails signals for us to wait: no one must enter during the execution of the pieces. A second man in tails hands out with a smile a collection of the thoughts inscribed on the walls. A third gentleman in tails, radiant and cheerful, slips me the schedule of concerts and conferences: admission is free. A fourth gentleman rejoices like a man blessed as he slides into my hand a list of excursions outside the city from $1.25 to $5 per person, exclusively in Lincoln sedans.

I go to the Capitol, where a Senate committee is holding a public meeting. A law of the State of Massachusetts requires the teaching profession to take an oath of loyalty to the Constitution. Teachers and students, intellectuals and workers are calling for the repeal of this law that allows the dismissal of teachers who mention the name of Marx or the existence of the Soviet Union. The Senate Education Committee is weighing the arguments of opponents and supporters of the oath. Today it is the supporters' turn to speak.

Imagine a large room. Common people—professors, teachers, and students—are crowded on the balcony. The Committee members are seated on a platform.

But the sight not to be missed is the orchestra. Thin-lipped, flat-breasted women, gloved for fear of germs and of sitting in such close quarters, all dignified, all malignant, all Daughters of the American Revolution.** These old ladies, dressed in dark colors and black hats, stiffly ensconced in their lives, their prejudices, their armchairs, as proud today, twenty years later, as on the day they sacrificed their sons on the altar of the Fatherland: the Gold Star Mothers. The men who prefer uniforms to civilian clothes because they hide their bellies, or almost, who know how to read but do not

---

* Mary Baker Eddy (1821–1910) was the founder of Christian Science. In 1908, she founded the *Boston Christian Science Monitor*. (French editor's note.)

** Reactionary organization, like the other three mentioned below.

like to do so and read nothing but the Hearst press: members of the American Legion. And the others, wounded or maimed for absolutely no reason, as if there were an impenetrable barrier between themselves and their amputated limb, lashing out with empty words to defend themselves against subversive memories, just as the body forms protective tissue around a bullet that surgeons have not been able to extract: the Veterans of Foreign Wars. Throw in some church ministers, a few old maids, a few human wrecks, and the picture is complete. From its glorious past, this crowd retains only the memory of witches burned near Boston two and a half centuries ago.

As at a baseball game, fans cheer for their favorites. Daughters, mothers, Legionnaires, and veterans applaud the speakers. What a burst of enthusiasm when Reverend Hayes takes the floor to denounce the sneers of his enemies.

"Behind this laughter," he exclaims, "beats the rampant black atheist heart of communism. I will fight to the last drop of my blood to eradicate this vile cancerous growth in society. Why do these teachers refuse to make the oath? Because their refusal is a smokescreen that hides their insidious communism."

The yelling is twice as loud when Frank Doyle appears. Frank Doyle of the American Legion, who declares himself "Frank in name and frank by nature," who proclaims that educators have sick minds, "I can prove it and I know the cure," who tells it like it is to the Harvard professors—"damn liars, pardon my language, ladies"—who says where there is smoke there is fire and good seed produces a good crop.

But what is male reasoning worth compared to female eloquence? Listen to Mrs. Hickey, whose only claim to fame is being the mother of six children whom she hopes can go to school knowing the law requires the pledge of allegiance to the flag. Listen to Mrs. Knight's assertion that universities and professors have been treated well in the state of Massachusetts. Were they grateful? No! Why? It is because all American universities are Communists! And here's the proof: they receive subsidies from the Carnegie Foundation,* whose avowed aim is to destroy the independence of the United States!

Convicted for inciting soldiers to disobedience, the patriots of 1775, who distributed leaflets inviting English soldiers to desert. Convicted for armed resistance to police, the Minutemen of Lexington and Concord. Convicted of high treason, Benjamin Franklin and George Washington.

Finally, I go to the opera. The new season is opening and limousines, furs, and jewelry are more abundant than ever. The boxes are full of celebrities. Mrs. Charles Sumner Bird, wearing a black and dark green dress, is accompanied by her brother-in-law, Mr. Oliver Wolcott, and Madame, in a brown dress trimmed with velvet of the same color. Mrs. Dudley Pickman has pinned a purple orchid to her ermine mantle, while Mrs. John S. Blyth has brightened up her chartreuse chiffon gown and sable cape with a bouquet of gardenias.

But all these glories fade in comparison with the spectacle in the great central box. A woman adorned in a dress from Paris, white and silver with scarlet silk fringe, cut very low in the back, who has settled in the back seat beside a young girl wearing a turquoise tunic that pleasingly contrasts with the orchids woven into her brown hair. They came with a man; all eyes are upon him. Mr. Alvan T. Fuller, his wife, and their eldest daughter whose presence adds vitality to this gathering, all elegance and beauty.

Alvan T. Fuller—surely you know of him? And Fuller, just Fuller? No? Come on, the director of the Museum of Fine Arts, Boston, lover of painting, happy owner of an entire gallery of Zoloaga paintings, whose reds he especially appreciates, so they say, for which he paid $100,000? Still doesn't ring a bell? What about the owner of the Packard Motor Car Company of Boston, a serious

---

* The Carnegie Foundation for the Advancement of Education, created in 1905 by Andrew Carnegie, the first king of steel.

company if ever there was one? No? And the governor of Massachusetts, who one morning, August 22, 1927, to be precise, greeted
the journalists who had come to interview him with a "Beautiful
morning, isn't it, boys?" while an honest shoemaker and a poor
fishmonger died in the electric chair? Have you by any chance forgotten the names of Sacco and Vanzetti?

"They should destroy that house and put up a factory or school,
to teach many of the hundreds of poor orphan boys of the world."
They have not destroyed that house, the Charlestown prison, as
Sacco desired. It still stands, not far from the spot where Paul
Revere took the start. We are driving along by the railroad tracks.
A bridge, then the gray building. High-barred windows; on the
far left, the cell that housed the two condemned men on the eve
of the execution ". . . here where life is buried and you can't see
anything but four sad walls and lap of sky that disappears under a
wing of a bird," wrote Sacco. "They've started running the prison's
electric motor . . . Now I can hear them preparing it for an execution, maybe mine—and that noise tears my entire being," wrote
Vanzetti. We stay close to the wall, turn left, go past the prison
entrance, and turn again. At the end of the compound, posters
have been pasted up, ads for cars, gasoline, and canned food. Here,
in the corner of the yard, was the electric chair. At the top of the
wall, the silhouette of a guard against the gray sky.

One evening, I meet Dr. A. M. at the home of friends, a psychiatrist, a man with a high forehead and receding hairline, round dark
horn-rimmed glasses, and an expression both skeptical and cynical.

"Yes," he says, "I knew them very well, especially Sacco. I saw
him . . . a hundred . . . hundred and fifty times in prison. He
hadn't been convicted yet, and he didn't work like the others. We
managed to find him an occupation. He was extraordinarily skilled
with his hands."

The doctor is silent, thinking, starts again:

"The guards were nice to him. He was even allowed to walk alone
because he had fights with the other prisoners. At the Dedham jail,

where he was being held at the time, there were only men con-victed of petty theft, desertion of the marital home, etc. They made fun of Sacco, who was charged with murder, and that's how the fights got started. Vanzetti, who was in Charlestown Prison, had no trouble with his companions, whose crimes were of a larger scale."

He pauses again, chooses a cake from the plate his hostess offers him, goes on:

"Sacco read a lot. He had a small bookcase: books on political economy, sociology, books on anarchism, socialism, communism, Marx's *Capital,* American writers: Jack London, Russians: Dosto-evsky, Tolstoy. He often asked me the meaning of words he didn't understand. They learned a lot in prison, especially Sacco, who was intelligent, but naïve and didn't have much education."

I do not ask the doctor any questions, he is talking to himself, like a sleepwalker.

"From the medical point of view, they were in good condition, both of them: detention didn't affect them too much. Except that, from time to time, they went on hunger strike. They did it inten-tionally, not because their morale had suffered. One day Sacco, who refused all food, began to rave. I saw him: he said he was being hunted, that they were putting poison in his food. He was trans-ferred to the infirmary and fed through a tube. Then he started to eat: hunger he could stand, but not the tube."

The doctor takes the drink someone hands him, examines it curiously, sets it on the table with a mechanical gesture.

"Often he had to sign official documents," he says, "but he refused. His lawyer came to see him, and people from the defense committee, but he said: 'we declared war on them, and they declared war on us. They don't want peace, and we don't want it either. What's the point in writing them?' Vanzetti also repeated: 'We are at war. They caught us. And that's that.' They were both very aware of the political implications of their case. Sacco did not believe they would ever be executed. He was convinced that mil-lions of men would rise up to free them. But Vanzetti said: 'No,

Nicola, they care more about their Fords than about us. They won't do anything.' When Sacco was convicted, I went to see him. 'This grieves me, Nicola,' I said.—'It's nothing, doctor,' he replied. 'They got me. That's it.' I loved them both: brave men who accepted their fate peacefully." He falls silent again, tells me about our host and the bookcase, suddenly says:

"One day I was smoking in Sacco's cell and threw my cigarette butt quite a distance through the bars. Sacco asked: 'You played baseball, Doctor?'— 'Why?— 'I can see you have a good arm.'— 'Just luck.'— 'No, no!'— 'Do you think you can do it?'— 'I don't know. I'll try.' He tried three times, without success. All this to say, he was interested in the smallest things."

The doctor goes to mingle with the other guests, very worldly, very self-possessed. Suddenly I hear his voice near me:

"Sacco got the newspapers, but they were censored: all references to the case were withheld. Otherwise, he could read everything and be interested in events. He had strong Italian features, and was more like a craftsman or an artist than a worker. He had a beautiful child, and a nice little wife. Vanzetti was single. When they were transferred to death row, I never saw them again. All the guards were saddened by the verdict."

It's late when we get up to leave. In the front hall, the doctor tells me:

"I never completely made up my mind about them. I'm sure they were able to kill someone for the cause, but they would never have done so to steal. I've known a lot of killers, real or suspected—a hundred or a hundred and fifty—but these two men left the strongest impression on me. They were so different from the others."

"Be a vanquished man," wrote Vanzetti, "but a formidable shadow."

Dana and Jessica Henderson take me to Watertown, a Boston suburb. Telegraph lines rake the gloom of a low-hanging sky. Bunches of washing hang between the bare trees and the black wooden houses.

The front porch is a few steps up. The door opens onto a drab interior: no bright colors, nothing new in sight.

A woman is there, small and plump. She has a high forehead, black eyes, short chin, thick blond hair. She smiles often, a polite smile but not a happy one, exposing a double row of small, straight white teeth. Wearing an apron and a little printed dress, she sits very quietly. Hers is a social manner common among the petty bourgeois; she listens in silence as others speak. Her hands are crossed on her lap. She is close to forty, soon her skin will grow red and blotchy, but for now it is pink.

Facing her, leaning against the wall, a tall slim boy, solidly built, wearing blue coveralls. An aquiline nose, white metal–rimmed glasses, an intelligent, austere scholastic face. His smile very faint. Monk or craftsman. A young girl in an armchair, she is fifteen or sixteen, the only one of the three with a pronounced, almost conventional Italian face: black curls trailing down her back, large black eyes, bushy eyebrows that look glued to her forehead. She is not pretty.

Rosa, Dante, and Ines Sacco: the widow and children, all silent.

The day before, Mrs. Henderson came to ask them if I could visit. Believing that I was going to ask about her husband, Rosa Sacco refused. I insisted, promising not to ask questions. I just say:

"You cannot know how grateful I am for your agreeing to see me. The names of Sacco and Vanzetti mean so much to us all."

"Why? I don't understand. That was nearly ten years ago."

She speaks in an even and colorless voice and then falls silent.

Jessica Henderson says:

"We just did a play in New York inspired by the Sacco-Vanzetti trial."

I continue:

"A French writer recently published a novel about the Sacco-Vanzetti case."

Dana says, "The Sacco and Vanzetti letters have been translated into every language."

We recite one after the other:

"I remember the demonstration in Paris in 1927."

"In the port of Leningrad, I saw the *Sacco-Vanzetti* Soviet steamship."

"There are a lot of streets called Sacco-Vanzetti in the suburbs of Paris."

"In Moscow, I went to the Sacco-Vanzetti cinema."

Rosa, Dante, and Ines Sacco remain silent. It looks as if they are only listening out of politeness. And that only politeness makes the little blond woman say "yes" from time to time.

"Did Vanzetti leave any relatives in America?" Dana asks.

"No."

"And have you heard from his sister who came here?"

"No, I have not heard from her since."

"I saw her when I went to Europe," said Dante.

"When was that?"

"Three years ago."

"Where did you go?"

"To Villafalletto, where the Vanzettis live."

"I went there too," says Dana, "I promised Bartolo. He gave me a letter for his family, so kind. He told them exactly what they must do. They were to give me red wine and white wine, but insist on red, because white is stronger and I do not usually drink. Did you also go see your family?"

"Yes," says Dante, "I was in Torremaggiore."

"Were you happy with your trip?"

"Yes," he says reticently.

"Not me," says Rosa. "I didn't have him with me."

Dana turns to Ines.

"And what do you do now?"

"I go to a business school. I love it."

"Are you learning to type?"

"Yes, that and other things."

Silence again. Mrs. Henderson starts talking about France. Rosa listens politely.

"The Popular Front can prevent war and fascism," says Mrs. Henderson. "Dante is very opposed to the war. Aren't you, Dante?"

"Yes," he says.

Silence once more.

"What happened to Bartolo's ashes?" asks Dana.

"His sister took them to Italy," says Dante. "They are in Villafalletto cemetery. The family had another funeral."

"A religious funeral probably," says Rosa, and a hint of contempt enters her toneless voice.

"And Sacco's?"

"Nic's ashes? I always keep them here."

Her face is closed. The children are silent. Dana says:

"Did you ever see . . . what was his name, that boy? Bini?"

"Brini," Dante says immediately.

"That's it, Brini. Have you seen him lately?"

"No," says Rosa. "I haven't seen anyone since . . ."

She pauses, and on her lips we read the word: murder.

". . . let's say since the execution," she says.

On the way home my companion says:

"Brini was a little boy at the time. He was one of the people who'd bought fish from Vanzetti on the day of the crime. They didn't let him testify. He'll be grown up now. Vanzetti was selling fish in Plymouth. In one of his letters he writes about the 'good shoemaker and the poor fishmonger.' It wasn't humility. He was proud that his friend was a good shoemaker. On the anniversary of the execution, I've often been tempted to send Governor Fuller a card with the words: 'From the good shoemaker and the poor fishmonger.'"

The car drives along the Charles River. We are heading for the last commemorative site of the revolutionary era: the Bunker Hill Monument. This is where, on June 17, 1775, the British launched an attack on American positions. The insurgents were armed with shotguns. Among them were Indians and Blacks. The best shooters were sent to the front, their comrades loaded the weapons with pieces of scrap iron, metal buttons—anything. Three times the regulars attacked the stronghold, and the third time they took it, but they had lost more than half their men and this victory was their first defeat.

At the foot of the obelisk on the hill, a boy recites in a monotone:

"This is the Bunker Hill Monument, erected in memory of the battle . . ."

From the top of the obelisk, we can see all of Boston—the river, the docks, the sea, and in the foreground, a few thousand feet away, the prison yard where Sacco and Vanzetti were executed.

In this land so many roads intersect, so many memories and voices intertwine: the hoofprints of Paul Revere's horse and the footprints of the workers from the Ford Plant, the fleeing soldiers of Colonel Francis Smith, and the arrival of Robert Elliot, executioner for the State of Massachusetts, the tread of George Washington and the slide of Governor Fuller's car, the first cries of Edgar Allan Poe and the murmur of teachers taking the loyalty oath, the loneliness of Thoreau and the solitude of Sacco and Vanzetti, beginning and end, beginning and end.

At the far end of the city, in Kneeland Street, picketers mill around the deserted workshops. Police on horseback ride up on the sidewalks to protect the scabs, shouting workmen surge toward them, throw a punch, fall, get up, throw another punch, keep advancing. Beginning and end, and beginning again.

NOTEBOOK

MAY 1936 (END)

May 16. William Wells, sixty-five, black, and his sister Cora lived in a hut in Gordonsville, Virginia. A white woman accused the old man of threatening her with his gun. Last night the police came to arrest Wells. Terrorized, he shot and killed a sheriff. Then he barricaded himself in his shack, knowing the fate that awaited him if he let himself be taken alive.

And indeed, all the area police and three hundred neighbors had surrounded the place. The siege lasted late into the night. The firehouse spotlights swept over the shack, doused by police with machine gun fire. Finally, an officer slipped up to a window and threw a burning torch inside. Between the waiting crowd and the suffocating fire, the two old people did not hesitate. They let themselves be burned alive.

May 17

The pioneer tradition.

Three unrelated items: Curley, governor of Massachusetts, has expressed his intention to establish an age limit for judges: seventy years. Judge Patrick Duane of Boston, seventy-four, has risen to the challenge. He has invited the governor to join him in a boxing match in the Great Hall of the House of Representatives.

Judge Owens of Baltimore pronounced a very light sentence

for a young man accused of attacking two girls. The girls' mother appeared before the magistrate and beat him up. In spite of his seventy-three years, the judge ended up having the upper hand. "It was an exciting fight," he said.

In Nashville, Tennessee, lived the three Lane brothers, Harrison, sixty-five, Henry, seventy, and Bud, ninety years. The two younger ones quarreled and began to throw stones at each other. The eldest went for his rifle and wounded Harrison.

May 19. Brooklyn jurors have just acquitted Benedict Parnigiani, accused of attacking a passerby. And yet the state prosecutor had a fully signed confession from the accused.

Parnigiani testified that two detectives had taken him to the basement of a Brooklyn police station, forced him to strip to the waist and tied his wrists to a central heating pipe above his head. The heat was so intense that Parnigiani agreed to sign a "confession" dictated by the police. Later, at the hospital, he required skin grafts on his wrists.

May 23. The Florence Crittendon League, a charitable organization, recently conducted a survey of 561 prostitutes in New York. One hundred and seventy women were domestics, eighty-two factory workers, and fifty-eight waitresses. The average weekly wage in their previous occupations was eight dollars. Thirty-three of the women had never before earned more than two and a half dollars a week.

A Washington Scene

There are trees in Washington. After New York, we are dumbfounded.

Washington is proud because there are few "poor Whites." There are very few Whites, say, who live in the slums: poverty and slums are for Blacks, whose population is close to 160,000, three-quarters of whom are unemployed.

Walking in the streets of the capital, it seems that sidewalks are made for Whites and the street for Blacks. Whites stroll, gawk, hail acquaintances, or hurry along to government offices. Blacks repair the pavement, lay the tram rails, maneuver shovel, spade, welding torch, saw, and hammer.

There are flags everywhere in the city. Starred flags on the walls of houses and on rooftops, large stylish flags designed to unfurl in artistic folds, lifted by the wind. Also, a multitude of little red pennants, flush with the asphalt, not ironed or hemmed like the others, impatiently flailing the ground at the entrance to construction sites, signaling men at work.

A small silver airship hovers over the city, whose center is composed of official buildings. Columns, everywhere: Doric, Ionic, Corinthian, and most of all hybrids, topped by pediments scrolled with long lofty inscriptions. Sitting in a small temple, a gigantic Lincoln strains to see the Capitol, but it is hidden by the obelisk in honor of George Washington.

In the evening, the Lincoln Memorial, the obelisk, the Capitol, and the airship light up, the first three for the sake of beauty, the last for the sake of utility: along the hull, flowing red letters invite airship enthusiasts to take a spin and motorists to buy only Goodyear tires.

Washington is the southernmost city of the North: Blacks live in designated areas, are not allowed in white hotels or movie houses. Not long ago, a Black, a university professor, ventured into a hotel elevator and was beaten up and kicked out of it.

I take a wrong turn on my way to the Senate. My mistake isn't serious because above the low houses I see the pale building where the senators' offices are located. I take a shortcut through the alleys. Small corrugated iron huts, smashed windows, ominous staircases, pens where no dog would ever lie, tiny courtyards too small to contain the few rags that housewives hang out to dry on raveling ropes, fences made of motley planks bearing inscriptions from their days as crates: "Fragile," "Pennsylvania Railroad," "Fresh eggs," yappy little dogs with protuberant ribs, toothless black women, filthy barefoot brats wallowing in heaps of cans, rusty metal, oily paper. A few yards away, the last tenements just manage to preserve the alignment of the street whose opposite sidewalk is lined with the offices of the Senate.

The Capitol is no different. From the main terrace, the view is of trees and ponds, the obelisk in the distance, and the Lincoln Memorial. But off to the side, one looks down into teeming streets that twist and turn between squalid buildings where raggedy black girls in doorways offer their bodies to passersby.

The "hill" (one says "go up the hill" for "go to the Capitol") is like those forest women of Galician legend, beautiful from the front. But from the back, all naked entrails.

CONVENTIONAL AMERICA

V. DEATH

When I open the office door, a gray man is just finishing a dictation to the stenographer:

". . . Forty dollars a grave, in lots of ten."

Mr. King is tall, stout, pink, blond, placid. Mr. Harris is thin, medium height, with graying hair. Mr. King is smoking a cigar, Mr. Harris prefers a pipe. Mr. King and Mr. Harris are business partners. Their job is reducing men to ashes.

"No, no," says King, "funerals do not concern us. We maintain perfect relations with the major funeral homes that I urge you to visit. But we ourselves work in cremation. I'll give you an example. If your mother dies, we will cremate her and take care of all the arrangements at the cemetery. As for the choice of coffin, the funeral, etc., you'll have to speak to someone else."

"Some technical details? Well! There are two methods of cremation. Gas. And oil. We adopted oil."

"During the procedure, a metal plate with a serial number is placed alongside the body, so there's no risk of error or substitution. It takes an hour and a half. Then you must wait four hours for it to cool. When the ashes are removed, all that's left are the large bones."

Mr. King jovially slaps himself on the thigh to show what he means by large bones.

"Here again, there are two processes. You either put the bones in a mortar and grind them, or crush them with a millstone. The grinder or the millstone. We adopted the grinder method."

"I forgot to mention one of the advantages of our system: there is no smoke or odor. That's important, write it down."

"The ashes are then locked inside a tin box. The serial number is stamped on the bottom and the lid of the container: once again, no danger of error, because except for this number, the boxes are identical and so are their contents."

"And then what?"

"It depends. There are six solutions. Sometimes the ashes are simply destroyed. There are two variations. Some prefer to throw them into the sea. Others prefer to disperse them among the trees. We support the tree solution. Second method: the family comes to pick up the box. Or we personally deliver the ashes to the relatives. Or the undertaker makes the delivery. Unless we send the parcel by registered mail, insured, for thirty-five dollars."

"What for?"

"Well, think about it. If the package is lost, the post office will reimburse our thirty-five dollars, which we return to the family. Sixth and final solution: the ashes are placed in our columbarium. Each delivery comes with a certificate attesting that the operation has been conducted in accordance with the law."

"And this costs . . . ?"

"Thirty-five dollars for adults, twenty dollars for children of five to ten, and fifteen dollars for children under five. The price of the certificate is extra. Any other questions?"

"If I am not mistaken, you have a private cemetery?"

"Sixty acres of land around our mausoleum. Customers can choose the location that suits them. By the way, we avoid the word "cemetery." In some countries, a funeral is a terrible thing. In Chile they harness the hearse to horses with feather headdresses. There's something morbid about it. Here we consider a funeral a natural phenomenon. There is a strong tendency to avoid monuments. A simple plaque is enough. Cemeteries become parks. Ours is big enough to receive you, but small enough to ensure privacy, far enough from New York to be in the middle of nature, but close enough to get to easily by road or rail. If you want to take a look around, come with me."

We're leaving.

"Any other questions?" asks Mr. King.

"How much is a place in your park?"

"Five dollars and above."

"And who are some of your clients?"

"Rockefeller and below. A wide range. All religions. Yesterday, a Russian Orthodox priest came to officiate. Day before yesterday, there were three Armenian bishops. Just to show you the diversity."

"Many believers among your customers?"

"They all are."

"Isn't cremation contrary to the principles of religion?"

"Yes, among Catholics and Orthodox Jews. For others, it's okay."

"I mean, from the point of view of resurrection."

Mr. King lets go of the steering wheel and throws my objection over his shoulder:

"Oh! You know!"

"So we were saying, among your customers . . ."

"Look, here's our list of subscribers: only a few of them. Some have been availed of our services, others are still alive."

He hands me a luxuriously produced booklet. I leaf through it at random.

"Take the letter A," Mr. King says. "Charles L. Allen, treasurer of the Westinghouse Co.; Isaac Alzamora, vice-president of Peru; Leopold Auer, the well-known violinist. Et cetera, et cetera."

"You have clients of all nationalities?"

"Oh, yes! English, Germans, Russians, Austrians, French, South American. We also have Chinese and Japanese. We cremate them but don't keep them."

"And Blacks?"

"No Blacks! Sometimes we incinerate one, but they're buried in their own cemetery."

"How do you find customers?"

"We use the press, mail, radio, and telephone, and we make home visits."

"The phone?"

"It's simple. We have the numbers of telephone subscribers, street by street. We phone them one after the other."

"To say what?"

"'Sir' or 'Madam,' it's a painful but necessary step, so why put it off to the last moment?' Of course, I'm summarizing here."

"Does it pay off?"

"Oh yes."

"And radio advertising?"

"The usual method. An artistic broadcasting cut with ads for our establishment. It's over for the moment. The best season is winter. No radio in the summer. People take vacations to the beach, they don't want to hear about those kinds of things."

"Don't as many people die in summer as in winter?"

"Oh, no! Ask any bureau of statistics. They'll tell you there's a smooth curve of deaths by month. Of course, for us, the average varies little: about 1,200 customers, more exactly, 3.1 per day. And you know, the Depression had no impact on our revenues. People die as much as they did before the Depression and they spend as much money on funerals."

A large park surrounds the mausoleum. Here and there, slabs of marble or bronze are inscribed with a client's name. A gardener is in the process of trimming the grass around the sides with the affected gestures of a hairdresser. Two stone women with a Greco-Egyptian look have pride of place on a marble architrave above a forged copper door. We enter the mausoleum.

Palm tree to the left, palm tree to the right, stained-glass windows to the left, stained-glass windows to the right, lilies to the left, lilies to the right, a wall full of boxes to the left, an identical wall to the right, men's room to the left, ladies' room to the right.

"These bronze lamps," says Mr. King, "were designed by Messrs.

Caldwell and Co., inspired by the oil lamps of the Greek villa, but of course, these run on electricity. The walls are cream Alabama marble. As it says in our brochure, 'this collective twentieth-century mausoleum unites the permanence of the Pyramids with the beauty of the Taj Mahal, the dignity of Westminster Abbey, and the comfort of our modern times.' This masterpiece is the work of the architect who built the tomb of the Unknown Soldier. Electric lighting, heating, ventilation, everything is perfect. Each recess is provided with its own lock. Uniformed guards are on duty night and day. Guides trained in the delicate understanding of human nature are available for consultation.

The mausoleum is filled with compartments, some of which are occupied or spoken for by future customers, and others are still for rent. I remember the company's caption from their ads: "You know who your neighbors are." You, the dead.

To go up to the second floor, you can take the elevator but there is also a staircase. On the landing, three naked Cupids hold up an alabaster lamp. A young marble woman dressed in veils absently squeezes a flower between her fingers. The stained-glass windows in purple, orange, and green depict landscapes and different symbolic signs. A fake parchment scroll explains that these are symbols of immortality not associated with any particular religion.

A somber melody, like an old clock chime, echoes through the mausoleum.

"You have an organ?"

The supervisor I am addressing eyes me with contempt.

"No! This is a phono amplified by acoustic devices. We can make it work at any time when there are visitors or a burial. You can hear it perfectly wherever you go in the mausoleum. We have no organ here."

Seeing that I am a foreigner, he relents and says:

"You know, a phonograph. You put records on and it spins. It is suitable for clients of all faiths."

THE COAL MAN IS LORD OF THE LAND

To Mal

The electrical stars of the Bethlehem blast furnaces sink into darkness. And Emmaus to the south, Nazareth to the north. To the south, Dublin, Veracruz, Palmyra, Strasbourg, and Gibraltar. To the north, Belfast, Moscow, Damascus, Lucerne, Tripoli. And here is Hamburg.

The lone neon signs keep vigil over garages and diners, those streetcars without wheels set down along the roadside, where coffee, sausages, and pancakes are on offer. Sometimes a level crossing post rises to advise: "Stop. Look. Listen."

A truck glides through the darkness: two white headlights at the front, the driver's face in shadow, two red lights at the rear.

You can hear them more than you can see them, those big winded beasts, panting with effort. They follow each other at five-minute intervals, each crowned with a dark cone. We pass one that is barely moving. Standing on the footboard, a man inspects the road. In the distance, two headlights blaze, go dark, light up again. The man nods as if he had heard a signal, shouts something to the driver and the truck, with its lights off, pulls over to the side of the road.

We're driving on a road that has suddenly become deserted. A patrol appears at a junction: the police look us up and down as if they were going to arrest us, then let us pass without saying anything.

The night grows heavy, the land has become more compact, it bulges out on either side of the road, darker than the starless sky. You'd almost think we'd changed countries, or nights.

Trucks again. We only see their headlights, brief, without luster, and sometimes the glowing end of the driver's cigarette. They move in single file, silently, as if bringing reinforcements on the eve of a great offensive. We must be very near to the front.

Colorless daylight breaks over the plain. The sky spits gray drizzle. Now we can make out the signs, black on white. Pennsylvania. The towns with Indian-sounding names: Tamaqua, Shenandoah, Catawissa, Tuscarora; or names with hues of work: Coaldale, Glen Carbon. Carbon Port. Minersville.

A sign: *Shamokin, 34,000 miles.* "Ask Fritz or Andy to take you to Shamokin," a friend in New York told me. "Shamokin: S as in Seymour, H as in Henry, A as in Albert . . ."

The trucks have turned off their lights. You can see the drivers, White or Black, with similarly coal-smeared faces. Each car has its own name, scrawled on the side: Mickey Mouse, Popeye the Sailor Man, Betty Boop, and last but not least, Miss Anne Thracite.

Anthracite is everywhere. It stretches as far as the eye can see on both sides of the road. Its ashen shards fill the trucks, which move along like a procession of slag heaps. This is Pennsylvania, home of the largest anthracite deposits in the world, unique to the United States: five hundred thousand square miles of deposits.

People settled in this part of the country, built towns, canals, and railways, all in order to extract its coal. First there was the mine, then the villages and shops, schools, churches, taverns. It was the only industry in the region, and the miner was the only worker. The miner needed tools: he gave work to the craftsman and to the small businessman. The miner needed food and clothing: he gave work to storekeepers. The miner could not be sick, he wanted to send his children to school: he gave work to doctors and teachers.

The miner needed to hope and be entertained and so gave work to the pastor, the tavern-keeper, and the actor.

The goods arrived in crates and left again in nets; bells and anvils rang, the schoolteacher taught the ABCs, attorneys and journalists wrote page after page, the taverns were filled on Saturday and churches on Sunday. Money jingled on countertops and rustled in cash registers, and the entire machine was running so naturally that gradually people forgot they were there for the sole purpose of keeping the miner in just good enough health, fed, housed, and clothed just well enough to be able to mine, break, and load four tons of anthracite every day all for the benefit of the mineowner.

It lasted more than a century, and then one day there were fewer people in the stores, shops, offices, taverns, and theaters, and more men idle in the street. Puzzled, the country tried to find out what was happening and learned that the mines were closing and fifty thousand miners were unemployed.

People were hungry, and although there were as many goods as before, and as many skilled and muscular arms, nothing could be bought or sold because the money had run out. In winter, they froze in houses built on anthracite. All you needed to do was go outside, bend down.

Some miners did bend down, at night, by the light of their carbide lamps. In that part of the country, people were still freezing, but the miners were no longer cold. However, they were always hungry, and their clothes were falling apart. They had the idea to take a bag of coal to the grocer and milkman, who also needed heat. And so it was that no one froze, and miners were able to eat and drink. A new currency came into circulation, black, hard, and bulky. Abandoning their own backyards, the miners started digging holes on the outskirts of their towns. They were nicknamed bootleggers, like their forebears during Prohibition.

Even a very rich butcher had no use for more coal than he needed to heat his house. He was willing to barter his meat against a hundred bags of anthracite, but refused to take any more. And as the miners had only coal to offer him, some went without meat. They remembered that anthracite could also be exchanged for money. All they had to do was load it on a truck and take it to town.

Truck drivers arrived in the region, at first just a few and then in droves, and with them came money. The country started to live again, maybe not as well as ten years earlier, when everyone worked, but better than the neighboring districts. Already, the bootleggers had started digging their holes around the old, closed mines. They were making a living and supporting the craftsman, the small businessman, storekeeper, doctor, teacher, pastor, tavern-keeper and actor. The circle had closed and the mine owners had been left outside.

And so, between 1930 and 1936, a new industry had sprung up, giving employment to tens of thousands of men and throwing some five million tons of anthracite on the market each year: one-tenth of national production. Everything happened in a perfectly simple manner, simpler than ABC. A as in Anthracite, B as in Bootlegger, C as in Can't-get-work.

On the porch of a little house, a woman is swinging in a rocking chair. She is reading a big book and barely looks up when I come up the front steps. I put my suitcase on the floor and sit. The woman is still reading. Her bare feet are shod in big thick men's shoes.

I take out my notebook, ask:

"Does Fritz live here?"

She remains silent as if she hadn't heard, and suddenly a male voice says:

"He went to his hole."

"And when is he getting back?"

"Dunno. Maybe in six hours, maybe in seven."

The woman resumes her reading and the chair, its rocking. Without raising her eyes from her page, she says:

"Put your suitcase inside. Nothing will happen to it. I'm there all day."

She looks up and says:

"This is a medical book I have here. I'm sick," she adds with a fixed, proud smile. "I can't walk. I've always been sick."

With the tips of her toes, she pushes against the floor and the chair starts rocking again.

I wander through the mining town. The tallest of the wooden houses are only two stories high. Each little front porch is furnished with a rocking chair or a board hanging from the ceiling. Old women in bonnets, hard-faced old men gently rock.

The street goes up for about three hundred feet. A plaque on one of the last houses reads: "Beauty Salon." Why bother? Then the stones turn into splinters of anthracite and the dust into coal dust. I'm on a hill. From up here you can see the mining town, wedged between two large cemeteries, and the black dunes of the slag heaps. Miners live, work, and die in this area of just over half a square mile.

Tire tracks are deeply imprinted in the cindery powder of the road. All around the ground is riddled with holes. Small holes like the ones children dig to play Robinson Crusoe, then pits with cribbing—a timber lining—wide slanting shafts.

At the foot of the hill, a man leaning over a narrow opening pulls on a rope. An old bucket rises to the surface. The man upends it; a few chunks of anthracite and black dust tumble out on the ground. Two little blond children come crawling as fast as they can, greedily grasp the larger pieces and begin sorting the rest. In front of them a little mound of coal shines beside another one dull and sooty. The father lowers the bucket into the hole again.

Every thirty feet, a well. Some are abandoned. In others, men are working. Here are two men slowly winding thick rope onto a winch. A box on wheels comes up the incline, the bootleggers empty it into a rusty sieve that they shake to separate anthracite from coal dust: in ten minutes they've gathered three shovelfuls of coal.

One last hole, almost a mineshaft. It is dug at a slant and lined with thin tree trunks. An old man stands in front of the pit. He is wearing a Pennsylvanian miner's cap with an open flame lamp attached to it. A young man in a cap sits straddling a beam. On the ground, a blond boy wallows in a pile of coal. His body, bare-chested, and face are covered in black right up to the rims of his eyes and teeth.

"Bootleggers?"

"Yeah," says the old one.

Then he asks me:

"Where are you from?"

"New York."

"How's it going there? How much is the coal?"

We strike up a conversation. I want to know if there are a lot of bootleggers in the area.

"Everyone. Look."

With a quick gesture, the old man shows the plain, and the flame in the lamp on his cap follows suit.

"Who does this land belong to?"

"Reading Co. says it belongs to them. But it closed its shafts, didn't it?"

"Is the work harder than in the mines?"

"Either way, all the miner does is work and sleep," says the man in the cap. "You know, to be knocked out, you don't need to go into the ring, just down into the mine."

"I spent fifty-two years down there," said the old man. "I started when I was eight, and I'm sixty now. There were no machines then. Bootleggers work the way we did in 1885."

With voluptuous little movements, the blond boy buries his feet in the coal dust and slides it between his toes. He says:

"On the other side of the mountain, there's a woman who helps her husband dig holes. On our side, there are two girls who work with their father. They must be about twenty."

"This is old mining country," says the man with the lamp, "everyone's a miner. There are a lot of wells that have been abandoned for sixty years, and all these hills are slag heaps. Some begin to dig a hole and then one day, the bottom gives way into an old gallery."

"A lot of accidents?"

"It happens. The other day, a father and son were down at the bottom, the father saw it was caving in, he sent the boy out but got caught himself. We were on our way home, we saw his wheelbarrow in front of his hole. We figured he'd gone home to eat, but I went by to see anyway: his wife hadn't seen him. We dug him out, he'd been dead for two hours."

"And how is life in general?"

"It's like postage stamps, you see a bit of everything," the boy says with an endless smile. "Near here, there's an old man who lives like a king, everything belongs to him: the house he lives in, the vegetables he plants and the coal he breaks. And there in that hut that has just one wall, a man lives all year round with wild dogs, they keep him warm in winter."

He buries his arms in the coal dust and flexes his pectorals.

"Did you have a better life before?"

"The old miners get together in the evening to talk about the old days," the boy in the cap says. "I like to listen to them."

"I'm starting to get tired of it," the blond guy says. "Now, everyone is his own master."

I return to the sick woman. She is examining a plate in her book showing a naked man, chest artistically sectioned to reveal gray lungs and a bleeding aorta. She says:

"I'm watching over your suitcase. I never go out. I can't move."

Fritz returns from his hole. A Lithuanian who emigrated to America before the war, he is slow and stocky, flat-faced, his pointed nose disappears under a coat of dust. Beside him are two younger men: Andy, blond, skinny, wearing glasses, and Jimmy, tall, fat, furry like a bear. Behind them, Jerry, Fritz's black doggy. It must not be practical for a miner to have a white dog.

I say: "So?"

"So?" repeat Fritz, Andy, and Jimmy, and Jerry barks.

"I would like to know how you started."

"Tell him, Fritz," says Andy.

"You see," Fritz says, and he stops. English words fall heavily from his mouth. He makes up his mind: "Back then, we just did it for ourselves. I mean, we gathered coal for the house. Then the mines began to close."

"All three of you are unemployed?"

"Yes," says Fritz.

"Of course," says Andy.

"I've never worked," says Jimmy. "Too young. When I finished school, it was already the Depression. In my class, two buddies think they're journalists, two others are waiters, and all the rest are bootleggers. After we'd gone and learned all of Longfellow by heart."

"In anthracite, we could feel the decline in 1925," Andy says quickly, "because of competition from oil and coke. The general decline has made the situation worse. In ten years, production has decreased by 40 percent, labor by 44 percent, total wages by 59 percent. It's our region that has the highest unemployment. And it's also here that the veins of anthracite form an obtuse angle with the tip pointing toward the ground, and vein ends are just at the surface: it's easy to extract. Start with the economic situation, add the geological conditions and you get the bootleggers. Explain, Fritz."

"First, you see," says Fritz, "we exchanged the coal for food, clothes—everything."

"Barter," says Andy.

"In 1930," Fritz continues, "we began selling it. We worked at night and arranged with truckers to come get the coal before daybreak. On leaving, we covered the hole with branches and came back the next night. Private police blew holes with dynamite and drove away the bootleggers. When there were more of us, we drove away the police."

"Not far from here," says Jimmy, "they set fire to a hole. They rang the alarm bell and the whole town came running to put the fire out. There are thousands of us now. When the police are called, someone raises the alarm by shouting, by beating pots and pans. The bootleggers come out of the holes and form groups. So, you understand."

"That's right," says Fritz, "the police don't dare."

"And all the people are with us," says Andy. "Take places like Shenandoah or Minersville, the only men who work there are bootleggers: if they stop, there's nothing left to do but close everything down. There are nearly thirty thousand bootleggers, with their families that makes over a hundred thousand people. We sell twenty thousand tons of anthracite per day, paid in cash. That means nearly $100,000 a day."

"And how is the mining organized?"

"Explain, Fritz," says Andy.

"First we worked by hand," says Fritz. "You know, we had a pickaxe, a bucket, a rope, a lamp, a winch, and dynamite cartridges. We dug a shallow hole at the edge of the road. The truck came to pick up the coal and loaded it just as it was."

"Then," Jimmy says, "some small businessmen got involved. They built mills for crushing and sorting anthracite. Bootleggers began to sift it themselves by making a series of finer and finer sieves. Now we have special equipment made for ourselves."

"The machine has partially replaced manual labor," Andy adds. "Jimmy, let Fritz talk."

"A hole lasts about three months," says Fritz. "We've emptied fifteen thousand so far. Today we dig deeper and and farther from the roads."

"And the companies didn't say anything?"

"Yes," Andy replies, "they've tried everything: their private police, state police, the courts, appeals to the governor, to 'public opinion,' as they say. A company has filed a lawsuit forty-two times, and each time it was ordered to pay costs. The judges are local, they refuse to imprison people who make a living shearing coal that companies have abandoned."

"Well," Fritz says, and he pulls out a newspaper clipping. "'The erroneous assertion that thieves would starve if we put an end to their exploits,'" he reads heavily, "'is not a sufficient excuse for allowing their crimes to continue Stop.' This is a telegram from the Chamber of Commerce to the governor of Pennsylvania. And the thieves are us."

"One day," Jimmy says, "the bosses decided to launch a major press campaign and invited forty journalists from New York and Philadelphia. They were given food and lodging and shown around, and all the reporters but two wrote articles favorable to bootleggers."

"They also made a film about 'coal thieves,'" says Andy. "Bootleggers played in it, but without conviction. We chose one for 'a subversive speech,' as they say. At first, he stammered, but when he saw the crowd of comrades around him, he forgot the text he'd learned, the director, the cameramen, and burst out: 'Our fathers and grandfathers worked in these hills . . .' The film was ruined."

"But how do the bosses explain the closing of the mines?"

"They pretend," Jimmy says "that the market has shrunk."

"Hogwash!" says Fritz. "We have more markets than we can possibly supply! We could double our production."

"The fact is," Andy says, "last year, we sold nearly five million tons here in Pennsylvania, and in the states of New York, New Jersey, Maryland, Delaware, and up in DC and Virginia, three hundred miles from here. This year, we'll sell six million tons."

"The bosses say," Jimmy continues, "that they cannot compete with us: we still sell a ton a dollar cheaper than these gentlemen. They say they have fees that we do not: expenses for the safety of miners, taxes, etc."

"Safety?" says Fritz. "They put up posters on the pithead of the mine and they make speeches to workers every morning before work. They even rigged up speakers in the galleries so they can yell louder."

"Still, they do have costs that we don't," says Andy. "They pay a high price for coal transportation on the railways belonging to them. They distribute dividends to themselves. A ton of anthracite costs them $2.30 on the pithead and they sell it for $9. We make $4 per ton in the hole, and the consumer pays only $7 or $8 for it. But employers prefer to sell less at a higher price."

"Is that why they've closed the mines?"

"They have interests in oil," says Jimmy, "it brings in more."

"Where two men used to work," says Fritz, "now there's just one."

"Rationalization," Andy concludes, "faster pace, mechanization."

"Don't miners believe this is the fault of machines?"

"What?"

They exchange looks and all three burst out laughing.

"Great joke!" Jimmy cries, slapping his thigh.

Fritz laughs so hard he can only repeat, "Machines? Machines?" and slaps me hard on the shoulder.

"They should just give us the machines," says Andy.

"Who owns the mines?"

"You're from New York," says Jimmy, "you must have heard of Mr. Morgan. Well! Most of the mines are his. But now each bootlegger has his own special little mine."

And as I insist:

"If you know your Marxism-Leninism," says Andy, and he looks at me sternly through his spectacles, "you should know that trusts, as they expand, close the businesses whose performance is lower to exploit the ones that cost the least and make the most money. This is what happened with the mines."

"Why don't a bunch of you get together? In a cooperative?"

"The tools," says Fritz.

"For a large mine," says Jimmy, "you just need more tools. Where will the money come from?"

"We're condemned to being craftsmen," declares Andy. "That doesn't stop some of the richer bootleggers from renting their labor and even exploiting it. Capitalism is beginning again on a small scale. But the union is trying to fight it."

"What union?"

"The Independent Anthracite Miners' Association," Jimmy says, "the bootleggers' union."

"Let Fritz tell it," says Andy.

"You see," says the Lithuanian, "in 1930, some bootleggers from Shamokin got together to defend themselves against the private police in the hills. Today most bootleggers are unionized. The union sets the prices, and takes care of their safety."

"Does the union get involved in politics?"

"No, the majority of miners don't know anything about politics. They were Democrats, and for the most part, Republicans, like their fathers."

"When I left school," says Jimmy, "I didn't even know who Karl Marx was. I thought he was one of the Marx brothers: Harpo, Groucho, and Karlo. It's just that I didn't like the way things were going in the mine."

"The bootleggers," Andy says, "were the only workers in the world outside the Soviet Union to expropriate the capitalists, and they didn't even know it. Now they're starting to understand. Do you have the resolution, Fritz? The one passed at the last union convention?"

Fritz takes out a mimeographed sheet, reading slowly:

"'Considering that the coal companies have failed in mining and have abandoned the mines, causing the unemployment of thousands of men and forcing them to become bootleggers for their livelihood;

"'Given that the abandonment of mines was caused by the greed of coal companies who wanted to produce less and earn more;

"'Considering that there are markets for coal that nature in its wisdom has placed in the earth for the use of the people of our great country; and that these markets were plain to see for the sellers of these powerful companies, who did not want to see them, and they were served by bootleggers;

"'Be it resolved that our organization, meeting in convention, calls on governments of state and country to take the necessary steps where private employers are unwilling or unable to operate their businesses, in order to reopen closed mines and rehire dismissed staff at union wages.'"

"Enough," says Andy. "Bootleggers began by picking up a bucket of coal in the backyard of their house, and now they are demanding the nationalization of mines."

Fritz's little black dog sneaks into the room and gives the men a look soaked in gratitude. Andy sits down and starts shouting. Jerry barks, and they both roll on the floor, growling with delight.

Then we eat bread without butter, dry sausage, and drink black tea that Andy has gone into the kitchen to prepare. He tells me he worked in the mines of Donbass, where he learned Russian. Jimmy understands a little, too: his parents are of Ukrainian origin. The region is populated by Germans, Irish, and also Poles, Lithuanians and Ukrainians, the first called "flat heads" and the others "round-heads."

"At home," says Jimmy, "we celebrate weddings Galician style. The whole village gets together, we dance the czardas, the mazurka. Everyone is drunk for three days, and six months' salary goes up in flames. Same for baptisms. Take me, I was baptized, I had eleven godfathers: one real and ten honorary."

I take out my bottle of whiskey. Andy brings a chipped glass, a teacup without a handle and two metal tumblers.

"*Za Radianski Soyuz!*" Jimmy says in broken Ukrainian.

"*Za Sovietski Soyuz!*"* Andy says in hard and melodic Russian.

Fritz desperately searches for the words of Russian he brought from his Lithuanian village as a boy. He reddens under the stress, a vein swells on his forehead, and he says in a guttural voice, butchering the endings:

"*Za proletarski Revolutsia!*"**

---

* To the Soviet Union!

** To the proletariat revolution!

I share a bed with Fritz, the dog sleeps between us. The next morning Jimmy takes me across bootlegger country in an old car.

We cross the mining towns with their low houses, where only the churches are higher, streets where little herds of children in overalls are camped out, villages where there is no noise but the sound of bells, no movement but the rocking of chairs on porches. We travel over countryside that is all hollows and mounds, as if inhabited by mole people.

From time to time we stop, walk to a mineshaft, talk with the bootleggers. I go down to the bottom of a hole, sitting astride a branch attached in the middle to a rope that is wound around a winch: the mine cage, six and a half square feet, barely big enough for three men.

The road along the valley of Hecksherville is full of potholes from the trucks. The huge headstock of the mine rises on our left.

"Come," says Jimmy, "take a closer look."

The air is shot through with cables and the ground with rails. Dozens of railways converge on the pithead. Convoys of coal carriages stretch as far as the eye can see. Huge buildings surround the mine head frame, which stands one hundred and sixty five feet high, encased in stairs, treadmills, iron cables.

All that is metal is covered with rust; everything wooden is rotting. The tiles are broken, sheet metal corroded to nothing, beams eaten through. The empty coal carriages are overturned and scattered all over the rails. The courtyard is covered with tiny pieces of coal unmarked by a single footprint.

"Six years ago," says Jimmy, "thirteen hundred men worked here."

The car moves onto a rutted hillside road. We climb the hill, and suddenly, beyond the next turn, we come upon the bootleggers' miniature head frames, in a straight line, all the way to the horizon. Pulleys creaking, winches turning, buckets moving up and down, engines backfiring, shouts, laughter, the shrilling of whistles. Eight thousand men are working there.

The holes are dug at a slant. Jutting out of them are a pair of rails on which a little carriage slides, attached to a cable that climbs to the top of the head frame, winds itself around a pulley and returns to the ground to attach itself to the rear wheel of a car, stripped of the tire. The car is set up on planks and does not touch the ground. A whistle blasts at the bottom of the shaft, a man gets behind the wheel, turns on the engine, shifts into first gear and the drive wheels spin in the air, the cable wraps around the rim and drags the carriage to the top of the head frame. Second whistle: the driver cuts the gas, and the engine, still running, holds the load in the air. Another bootlegger empties the carriage, which comes straight down: the gear stick is in neutral and the hand-brake prevents the cable from going slack too soon.

The head frame is constructed of large planks assembled with bolts. When the hole is worn down, the bootleggers will simply have to unbolt the tower and replace the tires of the car, which will transport them and their installation a little farther. There, they will dig a new hole with blasts of dynamite: an electrical wire attached to the magneto will trigger the explosions. And the trucks that will come to remove the anthracite will forge a new trail through the brush.

I ask the driver of the motionless car:

"Does the system work?"

"We get an average of nine tons per day," he answers. "But it took us two weeks to dig the hole. Right now, we're good for two months."

He presses the starter, switches gears.

"There are two guys in the hole," he says. "The mountain is gouged in every direction. One day something's going to happen. We'll have to dig people out. It's dangerous work."

We watch the carriage move up into the sky. I ask:

"Where do you get wood for the head frame?"

"At the company," he says. "We need wood, it's got to come from somewhere. If you get caught, you get caught. They send you to jail; you don't work anymore and you're fed."

"And all this equipment?"

I gesture at the carriage, the rails, the cable.

"Bought, borrowed, stolen."

He is silent for a moment and then says firmly:

"Not stolen. Taken."

Again he thinks before speaking.

"We work like hell," he says. "Our heart is in our work, and we go at it with all we've got. If we were stealing coal from the company yard, that would be different. But come on, we work hard to get it! Each man is his own bulldozer, his own getter and blaster. It's much tougher than the mines. But here you have no one keeping an eye on you."

He cannot express his thoughts. He looks around, as if looking for an argument, and finally satisfied, says:

"Well, see for yourself."

I look in the direction he is pointing in. At the bottom of the valley, among the red streaks of rails and a motionless clutter of coal carts sprawls the abandoned mine, immense and dead.

We leave. The slag heaps loom close to the miners' cabins. In a sad little slate-colored yard, a lone shirt dances in the wind.

"Locust Gap," says Jimmy.

Tree stumps petrify at the surface of a river of coal that turns upon itself, an ashen soup with slabs of cinder. Water without fish, branches without birds.

"Jesus," says Jimmy, "everyone I knew has been killed. Andy's brother was crushed in his hole last week. I could start naming all the ones who've died in my time and I wouldn't stop until night. And I'm only twenty-one."

We are approaching Shamokin. On the horizon, a line of excavations marks an old anthracite vein, now exhausted. Men who appear very small build trestles; others walk back and forth, sniffing the ground. And on all sides, blond kids smeared with coal gallop around, flying kites, and a woman, disheveled and grotesquely pregnant, yells at her son, calling him a bastard. In a muddy low-hanging sky, red kites fly above the plain.

We meet two miners, stripped to the waist.

"How many bootleggers around here?" Jimmy asks.

"Dunno," says one.

The other one says:

"Everyone."

Night has fallen, black as coal. Along the way, we guess the presence of heaps. A low light flickers in the sky.

"That's the Saint Nicholas coal breaker," says Jimmy. "It serves eleven mine shafts. It's the largest coal breaker in the world and it is in our district.

"Are you proud of it?"

"We will be one day."

That evening and the following day we visit the country and talk to people. I see a businessman in Pottsville, a pastor in Tamaqua, a newspaper editor in Shamokin, a justice of the peace in Brandenville; they are all supporters of bootleggers, and the magistrate is the union treasurer. I see mostly bootleggers, old ones with half a century's experience of work in the mines, and very young ones, who go to school in the morning and to their hole in the afternoon. They eagerly ask me about the life of French miners. Some are Republicans or Democrats, some are Communists, but most have no political opinions. They're for the nationalization of mines, some say "because the land belongs to no one," others "because human rights come before property rights," and still others "because bosses, who dare to call themselves businessmen, have failed miserably," all because in their holes, without knowing it, they sniffed the smell of free labor. When asked about expropriation, they do not understand, or they exclaim: "The mine and the factory aren't the same," but five minutes later, they shrug their shoulders and say: "After all, why not?"

Then comes the evening of my departure. A truck driver who transports anthracite to New York every day, takes me along. My friends accompany me to the footboard of the truck. Jimmy asks me to write down the words of the "Carmagnole" in English. Andy says, observing the garlands of electric lights blooming in the sky, in a grid of high-voltage wires:

"Communism is electrification plus the power of the Soviets. We already have electrification."

Fritz is silent and Jerry barks.

We leave in the middle of the night. Again, the caravan of trucks on the highway. The driver peers into the darkness.

"Sometimes the police are on the lookout," he says. "The first of us to spot them turns his headlights off and on again. That way we've been warned and we make ourselves scarce."

I sleep. Pennsylvania fleets by on the other side of the windshield. Our truck is called Miss Anne Thracite.

The lights of Bethlehem pull me out of my torpor. I ask:

"And other than that, the authorities don't do anything?"

"Nothing," says the driver. "If people are prevented from working, you have to feed them. It's simple."

Easier than ABC. *A as in America, B as in Backbone, C as in Communism.*

NOTEBOOK

JUNE 1936

June 2. It happened yesterday in Dayton, Ohio. Horace and Wilbur Johnson got home from school at 3:30. On the doorstep, their father was waiting for them with a gun. He told them: "I just killed your mother, your sisters and your brother. Do you want to join them or would you rather live?" The boys preferred to live. "You'll hear a bang," the father warned, "then you can call the police."

Officers found six bodies and a letter: "I killed this family except for two sons. I intend to kill them and then kill myself." There was a postscript: "The wife died Sunday at 4:00 in the morning, Rose-Marie on Monday, 10:45 a.m.; Walter, Monday, 11:45, Elsie-May, Monday at noon; Marietta, quarter past twelve. Goodbye."

The children who survived the massacre say that their father lost his job ten months earlier. The family sometimes went for days without eating.

The workers' housing estates of Mellon, Pennsylvania, are infamous. As an example, here are the terms of the lease that must be signed by any worker who comes to live in one of these estates. They are required to prohibit entry on the leasor's property to persons other than "doctors treating the tenant and his family, truckers and movers carrying objects belonging to the tenant and his family upon arrival and departure, and the undertakers with the hearse, cars and drivers, as well as friends, in case of death of the tenant or a member of his family."

A New York social club organizes a big party on a boat. It offers many attractions. The highlight: a cake-eating contest. Six black children must stuff themselves with lemon meringues and chocolate whipped cream (the richest treats are purposely chosen). The child who gobbles down the most will be declared the winner. A pari-mutuel betting system is set up for the contest. Prizes go to audience members who have bet on the biggest eater.

A police officer in the district of Queens, New York, sees three boys hanging onto the back of a rolling truck. He shouts, the kids flee. Seeing that he is not going to catch them, the officer shoots and injures two children.

Shoot to kill.

June 6. Daniel Cohalan, a former judge of the Supreme Court, spoke day before yesterday under the auspices of the Defenders of the US Constitution. He proposed, among other things, that the unemployed be denied the right to vote in the next presidential elections.

Today it gets even better. The Eugenics Research Association, which is opening an exhibition at the Museum of Natural History, learned from the report of the president Mr. Goethe that the unemployed had more children than people with a livelihood. Given this situation, Mr. Goethe advocated sterilization of the unemployed.

Mrs. Kasper, of New Jersey, has given birth to four children. All the newspapers report that the Key sisters, the Texas quadruplets, after visiting the Dionne quintuplets, came to Passaic to meet their Kaspers colleagues. A news agency reports that a deer in a Pennsylvania zoo has given birth to three fawns.

I get out at the little Mount Kisco train station with its employee with his peaked cap, it's black shoeshine, a scattering of onlookers absorbed in the act of gum-chewing. I follow a path and suddenly a gingerbread house appears, reminiscent of a Swiss chalet and Grimm's fairy tales.

Theodore Dreiser is waiting for me. He is tall, stout, thick-lipped. Fleshy nose, jowls, and under thick low-hanging eyebrows, small and somewhat melancholy and disapproving eyes. He speaks the way he writes: going into detail.

"I led the fight until 1932. I still lead it. I wrote, I talked. I went to Kentucky during the miners' strike. Because I wanted to ask a witness a simple question, a thug pressed his gun to my gut and ordered me to clear out. And he would have pulled the trigger. Who can you complain to? It's ridiculous. Press, justice, it all belongs to the trusts.

"I wrote a book: *An American Tragedy*. It was all but destroyed. A terrible country where mysterious things happen. Where a group from Wall Street controls movies. Where it is impossible to talk about politics or social issues on the radio. In fact, it is impossible to speak of anything except nonsense. I was once asked to talk into a microphone. I could have prepared a series of lectures on topics that mattered to me. I inquired if I would be free to say whatever I liked. They said that my talks would be read beforehand. 'If that's the way it is,' I replied, 'then goodbye!'

"I gave a multitude of interviews to the *New York Times*, *Herald Tribune*, and other newspapers. Whenever I happened to say something significant, it was ignored.

"I do of course want communism to bring us an era of peace. You see, I myself went from nothing to too much. But if I was sure that with communism established in the United States, I'd have a room and the ability to work and live off the fruits of my labor, I would say: 'Let's do it, starting tonight.' Provided that it gives everyone equal opportunity. Today, I have nothing more than I did when I lived in one room and wrote my first short stories. If it is certain that the communist system will not create bureaucracy, then let's instate it. Anyway we should try it. It can't be worse than our present reality, and it could be much better. There are so many people suffering, who have nothing, who are desperate, and others who live so well. There must be luxury, games, and entertainment, but they should not be reserved for the use of an exclusive few. It is unfair and unnecessary.

"I would like to witness the coming changes myself and see if they will bring about, as some claim, the death of adventure, the death of tragedy.

"There will always be tragedy. But it will change content too. So much the better. Just look what's happening here. American financiers are quickly learning the practice of fascism. They would like to replace liberal oligarchy with tyrannical oligarchy. They already control the press, radio, movies. They would take over the schools, condition the individual. Teach only slogans to keep men in bondage. I'd like to see a more diverse, freer world. Fascism is deadly. They produce ten thousand soldiers of wood. And then? They're like toy manufacturers. They seek tranquility. Wooden soldiers are safer than men. My father was one for years, almost his entire life. A practicing Catholic, he deprived himself to give to the Church. The power to instill illusions in the mechanical creatures that we are is very dangerous.

"I have always fought against fascism, myself. If it triumphed, I would have to take refuge in Mexico, no doubt. And there, I wouldn't be alone. You know, my books are banned in Germany. It's because today finance is the exclusive ruler of the world. Oh! Don't think I have no hope. But I see things as they are. It's like a cancer that's killing millions. We try to find the germ, to fight it, but in the meantime, cancer kills."

"And what will bring about the discovery that will put an end to cancer?

"Fear. I believe that life is a mechanical phenomenon, that men are mechanical beings. I am part of a flock of birds. No flock, no birds. I, Theodore Dreiser, writer, I attract people who are realistic, sensitive. Those who read me are against the injustices of life. I've never had any other kind of reader. I'll never write for the upholders of the established order. Life is something essentially changing, sad, tragic and beautiful. And I love it."

Tonight's Central Park is ornamental trees and automobile headlights. At the zoo, seals and a polar bear are recovering from the heat wave. Close by, on Fifth Avenue, revving engines, horns, a police car siren, the huffing and puffing of firefighters' vehicles. To the south, horizon of skyscrapers: chessboard of lighted windows in the night. Breathing of the neon signs. On the Columbus Circle side, at the top of the General Motors Building, letters roll by: "Drive Oldsmobile. Oldsmobile gives you super-hydraulic brakes. Oldsmobile gives you an all-steel body. Oldsmobile gives you everything. It is: 10:47."And again: "Drive Oldsmobile . . ."

A storm rises above the false park, drowning out the sounds of people, cars, the city. In its cage, a lion roars.

Every American, wretched though he may be, can become a billionaire or president, if he is frugal, industrious, pious, etc. If you are poor and old or young and unemployed, you have only yourself to blame. You should have worked and saved money. Hence the natural conclusion: a poor man, particularly if he is unemployed, is just a failure, and the unemployment benefit is an act of charity.

Because Ford is a billionaire, people listen to him as if he were an oracle. Ford is in favor of high wages. Ford attributes unemployment to laziness. Ford recommends a return to the earth. Events have proved him wrong, but he's proved wrong every man less rich than him, according to the same principle that maintains if you want to learn the secret of longevity, you talk to people who have lived to be one hundred. As for the maxims of Ford and his ilk, they are easy to recognize. "The only thing of value that I own is my experience, and it is the one thing no one can take away from me" (Ford). "Destroy the leisure class, and you destroy civilization," (J. Pierpont Morgan).

Yes, yes I know. In the United States for every one hundred inhabitants, there are six and a half feet of pipeline, 120 feet of airway, 485 feet of submarine cable, over one thousand feet of railroad track, almost two miles of telegraph wire, two and a half miles of road, twenty-one cars, fourteen telephones, fourteen radios, and ten unemployed.

REAL AMERICA

To Gíska

Weep no more, my lady,
Oh weep no more today,
We will sing one song, for the Old Kentucky Home,
For the Old Kentucky Home, far away.

"My Indian grandmother was called Delpha Lucas, and my father's father was a Garland, of English blood, but they'd been settled in Kentucky for several generations. My family is descended from the first pioneers to settle in the mountains of Kentucky. Have you heard of the Daniel Boone caravan? It was the first caravan, and my ancestors were among the first pioneers.

"My grandfather was a farmer. There were no mines in Kentucky yet. They didn't even know there was such a thing as coal under the ground. In Kentucky farms, after corn harvest, the boys all go away until the next spring to look for work in the neighboring regions and states. My grandfather Garland had heard that in Oklahoma, they split wood for fences and cleared the land. And so he went to Oklahoma. He was hired by his future father-in-law, a pure-blood Cherokee Indian chief. My grandfather Garland had asked him for work, and the chief kept him on at his farm. That's when my grandfather Garland fell in love with my grandmother Delpha Lucas, the daughter of the Cherokee chief, and she fell in love with him. She was only fifteen, and my grandfather Garland told her: 'Now I have to go home and help my father bring in the harvest.'

"She said: 'If you leave me, I will die of a broken heart.'

"And he said:

"'I can't take you with me, you're too young. If they catch me, they'll put me in jail for the rest of my life.'

"'Don't be afraid,' she said, 'we won't be caught.'

"She promised to meet him outside the next day and stole her clothes and put them in a game bag she hid in a corner of the yard. The next night, at one thirty, she tried her luck and slipped through the window; they fled and married, and raised their family in Kentucky. That's how I have Cherokee Indian blood in my veins, and you can see it from the way I look.

"Yes, my dear child, this was before the Civil War. My grandfather Garland was a captain during that war, and my grandfather Robinson, my mother's father, was a sergeant. And that makes me think of a funny story.

"My father was the first love of my mother's life, and one day they went to church, and my father was considered one of the most intellectual boys in our part of the country: I have already told you he was the son of a captain in the Civil War. The house was a mile and a half from the church, and my father and mother crossed the mile and a half without speaking once. My father was waiting for her to speak first and she was waiting for him to start.

"'Do you think,' he said, 'that your parents would be glad to see you with me?'

"And she said:

"'For sure, they like you very much, you and your family. You know what people think of your family and my family, because I am the daughter of a sergeant in the Civil War, and your father was a captain.'

"These were the only words exchanged before they entered the house.

"My mother's parents were farmers, too. My grandmother Robinson was pure Irish, and my grandfather Robinson was a mixture of Scots and English. When I arrived in New York for the first time, a journalist came to see me. She came and she said:

"'Aunt Molly, what nationality are you, if you don't mind me asking?'

"'I am,' I said, 'a mixture of joy and sorrow.'

"'What do you call a mixture of joy and sorrow?'

"'I mean, I'm a mixture of so many races that I feel too sad to explain. Think of me as a true internationalist.'

"Well! My father and mother went out together for almost a year and they got married. My father bought a farm of one hundred and fifty acres, next to his parents'. I was born on this farm. My mother was seventeen when she gave birth to me. My father was going to be nineteen in February, and I came along in October. When I was three, my father sold the farm and we went to Laurel, Kentucky, and he started to shear coal in the very first mines that opened. My father was one of the first miners to extract coal from the mines of Kentucky.

"With his first wife, my father had four children: two girls and two boys. A boy and a girl died during my mother's lifetime. Then my mother died, and that left me, and my brother John Garland. I was six years old, and my brother was three. My father's parents kept us for eleven months, and I was entering my eighth year when my father took a new wife. She was my mother's cousin, and she was very good to us. My father had eleven children by his second wife, and fifteen in all with his two wives. Three sons and two daughters of the second marriage are still alive, and I am the only survivor of the first.

"All the others are dead. If you have a lot of children in the mountains of Kentucky, there are quite a few who die.

"My brother John Garland was a miner. He was active in the United Mine Workers of America. In 1919, his employers hired an assassin and stole the life of John Garland. It was the first great sorrow of my life. When she was dying, my mother had called me to her bedside and told me to take care of my little brother. And she said to my father: 'I cannot live anymore, but never separate my two children.' My father promised, and after that, we grew up together and John Garland was my idol. When he was fighting with a guy bigger than him, he called me and together we walloped him. He could always depend on me, John Garland. I was his big sister. And when the bosses sent an assassin to kill my brother, it almost killed me, too. And since then I have never been the same.

"Three years after my brother's murder, it was my half-brother, Richard Garland's turn. He was a miner, all my brothers were miners, my father raised his sons in the mine. A piece of slate fell on my half-brother Richard Garland at the bottom of the mine, and killed him. He left a wife and four children. His son Vernon Garland was four years old when his father was killed. We opened the coffin in the cemetery for all to see, and Vernon passed his hands through the dead man's hair, which was silky and curly, and watched the crowd. He looked at my brother's mother and he saw she was crying.

"'Calm down, Granny,' he said, 'I have something to say. The bosses are responsible for my father's death. They were too stingy to put cribbing in the mine and prevent schist from falling, and because of that, I have to do without my father.'

"He did not shed a tear. Everyone talked about it at the cemetery. Old miners themselves were unaware that the bosses had killed his father, but this little boy knew.

"He is fifteen now, Vernon Garland. He's deliveryman around Pineville, Kentucky. He takes any job. He would rather steal than be a miner, and how he hates the mine owners! He always thinks of how they orphaned him. His mother cleans houses and does the laundry. She received $400 for the death of her husband, and that money is long gone.

"At the death of my half-brother Richard Garland, I composed the song 'The Miner's Farewell.' Everyone sings and composes songs in the mountains of Kentucky. And this is how the song goes:

Poor hardworking miners, their troubles are great,
So often while mining they meet their sad fate.
Killed by some accident, there's no one can tell,
Their mining's all over, poor miners farewell!

Only a miner, killed under the ground,
Only a miner, but one more is gone.
Only a miner, but one more is gone,
Leaving his wife and dear children alone.

Leaving his children thrown out on the street,
Barefoot and ragged and nothing to eat,
Mother is jobless, my father is dead,
I am a poor orphan, begging for bread.

"My father died in 1925. He was a preacher, but he believed in the organization and the workers who banded together. My dad, had he lived long enough to see communism develop in Kentucky, would have been the greatest fighter we'd ever had. All my grandparents are dead, too: grandfather Garland and grandfather Robinson, grandmother Robinson and grandmother Delpha Lucas who was a pure-blooded Cherokee Indian. Only Aunt Martha White, my mother's aunt, is still living, and today will turn a hundred years old. My father has two sisters, the youngest is the wife of Sid Stacy, who was the first engineer of the first train that went from Knox County to Clay County, Kentucky. The oldest is seventy-eight, weighs eighty-five pounds and is the mother of fifteen children. All my cousins are miners.

"Yes, we do have a lot of children in the Kentucky mountains, and we get married young. I got married when I was fourteen, and if I don't have many children myself, I have helped many to be born. Cause I took courses, I'm a midwife and registered nurse, and to this day, I have made 918 deliveries, and I never let a single mother or newborn die.

"I told you that my father died in 1925, and that same year, the president of the United Mine Workers of America sold us out for the first time. Miners had never led a viable existence, but until 1925, they had not starved because the union protected them somewhat. They earned $1.25 for five feet of clean coal: there was dirt in the coal, and they had to separate it out. Then they received $1.10, which was the union rate until the union was broken. Sometimes they earned up to $11.00 a week, but if you count the deductions, it came down to $5.00. Deductions, that's the way it was. Each miner pays 50¢ a month to a blacksmith to sharpen his pickaxe. He pays 25¢ to the burial fund. They deduct $2.00 a month for the doctor and $5.00 for the old shack where he lives, just big enough to sleep in and a corner just big enough to cook in. In addition, miners have to pay the company for the powder to blow up the coal, and carbide for their lamps. They have to buy their own tools: a dollar and a half for a shovel, 75¢ for the pickaxe, and 15¢ for the pickaxe shaft. We live on beans, bacon, and corn bread, and we are proud when we can get it, because we often have nothing. In the mountains of Kentucky, the children go to school in the summer, when they can walk around naked, but they stop going in September when it starts getting too cold. They wear little blue overalls, lined with wind, and go barefoot. In winter they cover up with a nasty cotton shirt or a flour sack.

"And so when the union sold the men in 1925, the bosses agreed and vowed never to hire union members. And they began to slash wages, so that around 1931, they were paying twenty-eight and thirty-three cents per ton of coal. In the morning miners could go to the company cash and get an advance of a few pennies for powder and carbide. Then the wife or the children went down to the company and prayed the employees to advance their twenty-five cents, enough for a couple of sandwiches for their man. After a few days, they would ask for a dollar—not money, just a coupon—and say:

"'We need to buy something to eat.'

"And the answer was:

"'Everything you earned today, you spent for your equipment.'

"And sent the poor people away.

"The strike began this way. The union president saw that he could strike another blow and extract a few hundred dollars more from miners. He called a convention in March 1931, and the miners attended—eleven hundred miners from the counties of Harlan and Bell—and paid him a dollar each to be members again of the United Mine Workers of America. Some had sold their last pig or chicken and the shirt off their back to raise the dollar. That day at the convention, the president collected $1,100 and he said:

"'Now, my lads, if you are blacklisted or sacked for attending this meeting, I'll take care of you, I'll arrange for you to be rescued immediately.'

"They returned to work, and every last one of them were fired and blacklisted so they could never find employment in the mines of Kentucky again. But their workmates came up to join them, and there were eighteen thousand miners on the surface.

"We elected a committee that told the union what had happened, and the union said it could do nothing. Only the Pittsburgh convention, they said, could help us. As for whether this Pittsburgh convention ever took place, I couldn't tell you, because we never got any assistance.

"We had nothing to give the children, except bean soup that stripped their bowels. Farmers brought us potatoes and tomatoes for the kids' soup, but we did not have enough to feed them all, and they were starving for ten leagues around. I did everything I could, everyone talked to me, I was a midwife, I had performed 918 births without ever letting the mother or newborn die, and I had godchildren in each miner's family. Since the beginning of the strike, there'd been thirty-seven children I tried to save without being able to get them food and they starved to death in my arms. How many times have I sat in a shack, by the light of a piece of twisted string dipped in a saucer in which there wasn't even ten cents' worth of oil—and even if there had been, in most cases there was no lamp— and the father and mother were there, having watched over their sick child for weeks, and when he passed, I stretched him out on a board or on the table and sat alone with the little corpse, and if the father and mother had fallen asleep in the meantime, I didn't wake them, knowing that for as long as they slept, they would not weep.

"Small children died one after the other, and as I'd been into town a few days earlier, almost everywhere I'd seen posters saying that the Red Cross had been helping people for fifty years. I'd visited churches before and tried to take up a collection to buy a few bottles of milk. I explained that I was a nurse in Straight Creek where children were dying of hunger and that I would be grateful for any small coin, but nobody gave me anything. So I went to the Red Cross and told them that I was a registered nurse and had seen their posters advertising themselves as a charitable organization. The woman says:

"'All the miners have to do is go back to work.'

"I say they could work from morning to night, but they still had no money to bring home a bottle of milk for the children at the end of the day.

"'We promised the bosses,' she says, 'to have nothing to do with those men on strike.'

"I threw her down on the floor and the first time I hit her in the stomach, and the second time on the mouth, and I left by the service door before they could arrest me.

"For two days I'd been hearing a two-and-a-half-year-old kid crying in the shack next to mine, and went downstairs to ask the young mother:

"'What is wrong with the little one?'

"And she said:

"'She's hungry, she hasn't eaten for two days.'

"So I said:

"'Why don't you go find her something? Have you no shame? Is it possible that I do more for your children than you do yourself?'

And she did not reply.

"'Do you have a clean bag?' I asked.

"'Yes,' she said.

"And I picked up the bag. I went home, I took my .38 under my arm, I called my stepson and I went down to the shop, laughing. As I walked down the hill, I heard four of another neighbor's kids screaming.

"'What's wrong with your children?' I asked.

"'They're dying of hunger,' she answered, 'and I can't do anything about it.'

"So I went to the shop laughing heartily.

"I told my stepson:

"'As soon as they give me a twenty-pound bag of flour, pick it up.'

"The grocer gave me the flour and I said:

"'How much?'

"'$4.90,' he said.

"And I said:

"'I'll see you in ninety days. I need all this to feed small children who are dying of hunger. As soon as I've collected the money, I'll pay.'

"'Put the merchandise down,' he said, 'or pay for it.'

"So I threw the bag of flour to my stepson, I took out my revolver and stepped back.

"'If you take it back,' I said, 'I'll shoot you.'

"'Okay,' he said, 'I'll call Frank Bowman and have you arrested.'

"'They'll have eaten in the meantime.'

"I went to the first place and gave them their rations and I carried the rest to the others. And when the sheriff came, he said:

"'Aunt Molly, what's going on? Would you have become a regular bandit by any chance?'

"'Oh, no,' I said. 'Look over there, Frank Bowman.'

"And he saw a little girl tearing dough between her mother's fingers.

"'That,' I said, 'is what made me act as I did.'

"He looked at me, the sheriff, and he looked at the children, and said:

"'They sent me to arrest you, but I have grandchildren, and I can't bring myself to arrest someone who has enough heart and guts to help children who are nothing to her. I'll pay for the flour myself, Aunt Molly, and you can pay me back later.'

"It would have disgusted him to arrest me: he had a house full of kids, and I had helped all of them to be born, and they called me Grandma.

"So in March of the year 1931 when the bosses drove the miners out, the weather was cold and bad, and my little sister had her mother and two children who were all sick. The bosses had obtained an eviction order against the miners, to evict them from their shacks. They brought the sheriff and the police to throw the miners into the street, and my little sister went and stood at the door with a Winchester. And my brother-in-law went to the other door with his double-triggered rifle, and he told them:

"'My children are sick, and before letting them be cast out in the snow, I'll send each of these sixteen bullets right into your heads.'

"They were afraid, because they knew that my brother would have done as he said, and they left, but he suspected they would return and arrest him for resisting the police. And he left and walked fifty-three miles in the snow and caught double pneumonia, and now he is in the final stages of tuberculosis, and they get $1.75 a week, and they don't have a rag to cover themselves with, except the old castoffs that someone gave me, and I sent them.

"In May, the killers and the scabs came to Harlan County, and of course we were warned they were coming. The miners lined up behind their huts, and we fought the scabs. They had machine guns, three miners were killed and we shot down fourteen scabs, and we wounded thirty-seven. I had a .38 in one hand and a .45 in the other, and I stood between my two brothers. The miners came down the hill, they took the scabs from behind and seized fifty powerful guns and two machine guns. The oldest of the miners was Bill Hightower, he was seventy-seven. He was a trade union activist, and came down to tell us:

"'They've brought a truck to pick up their dead and wounded. Anyone have any objections?'

"'Not at all,' the miners said. 'It's a damn pity we can't load the truck to the brim.'

"This happened on the fifth day of May, and the police arrested Bill Hightower, who was White, and Jones, who was Black, and six others, and they were sentenced to the electric chair. They arrested me, too, and I stayed in jail for nearly three weeks. The best propaganda I ever made in the mountains of Kentucky, I made speaking through the prison bars. The crowd clustered under my window, and I talked. One day, an old codger of a guardian said:

"'Listen, it makes me sick just to think about it, but if you keep bringing the crowd here, I'll tie up your hands and put you on bread and water.'

"'As long as I can teach the working class what to do,' I said, 'you'll always find me yelling through these iron bars. So just try and keep me from screaming.'

"And after three weeks they released me.

"I do not know what happened in the meantime, but I remember that the twenty-second day of May 1931 an envoy of the United Mine Workers of America came to Harlan County and began organizing the men. And on the seventeenth of June, he arrived at the small mining village where we lived at the time, and that night, he went straight to my house and called my husband, Bill Jackson. My stepson was there, and the man told him:

"'I've come for the union.'

"'Wait a minute,' Joe said, 'you've got the wrong address. We've been sold and we just came out of a war, and a bunch of miners are in prison. I do not want to hear a word about the Mine Workers of America.'

"'But it's the grassroots organization that I represent, and you won't pay us a penny. All you do is sign this card, and we'll take care of you. We'll send you an emergency canteen and everything you need.'

"Joe's face began to shine.

"'Give me your card and I'll sign it,' he said, Joe, my stepson. 'I'll take you up the mountain.'

"There were three hundred miners that night in the mountains, and they held a meeting, and the three hundred signed their card in the light of their carbide lamps. That night my husband and stepson returned home late, and they told me:

"'Mom, there's a section for women now.'

"'Okay, okay,' I said, 'and what's it called?'

"And they said:

"'It's called the Women's Committee Aux . . . Something like that, you'll see.'

"Two or three days later, a woman came and she gave me lessons, an hour each morning, to teach me how to organize people, and my sister and I, we started recruiting for the Women's Auxiliary Committee. And shortly after, we had food for our emergency canteen and we were back on the picket lines talking.

"Before that time, I'd never heard of a base union. I was a revolutionary and didn't know it. All my people were revolutionary and didn't know it. Now the bosses called me a Red, and I said:

"'Well, well, if we are Red, it's you who forced us into it by robbing us of all our rights. And when the union president promised to take care of us so that we'd have something to eat and then left us with nothing, that's when the Reds took the lead. If the union president was a man and had kept his word, there wouldn't have been any Reds, but as for me, I'm proud of it.'

"So the envoy of the United Mine Workers had come the seventeenth day of June 1931. And, shortly after, they brought an emergency canteen. And this man, Jeff Baldwin, ran the canteen with Joe Moore. And the bosses sent Lief Hines, the sheriff, to kill them, and the police came and killed them at the door of the canteen. Joe

Moore had gone to the door to see what was happening and they wounded him in the shoulder, and now he is paralyzed. Baldwin left a wife and four children. And the sheriff is still free.

"The union also sent two women, comrade Michaelson and Ruth Decker, and the bosses were after them. I spoke and I organized, and I had tremendous success, me and my sister, the one who has thirteen children. In one place, the Carey mines, the strikers had asked if one or two of them could go back underground to pump water, and we voted on it and decided they could. And before we realized, there were fifteen of them going down into the well. The Female Committee secretary, Ruth Decker, came to see me and said:

"'Aunt Molly, what do we do? If we let them in the mine, the strike is lost. We have to arrange a meeting.'

"She gave me posters, and I went down to the pit-head of the mine, and I stuck posters on telegraph poles, and I put some up on the walls of the post office. When I got home, I was accosted by an informer. He had seen me talking with Ruth, but he didn't know where she lived or what her name was.

"'If you knew what was good for you,' he said, 'you'd go tell this little woman not to talk tonight. If she speaks, we will shoot her down right where she's standing.'

"'The little woman' is what he called Ruth, seeing as he didn't know her name.

"'We will defend her,' I answered.

"And in the evening, my brother Jim Garland and I arrived and took Ruth between us, and my little brother had his Remington pistol in the hand, and I had my gun. All of us were there, the whole family. The miners formed a circle to hear me and I said:

"'Listen to me, the first person who takes something brighter than his thumbnail out of his pocket, we'll shoot him.'

"And Ruth, 'the little woman,' said:

"'They said that if I spoke here tonight, I would be arrested and killed. Here I am. And if I am not arrested and killed, I will speak.'

"We stood at her side keeping an eye on everyone. So she spoke, and when she finished, she took my gun, and I talked. Then I took my little brother Jim Garland's Remington, and it was he who spoke. We told them that if they went down to the mine the next morning, we would take white hickory sticks and beat them and put salt in their wounds. Not one man went down.

"But at the Castro shaft, there were a few miners who hadn't joined the union and continued to work, and we decided to send down some strikers to organize them. Only there was no way. Then I saw that there was only one thing to do: gather the women and children and take them to the bottom of the mine and have them sing 'Kentucky Miner's Wife' ('Ragged Hungry Blues').

"But I must tell you how I wrote this song.

"Our canteen was in the home of a sympathizer, half a mile from the mine, and one morning there was a band of fifteen small kids in rags and tatters. It was raining and the tips of their feet were flayed and bleeding, it was a horrible sight. I heard the children crying and I went to the door and said:

"'Why are you out so early, in the rain?'

"'We come to the canteen for a bowl of soup. We haven't eaten for two days.'

"The eldest was nine, and the smallest was six. Never in my life had my heart ached so. And I put my head down and started to sing. Since my childhood, I sing what I have on the heart. And here is how this song began:

> I woke up this morning, with the worst blues I ever had in my
> life;
> Not a bite to eat for breakfast, a poor coal miners wife!
> All the women in the coal camps are sitting with bowed-down
> heads,
> Ragged and barefooted, and the children cryin' for bread.
> No food, no clothes for our children, I'm sure this head don't lie;
> If we can't get more for our labor we'll starve to death and die!

Some coal operators might tell you the hungry blues are not there.
They're the worst kind of blues this poor woman ever had.

"So I got the women together, and they took their children, and we went down into the Castro shaft. There was a gallery there and holes on both sides and in the holes stood miners. The only light was from their carbide lamps. We walked into the gallery, I in the lead, the others behind me, and we stopped at every hole, and every time we sang 'Kentucky Miner's Wife.' They were working, the men, and when I noticed a few in a hole—I stopped, and all the women stopped, and all the children stopped—I sang, and everyone sang:

> *Ragged and barefooted, and the children cryin' for bread.*
> *Ragged and barefooted, and the children cryin' for bread.*
> *Ragged and barefooted . . .*

"The men stopped working to listen to us, they came out of their holes, and we went on to the next hole, with the men behind us, and we sang louder:

> *No food, no clothes for our children,*
> *I'm sure this head don't lie;*
> *If we can't get more for our labor*
> *We'll starve to death and die.*

"Men in our part of the country us are very religious and super-stitious. They think that if women or children come down into the mine, something terrible will happen. Maybe a fire-damp explosion or something else. So I started screaming:

"'Get out, guys!'

"And they surrounded me and they said: 'Something is going to happen for sure.'

"'Oh, yes,' I said, 'something will happen. If you stay in the

mine, you'll die of starvation. If you do not throw down your tools
and go back up and declare a good strike for better wages, we'll stay
down here and starve to death with you.'

"They knew that when I say something, I do it, and they began
to plead with us to go back up.

"'We have nothing to do up there,' we answered. 'No clothes to
wash, no food to cook, no household to watch over. We're staying
in the mine.'

"So they gathered their tools and they joined in our singing,
and they dropped everything and they said: 'We're not working
anymore.'

"I told you about comrade Michaelson and Ruth Decker. Well!
The bosses were after them, to run them out of Kentucky, and they
had arrest warrants made out. They had to leave to avoid being
arrested, while I kept on organizing, me and my little brother Jim
Garland, and Norman Link Everett Smith. The bosses accused me
of being a Red agitator, and they wanted my head. One day I took
a crate to the pithead, I got up on the crate, and I said to the miners
who passed to wait, that there was going to be a meeting. While I
was talking, the bosses sent a scab into the woods nearby, he fired,
and the bullet went through my crate. I swore and shouted:

"'You missed. Shoot again.'

"And I kept telling miners to organize and not go down into the
shafts. Later on, I often set my crate on the floor of the mine, and I
started to sing. When there was a crowd of miners listening, I said:

"'Guys, I want to talk for fifteen or twenty minutes, if not more.'

"A commission of writers—Theodore Dreiser and the others—
came to us because people were starting to talk about the miners'
strike in Harlan County. They stayed at the house near the church,
and they asked us to come see them, me and my little brother
Jim Garland and many other miners, and they asked questions.
We answered and said what we knew: the truth. Then the police
came and chased out the writers and wanted to arrest me. But we
had learned that an arrest warrant had been issued against me,

and comrade Michaelson, who was in Tennessee, came to get me in Pineville, at the bus station, she bought me a ticket and I left. There was a trial after my departure and for telling the truth, I was charged with criminal syndicalism. And they sentenced me to twenty-one years in prison. I can never go back to Kentucky, where I was born and where all my family was born, and if I go, they'll put me in prison for twenty-one years because I told the truth.

"I went to New York and spoke at meetings about our strike and the miners' lives. Then I started to organize the unemployed. There were a lot of foreigners among them, and the police and that bastard Willy Hearst—Dirty Willy, I call him—always said that Communists are all foreigners. One day there was a demonstration of unemployed, and I told them:

"'Let me march in front, I'm one hundred percent American and I have Indian blood in my veins.'

"We went down to Union Square, and I walked in front singing the 'Internationale.' There was a big cop in front of me, and I came right at him, my clenched fist out, and singing: 'This is the final struggle . . .' And the Irish bastard looked at me and he said to me:

"'Dirty Pollack, go back to the Polish hole you crawled out of.'

"But I was not afraid. I looked him straight in the eyes and said:

"'As it happens, I am descended from the families that Christopher Columbus first met when he discovered this stinking country. This is *my* country, do you hear me, you Irish redhead? And you, where do you come from? Since when are you American? For two weeks, ham-faced bastard? Get out of my country, you dirty bastard.'

"He went away. He saw that I wasn't the kind to let myself be pushed around, and I'd have hit him in the balls if he'd dared to raise his dirty hand to me.

"I traveled from city to city for the International Red Aid and the union, I spoke at rallies and I sang my songs. I went everywhere, but I didn't go back to Kentucky. I wrote a song and I'll sing it for you:

I'm nine hundred miles away from home,
I'm nine hundred miles away from home,
I'm nine hundred miles away from my home,
I love coal miners, I do.

I love coal miners, I do.
I love coal miners, I do.
I've lived among them all their lives,
With their children and their wives.
I dearly love a coal-mining man.

My father was a coal-mining man,
My father was a coal-mining man,
Then it ought to be plain for you to understand
Just why I love a coal-mining man.

I love coal miners, I do.
I love coal miners, I do.
I've lived among them all their lives,
With their children and their wives.
And I'll love them till the day I die.

I've two brothers dead and gone,
I've two brothers dead and gone
One was killed by the slate falling down,
I love coal miners, I do.

I love coal miners, I do.
I love coal miners, I do.
I've lived with them all their lives
With their children and their wives.
I dearly love a coal-mining man.

I'm nine hundred miles away from home,
I'm nine hundred miles away from home,
I'm nine hundred miles away from home,
I love coal miners, I do.

"I send them all kinds of literature, and they pass it around. As I am here in New York, I can choose the most important brochures and place them where they should be. I know hundreds and hundreds of people, and the best of them, to handle the propaganda, and I know where to go. Even in the countryside, I have cousins and second cousins among the farmers, and I send them brochures and I organize farmers and miners by correspondence. When they write to ask me what to do, I answer them. They always send me stamps for my replies because they know that I could not buy them.

"This story of class-consciousness—being a comrade—means a lot of things. When you talk with someone who's really lived through it, you see how many important things you can learn. You cannot learn it from books, you have to learn from someone who's gone through it all. It's no miracle that we're Red, those of us who come to class-consciousness. No need to look for another explanation. If you're looking for a real Red, an honest, good Red fighter, take someone who's spent time in the largest industry in the world, and you will have the real facts and a true comrade, honest to his last breath. A Kentucky hillbilly with class-consciousness is worth more than two hundred men who've lived a normal life.

"Things are starting to move over there because wages are still low, and they are starving, and the police are paid by the bosses, and they're killing the miners. Companies dock the men's wages to pay the teachers and doctors, but they appoint these men. The only newspaper in Harlan County is owned by a friend of the directors: he keeps quiet. When election time comes, they get the missing and the dead to vote, and when they've exhausted all the names, they invent new ones with names of flowers, trees, animals. And it's also the bosses who choose the bank where men—the few who've put something aside—can bring their savings, and the gravedigger who will bury them.

"But that doesn't matter. You remember the fifty guns and two machine guns that we took from the scabs that came to attack us in the mining town? They've never been found those weapons. They're hidden somewhere, well hidden and cared for and coddled and they are waiting for the revolution."